Erasmus and the Process of Human Perfection

The Philosophy of Christ

Sylvia Fitzpatrick

Stauros

First Published 2012

ISBN: 978-0-9573171-0-9

Stauros

Diviner's End, Painestown, Dunshaughlin, Co. Meath, Ireland.

Acknowledgements

The Publisher would like to thank University of Toronto Press for permission to reproduce extracts from the Collected Works of Erasmus.

Contents

INTRODUCTION....1

ERASMUS' CONCEPT OF CHRIST....7

ERASMUS' CONCEPT OF THE HUMAN BEING....36

THE GODLY FEAST....87

THE CICERONIANUS....114

THE PERFECTION PROCESS IN SCRIPTURE....148

TERMINUS/IUVENTAS: THE IMAGE OF PERFECTION...179

THE PERFECT HUMAN BEING....199

NOTES....215

BIBLIOGRAPHY....261

INDEX....267

Introduction

John Colet said that the name of Erasmus would never perish. This has proven to have been prophetic: Erasmus is indeed still famous. Nevertheless, outside of the world of scholarship his name is far more well-know than his writings. History dictated that he would be overshadowed by the seismic shift that occurred when the Reformation exploded onto the European stage of his day. This schism in Christianity meant that Erasmus' audience was split into two opposing factions and this in turn meant that his writings have frequently been interpreted in the light of one or other of the two main confessions ever since. Erasmus does not fit neatly into the theology of either side and so, in many ways, he was left behind. And yet, there is something compelling about his writings which has ensured that he is closely studied to this day. This is not simply his immense erudition, his encyclopaedic knowledge of classical and Scriptural writings, his highly entertaining satire, his writings on educational and literary theory, but it is something more. There is an enigmatic quality to his work that still fascinates. I propose, in this book, to explore his view of the meaning of the Christian message in its totality in order to deepen our understanding of his true purpose in creating his immense body of work.

Erasmus chose to spend his entire life communicating his version of Christianity to as wide an audience as he could. He believed that the Christian church of his day had lost its way and had become clogged up with the human accretions of centuries of pointless, mainly, scholastic theology. To counteract this he wanted to use his scholarship to get back to an earlier, purer and, for him, more valid Christianity. He was an extraordinary human being whose dedication to this task was total and his output was vast. Many of his writings became bestsellers, earning him the title,

Prince of Humanists. Despite this, however, he was not the founder of any school or faction of Christianity. People on both sides of the great post-reformation confessional divide found Erasmus infuriating. On the Catholic side, he was twice offered a cardinal's hat but was nevertheless also castigated by the Inquisition censured by the faculty of theology at Paris and most of his works were placed on the Index of prohibited books after his death. On the side of the reformers, while many of the friends he had influenced became Protestants, he himself did not. He was severely criticized, most notably by Luther, for his apparent cowardice in not joining their ranks. While his religious beliefs are clearly Christian, the precise nature of those beliefs was the source of much speculation among his contemporaries and, despite a large measure of consensus; this issue is still being debated by historians today.[1] In simple terms this is due to the fact that, on the one hand, he never ceased to criticize institutionalized religion, while on the other hand, he steadfastly remained within the established Church of his day, despite the obvious option of joining the reformers with whom he shared some crucial beliefs. Nevertheless, the dominant trend in more recent studies of Erasmus' religious beliefs is to view him primarily as a biblical humanist whose main aim was a humanistic revision of the text of Scripture which he undertook in order to undo the medieval scholastic influence on theology and the Church. He is not perceived now as having been either an innovative or radical theologian, or a practical reformer.[2] Erasmus studies have more or less settled into this consensus and new research tends to concentrate on more specialized accounts of his philological and hermeneutical practices particularly in relation to his New Testament writings.[3] This view of Erasmus as being a fairly orthodox Christian is bolstered by his own protestations of orthodoxy in the face of the severe criticism levelled at him by a number of his powerful ecclesiastical contemporaries. He really had no choice in this matter, however, because in the sixteenth century persistent heresy was an offence punishable by death in many territories and Erasmus had no desire to let an untimely death interfere with his work. Any assessment of his beliefs must take this constraint into account. It is also crucially important to remember that he was determined not to be the cause any kind of rift in the Christian Church because he believed that religious schism would produce nothing but bloodshed and terror and that no good could possibly come of it. Consequently, he always wanted to find consensus and was willing to compromise to this end. Unfortunately for the people of Europe his fears on this score proved to be all too correct. Nevertheless, despite his necessary protestations of orthodoxy and his appeals to the authority of Scripture, close reading of his religious writings together with his scathing satire against the abuses in the church often leaves one with the whiff of the unorthodox and the possibly heretical.

Erasmus does not fit neatly into any Christian or philosophical category. The accolade 'a man for all seasons' that he conferred on his friend Thomas More was much more appropriate for himself. While he was not, in any way, intellectually eclectic there are, nevertheless, several difficulties in assessing his work as a totality. The first of these lies in the fact that he chose numerous and often very different modes in which to express his ideas. He used biblical philology, exegesis of classical adages, satire, comedy and classical translations, together with spiritual and educational writings, to expound his views. His writings encompass the modern disciplines of theology, classical studies, philosophy, intellectual history, as well as literary and educational studies. Since each of these fields requires a level of expertise it is naturally difficult for one person to produce an integrated assessment of them as a whole.[4] What tends to happen is that Erasmus scholars naturally assess his output from within the framework of their own particular discipline. These fall broadly into two categories: religious/theological studies and literary/rhetorical studies. With the result that, as Bruce Mansfield the major expert on Erasmian historiography has concluded,

> those who begin with the question about Erasmus and theology tend to finish with an orthodox and devout Erasmus, those who begin with the question about Erasmus and rhetoric, tend to finish with an Erasmus of dialogue and openness. The difference resides, not only in the evidence marshalled, but also in the structures of two traditions with distinctive orientations.[5]

However, it is crucial to remember that Erasmus himself did not see these writings as separate rather, for him, each glossed the other. He said that his viciously satirical *Praise of Folly* carried exactly the same message as his profoundly religious handbook: the *Enchiridion*.[6] It is not possible, however, to define his thought either as thoroughgoing theology or as rigorous philosophy. He did not consider himself to be a theologian, although he wrote widely on theological matters.[7] Nor was he an original or trained philosopher, although he expressed opinions on many matters, such as the nature of the human being, that lie within the expertise of the philosopher. Erasmus was a man of the Renaissance who must be assessed within his own terms rather than by means of any imposed modern classification. Taking him at his word, we must see his work as a totality rather than dividing it up into its modern categories.

Assessment of his thought has further suffered from the fact that he lived at the time of the religious upheavals we call the Reformation. The reformers are generally viewed as a dynamic force in opposition to the more static nature of the Catholic Church. Erasmus, who did not intentionally initiate any separatist reform movement and who chose to stay within the old Church, has been mistakenly identified as belonging to its stasis. His most important religious views were fully formed before the Reformation and, consequently, it cannot be seen as a conditioning factor of his essential thought. He belongs far more to the age of the Renaissance and to the milieu of Humanism than to the Reformation. The historiographical emphasis on the question of the position he took between the two great confessions can, therefore, be misleading. He conceived of Christianity above all as a religion of harmony and unity and thus his main view of the split was that it should be healed as soon as possible. This is what conditioned all of his utterances on the subject. The dogmatism of both sides was exactly what he thought had to be avoided at all costs. His religion was undogmatic, open-ended and tolerant of everything except division. The humanist author of the *Epistolae Obscurorum Virorum* described him as a man entirely on his own; this is precisely what he was. Moreover, it is precisely what he thought everyone else should be also. In true Renaissance fashion, the focus of his thought is always the individual.

He chose to call the message of Scripture the *philosophy of Christ*. This description is a crucial key to understanding his thought. For him, as for many of his humanist friends, philosophy was, as Socrates had described it: a preparation for death. What they generally understood by this was that it was a discipline or a practice that led the human being by degrees from the transient changeable material reality of this world to an understanding and knowledge of the eternal unchanging true reality of the divine realm. In this way it prepared a person for the perfection of the next world. Erasmus chose to describe the Christian message as a philosophy because for him Christianity was first and foremost a way or method of human perfection. It contained all the information that a human being needed in order to live the best possible life. This was not, however, simply a matter of moral righteousness. It was, rather, a way of internal transformation in which the aspiring Christian would become a perfect human being, changing their very nature, by degrees. Scripture was the instrument and means of Truth but this truth could only take hold totally in the hearts of aspiring Christians if they were transformed in such a way that they incorporated the truth of Christ into their own beings in a most profound way. Then, they would not simply believe in Christ but, in a sense, they would become the same as Christ. This, for Erasmus, was the summit of human perfection. His concept of human nature meant that, for him, true Christianity and true humanity at their highest levels were really one and the same thing. To be truly Christian was also to be truly and fully human. It was the pinnacle of human perfection. When he defined the term *philosophy of Christ* he said that it was what Christ himself had called a rebirth and that, in fact, it was nothing other than the restoration of human nature to its original perfect state. This was his version of Christian Humanism. Christ had become a human being in order that we might become perfect and incorporate the divine Christ.

Many of his Renaissance co-humanists, who like him were all Christians, had found that in addition to the Christian Scriptures they needed philosophical systems in order to augment their understanding of themselves and the world. The most famous of these men were deeply influenced by one or other of the Neo-Platonic or occult philosophies: Pico della Mirandola and Reuchlin by Cabbalism; Marsilio Ficino by Hermeticism; Lefèvre d'Étaples by Cabbalism; Cornelius Agrippa by Magic and Hermeticism. Francis Yates has shown that they were seeking a more powerful philosophy to bolster Christianity and replace scholasticism.[8] It is significant that Erasmus, who shared with these men an immense love for the classics and great respect for the writings of Plato, never involved himself in any of these systems. It was in this context that he named the message of Scripture the *philosophy of Christ* because, despite his admiration for his fellow humanists, he believed that Christ's message needed no man-made philosophy to bolster it. Everything necessary for the perfection of the human being could be found in the life and teachings of Christ. It was also clearly a negative comment on the scholastic dependence on Aristotelian philosophy which he thought had led to many errors.

Erasmian Christianity rests on the twin pillars of his concept of Christ and his concept of the human being. These two concepts contain all of the basic information for the interpretation of his thought. Thus I will begin by examining the richness of these two concepts in his writing.

Chapter 1

Erasmus' Concept of Christ

As with most other Christians, the term Christ had two distinct meanings for Erasmus. First, he used it to denote the historical Jesus, born in time into the physical realm. Secondly, he conceived of Christ as the eternal divine *Logos:* an entity that transcended both time and the physical realm. In both cases, however, his views differed subtly from the accepted orthodoxy. This, together with his concept of the human being, had profound implications for the way in which he believed humans achieved salvation.

His concept of the historical Jesus was of a being that had 'two very different qualities: divine majesty, than which nothing can be more sublime; and human weakness, than which nothing can be more abject.'[1] It was crucial to Erasmus' version of the *philosophy of Christ* that Jesus Christ was *both* human and divine. He wrote:

> Christ is a man in such a way that at the same time he is also God, not the God peculiar to this or that nation, but the God of the whole world, and a God who is one with the Father. He is in command of all, and all these things are carried out by his inscrutable wisdom.[2]

The precise elements of the nature of Jesus Christ, whether human or divine, have been the subject of heated debate among Christians from the earliest times.[3] Erasmus was aware of this and had no intention of entering the debate. While this was primarily because he hated dissension, it was also certainly because his terms of reference, if too clearly defined, would have been seen to lie outside the then current, or indeed any, orthodoxy. Erasmus' view of the historical Jesus over-emphasized the abject human element of his nature. If the implications of this had been elaborated it would have been seen as being dangerously close to the Arian heresy. The scholarly and erudite Erasmus was not about to fall into this trap. Nevertheless this view of the human aspect of Christ was vital for Erasmus because he believed that unless people knew that Christ, in his own nature, shared fully in their humanity they would not be attracted to his message. His view of the function of the human nature of Christ was that it 'first makes a contribution towards arousing men's love towards him (for we are more ready to love things which we know)'.[4] Then, if people could love Christ as something familiar, this in turn would provide a 'keener incentive to imitate him. For who would try to emulate what had been done by an angel in appearance only and not also in truth?'[5] The real value of Jesus' life was that it provided a model for the way of human perfection and not simply a moral guide. Christ, therefore, had to be a real man and not a disguised angel or other divine creature if he was to be useful to humankind in the process of perfection. Quite simply, if he were not truly a man, then human beings would clearly despair of imitating him. Erasmus was arguing in effect that it was not realistic to expect humankind to take a leap of faith and to accept something beyond the realm of their experience. The corollary of this was that just as the Erasmian Jesus is more human than orthodoxy, so also, the Erasmian human being is more god-like. The process of perfection is one in which God becomes human in order that humans may in some way become god. The imitation of Christ is truly meaningful when the human being can become Christ. Orthodoxy allowed that the human being should embody the spirit of Christ but in Erasmus there is such a close correlation between the perfected human being and the more human Christ that he appears to believe the perfect human being can become Christ. Clearly this did not mean that the human being would become the historical Jesus of Nazareth. What it meant was that each person had to unite the eternal spirit of Christ or the *Logos* to his or her own humanity as Jesus himself had. So just as God became a human being, each person could become God. Perhaps it would make more sense to say that Erasmus believed humans could attain Christhood. This is what Erasmus' Christian humanism meant.

Erasmus' Concept of Christ

In conformity with Christian convention Erasmus thought the best exposition of the *Logos* was to be found in the *Gospel of John* because he believed its main theme was the mystery of the Divine nature and 'its marvellous association with our own'.[6] He then gave a brief summary of the orthodox view of the trinity while at the same time expressing his belief that it was somewhat beyond our powers of comprehension. He asked:

> What human intellect can even begin to encompass how God the Father without beginning and without end eternally begets the Son? - into whom in the act of generation he pours the whole of himself, and yet loses nothing; and the Son is born from him, yet never leaves the Father who brings him into life? Or again, how the Holy Spirit proceeds from them both in such a way that there is a perfect community of the same nature between them all, with no confusion between the individuality of the three persons?[7]

While this was a consciously orthodox statement about the nature of the Trinity, Erasmus then asked 'who can embrace in his understanding the bond by which that supreme and ineffable nature bound man unto himself, so that the same person who had eternally been very God of very God was born very man of very man?'[8] Here, as elsewhere, Erasmus did not refer to God sending his only begotten Son to redeem humankind; instead he depicted a mystical union in which the divine nature bound the nature of an ordinary human unto itself so that it was born 'very man of very man'. There was no specific mention of Christ, just the bonding of 'that supreme and ineffable nature' with ordinary human nature. It is as if an ordinary person was united with the eternal spirit of the *Logos* and so was exalted, rather than the orthodox concept of God sending down his only-begotten son to become a human being.

Far from expounding a concise doctrine of the *Logos,* however, Erasmus believed that it was not possible to understand this mystery without first progressing on the way of perfection by imitating Christ. This was an essential factor in his thought. For him the way of perfection and the understanding of the nature of perfection could only be achieved in stages, gradually. He wrote that the earlier evangelists had

He went on to argue that: 'perhaps the time was not yet ripe for such an ineffable mystery to be made public in written form, for fear the godless might laugh to scorn what they could neither believe nor understand'.[9] In Erasmus' writings this correlation between belief and understanding is very common but he also argued that on account of the gradual nature of the process it was sometimes necessary to be parsimonious in the dissemination of the truth. In another letter he pointed out that Christ himself was often deliberately obscure. He wrote that Christ 'sometimes spoke as though at the time he wished not to be understood' and that 'Jesus so mixes and adapts what he had to say that he seems to me to have wished to remain obscure not only to the apostles but to us'.[10] In his opinion it was the rise of heresy that made John and the Fathers after him write more openly than they would have liked about the divine nature.[11] Thus Erasmus suggested that certain elements of Christianity should not be communicated openly because it might be detrimental to do so. While the idea of mysteries of faith is perfectly orthodox, Erasmus differed from the usual view in that he believed these mysteries could be gradually penetrated by someone who had taken on, and progressed along, the path of Christian perfection. Moreover, it is clear he thought that both the apostles and his own contemporaries were equally expected to find these things obscure until they had advanced in Christ.

There is an element of the unorthodox also in this notion that Jesus did not distinguish between pre-Redemption and post-Redemption Christians and that he set out deliberately to obscure the truth of certain mysteries from all but an inner circle. It could be seen as undermining the doctrine of the Redemption. Indeed, Erasmus was castigated by Beda, the Paris theologian, for saying this.[12] He expressed the same idea in a letter of 1521 where he described the method of teaching employed by Jesus. He said that he attuned himself to the feelings of the Jews and that 'he says one thing to the multitudes, who are somewhat thick-witted, and another to his disciples; and even so he has to bear with them for a long time while he gradually brings them to understand the celestial philosophy'.[13] This kind of statement could be interpreted as elitism on the part of Erasmus. It was not. He believed the path of Christianity was open to all men and women but it was so difficult that very few succeeded in attaining the highest perfection, despite the fact that all were capable of success. In the *Paraclesis* he said that 'only a very few can be learned, but all can be Christian'.[14]

Erasmus' Concept of Christ

Erasmus' Christology is the bedrock of his beliefs and as early as 1499 his Christological views were firmly established. In that year he had a dispute with John Colet, which illustrates the exact way in which he thought the human and divine parts of Christ interacted. It also demonstrates his fully-fledged belief in the efficacy of Christ's human dimension as an example of the way of perfection.[15] The dispute centred on the account of the agony of Christ in the garden of Gethsemane. Put simply, Erasmus argued that Christ, because of his human nature, had felt real aversion to the prospect of dying. Colet, however, on account of his own view of Christ's nature, would not countenance this. Erasmus argued that when 'Christ, speaking after the fashion of men,' said: 'Father, let this cup pass from Me; yet not as I will, but as Thou wilt', what he meant was,

> My Father, I am conscious within Myself of the nature I have taken upon me, a nature that violently dreads a cup so bitter; but let Thy will, not Mine, be done, since whatever is Thy will is Mine also. I am in no way moved by this anguish of spirit to be unwilling to drink the cup. Rather, I Thirst deeply for it; for, exceedingly bitter as it must be for Me, it is to bring salvation to those whom I love, and it cannot do so unless it be bitter for Me. Therefore I wish to drink it, but the will whereby I wish this is Thine, not Mine, for My steadfast desire to do so comes not from Myself but from Thee, by whose gift I am what I am.[16]

Erasmus asserted that Christ felt genuine human anguish but he did not let that anguish influence or determine his actions. He achieved this by being completely conscious of the disparate elements within himself. Erasmus believed that it was by means of this act of conscious introspection that Christ had subjected his human will to the divine will.

The purpose of Erasmus' elaboration on the nature of Jesus' condition in the garden was to demonstrate the complexities of true consciousness. Having first argued vehemently that Christ dreaded the prospect of death because of his lower nature he then argued that

> among the whole army of martyrs there never was such holy joy as Christ had in that hour when he sweated drops of blood. At that very moment he rejoiced with inexpressible gladness that the time,

> ordained by his Father before time was, had now come to pass, when he should reconcile fallen mankind to his Father by his death. Never was there any man who's longing for life made him wish as ardently to live as he wished to die. Never did anyone seek the kingdom of Heaven as passionately as he thirsted for death.[17]

While a belief in the human nature of Christ is quite orthodox Erasmus stretched it to edge of, and even beyond, orthodoxy. His Christ is very human. He was, nevertheless, aware of this pitfall and was careful to avoid being categorical about it. This was not difficult for him because he also believed that Christ contained a divine element. Throughout his writings the two natures always co-exist in a creative tension. Nor did he see any inherent contradiction in these conflicting emotions. He explained that:

> there is no reason why one soul should not experience different sense-impressions by way of different organs, above all in Christ, and.....the senses never obstruct the operation of other senses, nor the feelings other feelings. To this extent, Our Lord's soul, where it approached most closely to his bodily feelings, was sensitive to the agonies that torture the body, while on the other side, where it lay nearest to the Godhead, it exulted with ineffable joy. Yet that feeling of grief did not impede his joy, nor did that joy diminish or alleviate the experience of terror.[18]

The great joy that Christ felt was a result of the fact that he knew he was going to reconcile fallen humanity to his Father by his death on the cross. This understanding was reached by means of an interior process in which Christ, died to his lower human part and reconciled his total being to God by conforming to the dictates of his higher nature. Nevertheless Christ, even at the end of his time on earth, had not managed to eliminate the weakness of the flesh. He felt real terror. He had to do battle with his own human weakness until the very end.[19] The method he employed to overcome weakness was not to suppress his terror or try to stamp it out but, rather, to allow it expression, while at the same time being conscious of his higher aim. Erasmus was quite explicit in his belief that the two emotions could be experienced simultaneously and that a process of conscious introspection was necessary in order to choose the right course of action. Moreover, it is clear that he believed right action would *necessarily* follow from proper understanding.[20] In the case of Christ, he believed that his soul was in a state of earthly perfection, which meant that despite a very real struggle he was always going to choose the good. This was not the ultimate state of perfection that was only achievable in Heaven. The importance of the agony in the garden, for Erasmus, lay in the fact that it functioned as a very important a lesson for humanity. The process of reconciling the two natures in Christ was precisely the same process that each individual had to engage in if they were to achieve perfection.[21] What he described in the Gethsemane incident was the psychological condition of true Christians who have united within themselves the two warring natures described throughout the *Enchiridion*, in such a way that the spiritual nature triumphs over the earthly one to produce a state of joyous harmony.[22]

Erasmus' particular emphasis of the human aspect of Christ's nature did not mean that he dismissed or even diminished the divine nature. He clearly believed in the divine nature of Christ and its importance in the salvation of the human race, but he thought that it was only possible for aspiring Christians to achieve a full understanding of this when they had progressed to the point where they could distinguish the warring factions in their own nature. In other words, our understanding is limited by our experience. Erasmus noted that Scripture portrayed the patience, gentleness and long-suffering nature of Christ rather than the joy he was capable of experiencing in the face of death. He argued that Christ did not exhibit the joy he felt in Gethsemane because 'that joy was not likely to be of great service to us, but his sorrow brought us gain; it was essential that he who paid the penalty of death for our sakes, might be held to be very man'.[23] If it was a mere pretence and not real sorrow and despair then how could it serve to enlighten us? People who had not yet progressed far on the path to Christianity had to be able to relate to the nature they shared with Christ in order to know how to imitate him. Erasmus made it very clear that he believed Christ had truly felt this very human sense of fear and despair when he said: 'there is none to doubt that he who stood in dread of death was very man'.[24] He then added that

> he did not exhibit, in himself, that joy amidst great agonies which, since it is opposed to nature, he does not expect of us, but he sets us an example of the patience and gentleness which he bade us learn

> from him, and did so by the tokens that are most familiar to men's senses.[25]

In sum, For Erasmus Christ is above all our teacher. We learn the way of human perfection not only from the words of Christ but also from all of his actions and his very life. He values Christ's death and resurrection above all as an extraordinary metaphor for the process of perfection in which the human being must die to the world or the flesh in order to be born again as a new person. Perfection is a process that is learnt by imitating the very human Christ who overcame his abject human side, not by denying or annihilating it but, by identifying with his superior divine nature and always allowing it to dictate his actions. In the *Paraphrases* Erasmus depicted an even more wretched picture of Jesus in Gethsemane. He said he was

> a man destitute of all help, he began to be shaken by fear and robbed of his senses by anguish. Indeed he was truly man and significantly expressed in himself what happens to men who are nothing but men when such a storm is threatening.[26]

He then elaborated on this, using very colourful language to drive home his point, by depicting the state of utter despair in which Jesus could not even find consolation in God his Father.[27] He said that Jesus

> sought refuge in his Father's help, finding no immediate relief from his misfortune even in him. Thus, he fell down on the ground, lowered his face to the earth, and begged his Father to let the time of trial pass if it was somehow possible. His physical nature recoiled from suffering and imminent death.[28]

The intensity of this language depicts a very weak and broken human Jesus who was utterly lost and destitute of all hope. He was true man at his most abject. In his *Paraphrase on John* Erasmus said that Christ

> did not put on an imaginary body; who would love an empty ghost or a deceiving illusion? But he truly put on a human body; that is, he put on the whole nature of a man, not even disdaining the part by which we are in bondage to death and differ least of all from the race of dumb animals. And he did not put it on for a time, soon to

> lay aside what he had put on. But in order to confirm faith in his human nature, not put on in pretence, he dwelt on earth for a long while; He thirsted, he hungered, he was afflicted, he died; eyes saw him, ears heard him, hands touched him.[29]

Despite this insistence that Christ was truly human and full of human frailty Erasmus never portrayed him as being permanently defeated by the weakness of the flesh. The whole point of the exercise was that despite his true human weakness Christ overcame the flesh and thereby gave us the perfect example of how to engage in the struggle for perfection. This was possible because Erasmus believed that Christ's composite nature was, in fact, akin to the true nature of human beings. Each of whom was also made of human and divine elements. It was, therefore, vital that Christ showed both of these natures in his life.

> Although while he dwelt on earth carrying out the task of our salvation he preferred to show us a model of self restraint and gentle obedience rather than display his greatness, nonetheless everything he said, all his deeds, even his bearing and expression made clear that he was full of every divine endowment, full of eternal and inviolable truth.[30]

In describing the joy mixed with agony, the emotions under the sway of reason, the human and divine dynamic of Christ at Gethsemane, Erasmus was speaking in terms that could also be understood by those who were further along the path of Christianity. His intention of disseminating these views to a wide audience is evident from the fact that while this debate was initially conducted by means of private correspondence with Colet, he later amplified the argument and published it in his *Lucubratiunculae* of 1503.

Again the most notable element of this dispute was the emphasis Erasmus placed on the salvific importance of Christ's role as an exemplar for humankind. While he never denied the orthodox doctrine of Redemption, in which Christ redeemed us by becoming truly human and atoning to God for our sins by being crucified, he nevertheless did not emphasize the mysterious element of this doctrine.[31] In that doctrine there are many mysteries including the exact mechanism of Redemption. Erasmus was never very interested in mysteries. In the *Adages* he quoted a saying of

Socrates: 'the things that are above us are nothing to us'.[32] He interpreted this as meaning that Socrates 'discourages us from restless enquiry into heavenly things and the secrets of nature' and that the saying could be 'diverted also for use against those who talk loosely about...the mysteries of theology'.[33] He believed that we should start our search for knowledge and perfection with the things that are accessible to our own intelligence and experience and that it is only when we have mastered these that we can move to the next stage.

This emphasis of the human nature of Christ did not go unnoticed in Erasmus' own time and despite his desire to avoid conflict, he found it impossible to elaborate it without incurring the wrath of his fellow-churchmen. Some of whom thought he was sailing too close to the position of the Arian heresy. In his preface to the works of St Hilary Erasmus obliquely implied that he had some sympathy for the views of the heretic, Arius who was condemned for his belief that Christ was created by God and therefore being a creature was not the second person of the Trinity.[34] In the context of arguing in favour of tolerance for theologians who may make an error of judgment, he said that Hilary was wrong to rail against the Arians because 'it is probable that there were men in the Arian faction who were convinced that their preaching about Christ was true and devout'. He then went further and said that their doctrine rested on many authorities and that some of Holy Scripture gave the impression of supporting it.[35] In an age where the persistent profession of Arianism could have resulted in death, this was a very daring assertion. Erasmus would not have risked the censure this statement was bound to provoke for nothing. Nor would he have risked misleading his readers. Clearly, he had some sympathy with an Arian or semi-Arian position. When he produced his *Novum Instrumentum* he left out the famous Trinitarian source, 1 John 5, 7-8. This seriously undermined the Scriptural validity of the doctrine of the Trinity. Despite the fact that he often writes in an orthodox way about the Trinity, this omission was consistent with his emphasis of the human nature in Christ. Without the doctrine of the Trinity, which makes Christ a unique Son of God and a part of the divinity, it would be possible to argue that Jesus was simply a very superior Son of God who as a true man embodied the divine and human natures. While the Father the Son and the Holy Spirit are mentioned throughout Scripture the Johanine Comma is the only place where it is clearly stated that the three divine persons are one entity. Erasmus understood very well the seriousness of destroying this bastion of dogma but he did it anyway. At the same time the more orthodox editors of the Complutension Polyglot bible in Spain left the verse in despite the fact that they, too, were never able to show that it existed in an early Greek manuscript. Although Erasmus was forced to reinstate the Trinitarian clause when the Trinity college codex was forged in England containing it, he did so reluctantly and appended a footnote correctly stating that he thought the manuscript was very recent.

Various theologians and even some of his fellow-humanists attacked him for this over-emphasis of Christ's human element. In general, they criticized parts of the *Praise of Folly* and the *Enchiridion* but the attacks reached a fever pitch when he published his annotations on the New Testament in 1516.[36] The attack of the French humanist, and former ally of Erasmus, Lefèvre d'Étaples, is a prime example of this kind of criticism.[37] In a letter to Thomas More about the origin of this dispute Erasmus wrote: 'I touched him on the raw by saying "he is a man"'.[38] He was referring to his note on Hebrews 2:7 which he interpreted as meaning that Christ had been made 'a little lower than the angels'.[39] Lefèvre disputed this and preferred that it should read, 'a little lower than God', like the psalm to which it referred.[40] In insisting on the interpretation that Christ was a little lower than the angels, Erasmus appeared to diminish his divinity and place him on a par with humankind. While he could claim to be on safe ground here, insofar as Jerome had favoured this interpretation, his vehement defence in the form of an *Apologia* against a fellow-humanist illustrates both the validity of the attack and the importance of the point to his concept of Christ.[41] Clearly the *Apologia* did not silence his critics because a little later, on 6th December 1517, he had to write three letters defending the Christology he had presented in it. In these letters he tried to hold on to his own view while remaining within the orthodox tradition. The first of these was to Ludwig Baer in which he wrote:

> that Christ was not a composite being of two natures is a fact I learnt some thirty years ago...all through my argument I maintain the singleness of his substance, nor do I say anywhere that Christ is to be taken as having one rather than both, as Lefèvre says, by which I mean the divine nature, but a divine which has united the

human to Itself.[42]

The same argument was put forward in the remaining two letters, which he addressed respectively to Faber Capito and to Beatus Rhenanus.[43] It is clear from the fact that Erasmus felt the need to write to Capito again three days later that the above explanation was not sufficient to quell the latter's suspicion about his orthodoxy. Nevertheless, Erasmus stuck fast to his interpretation of the nature of Christ even in the face of fierce criticism. While he was willing to change the language he used to please his critics, he would not change his particular emphasis of the human element in Christ. The strength of his conviction is also clear from his remarks in a letter to the French humanist Budé.[44] He said that it had been necessary to refute Lefèvre 'unless I had preferred to imperil, or rather to betray, the citadel of my beliefs' for 'to admit a charge of irreligion is forbidden in the first place by religion itself'.[45] He also said:' I am unfortunate, I admit, compelled as I have been to plunge into this contest which I have always abhorred, and into which nothing but this one weapon could have dragged me'.[46] While it was indeed true that Erasmus could not afford to have a charge of irreligion hanging over him, he nevertheless would not back down in any way because to do so would have caused him to betray a fundamental and dearly-held belief. His particular Christology was absolutely central to his belief-system.

He also sailed very close to the wind in his desire to communicate his view of Christ in his annotation on Philippians 2, 6-7. These verses, which describe the nature of Christ, read: 'who, being in the form of God, thought it not robbery to be equal with God, but made himself no reputation'. Erasmus suggested that the clause 'thought it not robbery to be equal with God' should be understood of Christ inasmuch as he is man. If it were allowed that Christ, on account of his humanity, was equal to God then the corollary of this would be that human beings also could be equal to God. This was clearly blasphemous. Moreover, it was also a highly dangerous piece of exegesis because the Church Fathers had interpreted these verses as referring to the divinity of Christ and they had specifically used them to refute the Arians. So Erasmus' insistence that the verses referred to the human element of Christ weakened the orthodox case *vis a vis* the Arian one. Given the breath of his patristic knowledge, this cannot have been accidental.

Indeed, he was criticized in a letter by the staunch catholic, Hieronymus Dungersheim, for this.[47] There is no record of a reply from Erasmus to this letter but its significance lies in the fact that, again, it was his particular emphasis on the human element of Christ that gave offence. Erasmus' unwillingness to defend himself suggests that he was aware that he could not do so without prejudicing an essential belief.

Prior to the publication of the *Annotations*, Erasmus had portrayed the humanity of Christ in the *Praise of Folly*, in which work he went as far as attributing human folly itself to Christ and the apostles.[48] This aroused the ire of the Louvain theologians amongst others. In his famous letter to Martin Dorp, which was usually published with this work, he defended this portrayal against these attacks. He argued that Christ and the apostles were all credited in the Gospels with 'some kind of foolishness'.[49] His point was that because Folly rules supreme in all human affairs, if Christ were truly human, he would, of necessity, have had to embrace Folly in order to overcome it for our sakes.[50] He held, however, that Christ and the apostles were not foolish in an ordinary sense but that, nevertheless,

> in them too there was an element of weakness, something attributable to our natural affections, which when compared with that pure and eternal wisdom might seem less than wise. But this same folly of theirs overcame all the wisdom of the world.[51]

Here, again, Erasmus' Christ is depicted as fully human and sharing the same human weaknesses as the humble apostles. Indeed, in the *Praise of Folly* Erasmus outlines the importance of this very weakness as an instrument of our Redemption.

> Christ too, was made something of a fool himself in order to help the folly of mankind, when he assumed the nature of man and was seen in man's form; just as he was made sin so that he could redeem sinners. Nor did he wish them to be redeemed in any other way save by the folly of the cross and through his simple, ignorant apostles, to whom he unfailingly preached folly.[52]

It is somewhat unorthodox to suggest that Christ sinned, although Erasmus made it clear that he was following St Paul who also said that Christ was 'made sin'.[53] He interpreted this as being even stronger than saying that Christ was a *sinner* but he argued that the way St Paul meant it was in fact a pious tribute.[54] The orthodox view is that Jesus' work of Redemption entailed taking upon himself the sins of the world. Erasmus, however, suggested that, just as he was made man, he was also made sin. What he meant by this was that Jesus, being fully human, was also subject to all human weakness including the capacity for sin. Erasmus was aware that the Greek word for the verb to sin is *amartano,* which also means to miss the mark or target. Since, for him, the attainment of Christ or perfection was the target or goal of human beings, sinning would have meant missing this target. Thus sinning, rather than being a positive evil act, was instead a negative inclination away from the process that leads to Christ or perfection. More significantly, it was also part of the state of nature into which everyone is born insofar as Erasmus believed that 'birth does not create a man, but only something capable of having man's nature.[55] He thought that the attainment of Christ was achieved by means of an internal struggle between the two elements of the human being. In order to teach us the way of salvation, Christ had to be made man, and this entailed being subject to the condition of 'missing the mark' or sin, so that he could demonstrate the way to overcome this condition.[56] In the *Enchiridion* he asserted that the path to perfection is a narrow one along which few human beings have walked.[57] It is not, however, beyond our capacities. He argued that 'all those who were pleasing to God from the beginning of the world have trodden it'.[58] Most importantly, he maintained that Christ himself had walked this path.[59] Thus in some sense the incarnate Christ in the man Jesus had had to strive to achieve Christian perfection because if he had been perfect and purely divine he could not have taught us by example.

Again, not surprisingly, he was criticized for this, most notably, by the Englishman, Edward Lee. In 1518 he wrote to Maarten Lips defending himself against this attack. Lee had argued that it was wrong to attribute foolishness to Christ.[60] Erasmus stood steadfastly by his opinion and firstly defended himself in a typically humanist fashion by saying that he attributed folly to God and Christ because Paul and Augustine had done this.[61] Then, he asserted that

In order to show how Christ had brought himself down to the level

> of our weakness, I had said that there was in Christ something infirm, something subject to our affections; and the blockhead imagines that I attribute faulty passions to the mind of Christ.[62]

The distinction between 'something infirm' and 'faulty passions' is, perhaps, most clearly illustrated in Erasmus' exposition of the process that Christ engaged in at Gethsemane. The 'something infirm' was the weakness of human nature, which Christ had to struggle with right up to his death. This did not result in his giving in to 'faulty passions' however, because he overcame weakness through consciousness and subjected his lower human will to the will of God, or the divine will. This view is also expressed in the *Enchiridion* when he wrote of an incident in which the apostles asked Jesus 'where shall we go? You have the words of life'.[63] Erasmus said that the explanation for the phrase 'words of life' was that they flowed from the soul of Christ 'from which divinity never departed even for an instant'[64] Thus although Christ had to struggle continually and was subject to the same weaknesses as all humans, he nevertheless always triumphed over his lower passions. Christ had conquered sin for us. He 'was the first and only one, himself free of sin, to suppress the tyranny of sin'.[65] For Erasmus this immunity was not a result of detached omnipotence it was achieved by means of a struggle, which had resulted in victory over sin. He clarified this in his *Paraphrase on Romans* where he wrote of Christ that

> to such an extent did he adopt the mask of sin, so to speak, that through the form of sin he first conquered sin, then destroyed it, made a victim for our sins. And since he died in this way in accordance with the flesh which he had put on, he subdued death, which used to be our master through the passions of the flesh and the carnal law; and he brought it about that for the future the flesh of the law would be abolished and that the better part of the law, which we have called spiritual, would take its place.[66]

Christ overcame sin by becoming subject to sin and thereby putting himself in a position to demonstrate to us the method of conquering our faults. This is the Erasmian interpretation of the Pauline concept that strength is made perfect in weakness. He expressed this view in 1512 in a letter to his close friend Ammonio when he wrote that Christ tests 'most severely in misfortune's storms those whose discipleship he most desires to reveal'.[67] In this way, for Erasmus, human weakness and all the trials of life are the essential raw material for the process of perfection.

In tandem with his view of the nature of the incarnate Christ in the man Jesus, Erasmus also attributed a second meaning to the term Christ. This was a far more complex and multi-dimensional concept. It was a universal and eternal principal. This was the Christ, which was the ultimate goal of human beings. He wrote that St Paul was anxious over the Galatians 'until Christ takes shape in them'.[68] Clearly this Christ was not the historical figure of Jesus, the Christ of the first century, but the divine *Logos*, which was defined and described most clearly in the gospel of John. In his *Paraphrase on John* Erasmus described the two Christs and he criticized the stupidity of some people who thought of Christ only in terms of Jesus of Nazareth and did not understand the eternal nature of Christ the *Logos*. He wrote:

> even more stupid is the mistake of those who think that the Son and word of God came into existence only at the time when he was physically born of the Virgin Mary. Every created thing has a beginning in time, but the Son of God was born twice, once from his Father before all time, or rather without time, true God from true God, and again in time marked off from eternity, of the Virgin Mary, true human from a human.[69]

The Greek word *Christos* used in Scripture was a translation of the Jewish word *Messiah* and meant the anointed one, that is, the enlightened, or chosen, one. Christ, for Erasmus, was synonymous with enlightened consciousness. He said that Christ was Wisdom and the true Light who alone shattered the 'night of worldly stupidity'.[70] He thought that the term meant a deep and profound knowledge of the truth. Christ was the light of the world: the source of wisdom that dispelled the darkness of ignorance. He was

> the source of light, inasmuch as the Father through his eternal begetting pours into him the fullness of nature, so that he alone restores life even to the dead, and with his light scatters the darkness of souls no matter how thick it may be.[71]

This function of the enlightenment of humankind was the essential purpose of the spirit of Christ or the *Logos*.

Erasmus' Concept of Christ

> The word of God was the true light, forever pouring forth from God the Father, the source of all light, from whom everything that shines in heaven and earth borrows its brightness. Any spark of intelligence, any knowledge of truth, any light of faith, whether among mankind or the angels, comes from this source. Just as without the sun this world is blind, so without this light all things are in darkness.[72]

Christ, as illuminator, is the means by which we can come to know the truth about the nature of existence. The goal of this illumination is the perfection of human nature. There is no salvation without true consciousness and that is impossible without the light of Christ. Erasmus explained that

> this light goes on shining by its own natural power even in the thickest darkness of the world, offering itself to all so that they may live again and see the path of eternal salvation, which is open to everyone through the gospel faith.[73]

There is a great need for the light of Christ in the world because of the innate darkness or ignorance of the material realm. Material reality is an illusion, which Erasmus equates with darkness. Nevertheless this darkness is not inert. It has a grip on the human soul and is very powerful.

> The darkness of this world fights constantly against the light, which the world hates as the revealer of its works, and it quenches or dims the rays of many, but against this living and eternal light it has not prevailed. Tumults have been raised by Jews, by philosophers and men of power, by those who have completely surrendered themselves to transitory things, but this light wins out; it still shines in the midst of the world's darkness, and it will always shine, sharing itself with anyone who only shows himself capable of enlightenment.[74]

The truth is available to all but in order to achieve perfection each one of us has to struggle with the mundane forces of darkness, or identification with the material world. As a result of the difficulty of the struggle Erasmus asserted that many people never achieved victory over darkness. They did not recognize the light, or true reality. 'Accustomed to darkness, they shunned the light, and blinded by sins, they embraced death instead of life.'[75] Indeed, even when Jesus 'showed himself to the world in more familiar guise, dwelling in a human body and living among mankind, he was not recognized by those who had dedicated themselves entirely to this world'.[76] This was the human struggle: the forces of the world, which were very powerful, could only be overcome by clinging to the light of true reality. Although Erasmus believed that it was not possible for the light of truth itself to be extinguished by worldly darkness, nevertheless, many individuals were lost forever in the ignorance of the world.

Erasmus first elaborated on this distinction between the historical Jesus and the concept of Christ in the *Enchiridion.* In writing about the episode after the resurrection when Jesus was about to leave the apostles and he reproved them for their lack of faith, Erasmus pointed out that 'as long as the apostles enjoyed the physical company of Christ, do you not read how weak they were and how crass was their understanding?' He explained that their weakness was because the 'flesh of Christ stood in the way'.[77] He went on to say that Christ told them 'if I do not go away, the *Paraclete* will not come. It is expedient for you that I go'.[78] Erasmus then addressed his readers and asked how they could put their trust in corporal things if 'the physical presence of Christ is of no profit for salvation?'[79] While it was acceptable to point out that material and physical things were of no use in the process of salvation, this denigration of the physical presence of Christ himself, if it were carried to its logical conclusion, would have had very serious implications for the role of the sacrament of the Eucharist in the process of salvation. If the physical presence of the living, breathing, Christ were an impediment to perfection then the physical element or *real presence* in the Eucharist would also be detrimental. Erasmus went on in this passage to support his argument by pointing out that St Paul said he had advanced in the spirit beyond the mere physical knowledge of Christ. Thus he implied that St Paul also differentiated between the historical Jesus and the spirit of Christ. Moreover he said that Paul achieved this understanding because 'he had advanced to a higher state of grace'.[80]

While Erasmus never openly denied the doctrine of the real presence he nevertheless always emphasized the spiritual meaning of the Eucharist, often to the very point of heresy. Indeed

Melanchthon stated that Erasmus' views on the Eucharist would have caused much more trouble if Luther had not arrived on the scene and diverted opinion in another direction. Erasmus believed that the significance of the Eucharist lay in its secret meaning, which had been revealed to very few people.[81] He expressed this most succinctly in the *Praise of Folly* when he said 'it represents the death of Christ, which men must express through the mastery and extinction of their bodily passions, laying them in the tomb, wherein they can be united with him and with each other'.[82] In short, he believed that the Eucharist represented the way or method of perfection, which allowed human beings to overcome the pull of the world and in turn then united them to Christ and to each other. This was expressed by the eating of the body of Christ in the form of bread and wine. For Erasmus, the eating of the 'body of Christ' symbolized the fact that the participants were infused with the spirit of Christ, the *Logos*. He then became their centre, their aim and target. If they were infused with Christ, they were also one in the Body of Christ in the wider sense of all those who embody Christ. The spirit of Christ was something that all could achieve by dying to, or overcoming, worldly passions. This spirit had been embodied in a most perfect way in the historical Jesus who was *Christos*.

This concept of the Eucharist together with his emphasis on the pedagogic importance of Christ's human dimension meant that the death and resurrection of Christ took on a different perspective in the redemptive process for Erasmus. The redemptive function of Christ's life lay, first and foremost, in the fact that it symbolized the method by which human beings progresses from the imperfect state in which they are born to the state of perfection in which, ultimately, they can become one with Christ. We must die to our bodily passions as Christ died to the world. Then having experienced this death to the world, we will rise again in a renewed state just as Christ himself rose again. Christ, the most perfect teacher, was, in his life and in himself, the most perfect expression of the potential of a true human being. By his words, and especially, by his very life and death, he taught us all we would ever need to know in order to achieve perfection. Erasmus referred to this dual method of teaching in the *Adages*, when he wrote that 'just as the whole of Christ's teaching spelt tolerance and love, so his entire life was a lesson in compassion'.[83]

We are redeemed, first and foremost, by Christ's teaching. In conformity with this belief Erasmus spent the whole of his own life in imitation of the pedagogical role of Christ. Every line of his immense corpus was dedicated to this end. He wanted above all to help his readers to understand the only truth: the *philosophy of Christ.* He wrote 'I wish to be of use to all men, in such a way that if possible I hurt no one'.[84] Erasmus' diminution of the mysterious element of Christ's redemptive powers and his emphasis instead on the power of his teaching as the embodiment of truth placed a tremendous onus on each person to absorb this teaching and put it into practice. The individual's role in his or her own Redemption was enhanced in the Erasmian system and the sacramental role of the church was thereby diminished. Erasmus nowhere overtly condemned the orthodox doctrine of the Redemption and it was possible for him to speak of the redemptive role of Christ in a seemingly orthodox way because he believed that Christ, as embodied in Jesus of Nazareth, had indeed saved humankind by his life and death because these events had been consciously constructed by him, in line with the divine plan, to represent the perfection process and consequently, his life was the most perfect, and most efficacious, lesson in the method of perfection available to us. Moreover, it is also clear, that Erasmus believed in the redemptive power or function of Christ as the spirit of truth, or *Logos*.

This belief in the redemptive function of the eternal *Logos* led him to the conclusion that people who had lived before the time of Jesus had been capable of embodying Christ and were, therefore, redeemed. He made his character Eusebius, the host in *The Godly Feast,* say that

> perhaps the spirit of Christ is more widespread than we understand and the company of saints includes many not in our calendar. Speaking frankly among friends, I can't read Cicero's *De senectute, De amicitia, De officiis, De Tusculanis quaestionibus* without sometimes kissing the book and blessing that pure heart, divinely inspired as it was'.[85]

Here, through the medium of a fictitious character, Erasmus asserted his belief in the widespread nature of the spirit of Christ.[86] He believed that spirit was one a truly conscious human being embodied; that is to say, it was the spirit that informed a perfected human psyche. In his biblical writings Erasmus often expressed the view that the spirit of Christ was evident in Old Testament times, prior to the advent of Jesus. In his *Paraphrase on John* he portrayed John the Baptist as saying: 'he is the well-spring of all truth and grace...Whatever power there was in the patriarchs, in the prophets, in Moses came from his well-spring.'[87] In his paraphrase of St Paul's letter to the Romans he was even more explicit. He said that 'Abraham was righteous because he believed in Christ'.[88] The verses in Romans do not actually say this. St Paul wrote of Abraham's faith, but Erasmus changed that to faith in Christ. St Paul's reference was to Genesis 15:6 which states that God told Abraham his descendants would be numerous as the stars. Abraham's faith, therefore, would have been in God's promise to him but Erasmus chose to interpret it as faith in Christ because he believed that salvation came specifically through faith in the knowable Christ rather than the unknowable God. Erasmus believed that the method of perfection for all human beings was the incorporation of the *Logos* of Christ whether they lived before the specific Incarnation of the *Logos* in Jesus of Nazareth or after him. He returned to this theme in *Romans* when he said that Abraham's sons were all sons of God and that Isaac, in particular, was a type of Christ and 'the one and only son of faith whom God had especially chosen by his will'.[89] The function of the historical Incarnation of Christ was not the replacement of the Old Testament law, but the perfection of it. He wrote: 'our lord Jesus did not want to abolish the authority of the law; he wanted to interpret what had not been understood. He perfected rather than destroyed it'.[90] Christ, for Erasmus, was 'the central point of the whole law'.[91] Nor was this revelation confined to the chosen people. Erasmus said that God will regard the heathen as circumcised if 'he achieves what is the essence and goal of the law, namely, a sound and pure life; and if he trusts and obeys Christ who is the fulfilment of all laws'.[92] Erasmus believed that all of us, as God's creatures, have had access since the beginning of time to the truth of Christ. He argued that Christ the *Logos*

> the word of God has always been in the world - not that he who is immeasurable can be contained by any boundary of space, but he was in the world as the intelligence of the craftsman is in his handicraft, as the pilot is in that which he steers. The light was even then shining in the world, somehow making plain through what

> had been marvellously created the divine might, wisdom, and goodness, and in this way even then he was speaking in some fashion to the human race.[93]

This eternal spirit of Christ or the *Logos* was then the instrument by means of which God becomes manifest to us. In his *Paraphrase on John* he said that

> the term "Word" is used because through him God, who in his own nature cannot be understood by any reasoning, chose to become known to us; and he chose to become known for no other reason than that from knowledge of him we might attain eternal bliss.[94]

Later, in his work on the *Explanation of the Creed*, he said that human speech had been provided principally for the purpose of making God manifest.[95] He also thought that the *Logos,* or the eternal Christ, had a second function which was that it was the very instrument of creation and it continues through all time to be the guiding principle of creation. He outlined this function thus:

> through this word of his, coeternal with himself, the Father created all things that were created, visible and invisible; through it he governs all things, through it he has renewed all things, not as using a tool or a servant, but as a son of the same nature and the same power, so that everything that exists comes from the Father as the ultimate source but through the Son, whom he had eternally begotten equal to himself in all things and whom he begets without end.[96]

Christ, then, is the life-force in the sense of that vivifying force which allows all living things to reach their allotted end: the force of creation and perfection.

> And not only was there in this word of God the power of creating at his nod the entirety of things visible and invisible, but the life and vigour of all created things was also in him, so that through him every single thing would live by its own innate vigour and would protect itself, once the force of life was implanted, by continual procreation.[97]

In short, Erasmus believed that without the spirit of Christ we could not come to know God. Christ was the means of our knowing God.

'No one knows the Father as he really is except the Son and anyone to whom the Son has chosen to reveal him.'[98] The world and humanity itself was created through the mediating power of the Son for the express purpose of making God manifest. He asserted that God

> created all of this machinery of the world, and in it the minds of angels, and the human race, midway, as it were, between the angels and the beasts, so that from the wonders of creation and even from itself it might deduce the power, the holiness, and the goodness of its maker.[99]

The aim of our knowing God was that we would then love him and in that power of attraction lay our perfection.

> So the Father, truly almighty, created all things by means of his Son and word, And for this reason chiefly he first delivered his word, so that through it he might become known to us in speaking, as it were, and so that through it, having become known by means of our wonder at the beauty of the workings of the universe, he might wend his way into our affections.[100]

In his New Testament, Erasmus changed the preferred reading of Acts 17:25 from, 'he gives to all life and breath *and* all things', to 'he gives to all life and breath *through* all things'.[101] While this was based on a reading of the Greek original, it nevertheless accorded with his own beliefs about the way in which the Creator becomes manifest through his creation. The way to true eternal life is to advance towards knowledge of God. This knowledge is achieved by means of first knowing the creation. The things we can see lead to knowledge of the more real unchanging world of the unseen.

This Erasmian concept of the *Logos*, or Christ, provoked much criticism.[102] In the second edition of his New Testament version of the Gospel of John he used the Latin word *sermo* rather than the Vulgate *verbum* to translate the Greek *logos*. Despite the outcry this caused he stuck to his choice of term.[103] In an effort to calm his critics, he wrote a defence of his position: the *Apologia De in Principio Erat Sermo*. [104] In this he argued that *sermo* and *verbum* were used interchangeably by the Fathers, as well as in the Vulgate, to designate the Son of God.[105] It is clear, however, that Erasmus' own reason for using the term was not strictly philological.[106] He thought that *sermo* was a far more suitable way of translating the concept of *Logos*, or Christ. He said that

> the emanation of the divine word corresponds to our thinking. But when it is the eternal thought of the Father, it follows that the divine word is born in another manner, and in another manner produced than by assuming human nature. For what is born in a certain way, is brought forth in that way...By this third way God generated his Word, when he spoke by thinking within himself.[107]

Erasmus then added that 'he who thinks is in a certain manner talking to himself.'[108] Thus *sermo*, which connotes a dialogue, is more appropriate than *verbum*, which can simply mean a word. This element of Christ was the instrument of divine creation. The process of divine creation was one in which the Divinity engaged with itself in a dynamic way to produce the creation.

The two principal elements of Erasmus' concept of Christ, the human temporal and the divine eternal, come together in the function of imparting knowledge of the truth to humanity. The specific Incarnation of the *Logos* in Jesus of Nazareth and the eternal *Logos* both operated in this way. Understanding and knowledge were vital for faith, and faith was essential for perfection. In his *Paraphrase of Mark*, Erasmus depicts Christ as saying: 'he who does not believe does not understand'.[109] For Erasmus, Jesus' teaching was conducted verbally through the medium of the parable and also through the medium of his life itself. He thought that Jesus' choice of the parable, as the mode for his verbal instruction was most efficacious. 'Christ taught in parables that is in similes,...for this is the simplest and most suitable way of teaching uneducated men.'[110]

> The philosophers with their convoluted syllogisms enveloped their listeners in a cloud of darkness. The orators with their marvellous abundance of words twisted the minds of men. The Pharisees heaped up abstruse doctrines far removed from the people's grasp. But Jesus chose for himself that simplest kind of teaching which is a stranger to theatrical display.[111]

The value of the parable as a method of teaching was that it could be understood at whatever level of development the listener had achieved. Erasmus was always at pains to explain that Christ's teaching could only be understood gradually in stages and that it was detrimental to hurl it all headlong at someone who was not capable of understanding it.[112] Thus the parable was an excellent vehicle for the dissemination of truth because it could be understood on several levels depending on the state of the hearer.

The most potent form of parable, for him, was Christ's life itself. He believed that everything Christ did was consciously constructed to instruct us as to the method of perfection. When the apostles could not understand the parable of the sower Erasmus described Jesus chiding them thus: 'how then, will you understand all the other parables when nothing of what I say *or do* is without a deeper meaning?'[113] Thus, not just his words but also his actions were deeply allegorical. In Mark, when Jesus decided to warn the apostles about his forthcoming death and passion in case they would be overwhelmed by grief, Erasmus described him saying 'you must know and remember this...lest you think this is carried out by chance or without my knowledge and against my will, whereas everything is carried out according to God's plan'.[114] Erasmus then addressed himself to his readers and advised that they should take note

> not only of Jesus' words, but also how he conducted himself throughout his life. None of this was done by chance but rather by a divine plan and for the instruction of mankind, For there is nothing that does not have an exemplary character displaying godliness for us, nothing that does not reflect ancient prophecy or express a figure by which, in a dark manner, the law had designated Christ or a meaning forecasting future events.[115]

Throughout this paraphrase, in particular, Erasmus constantly read Jesus' actions allegorically.[116]

This idea that Jesus taught us by his word and he deeds is consistent with the fact that Erasmus believed that in order to know something properly it was necessary to grasp it with two senses.[117] His view of Christ as the perfect pedagogue is conditioned by this belief. When he wrote of the efficacy and appropriateness of parables he said that Jesus wanted his audience to both hear and see his words. They heard the parables and other sermons but they were also watching his actions. Erasmus believed that Jesus, the greatest teacher who ever lived, communicated to two senses of his listeners and that we, too, can learn from both his words and his actions. When he described Jesus talking to the apostles about their level of understanding he described him as saying that the apostles were allowed to know everything but that for those 'excluded from the inner circle, all is conducted in parables, whether I speak or act before them. For they do not have suitable ears or suitable eyes'.[118] He believed that 'just as Jesus words often take the form of a parable, so his actions, too, are frequently parables'.[119] The mystery of the cross had to be acted out by Christ in clear and simple events because it would not have been sufficient for the salvation of humanity if he had simply preached the truth in words.

Erasmus' objective was a very subtle and difficult one. He wanted to impart what he believed to be the true meaning of Christianity to all human beings. The contemporary church taught that we were saved by Jesus' death on the cross. Erasmus believed that the true meaning of the cross was that we had to save ourselves by dying to the world and our worldly bodies. For him, Christ, in one sense, was consciousness of the truth of human existence. It was like an inner voice that knew the way of salvation. We could only be perfected by acknowledging, and then following, this inner voice. In the colloquy, *The Godly Feast,* Erasmus has the character Timothy refer to this voice as 'the Master'.[120] The perfected human being would be led in all things by this 'Master'. The sacramental function of the church was thus severely limited by this concept. He did not see salvation depending on membership of any particular type of Christian church or sacramental system; he believed that the method of salvation was available to everyone in the scriptural accounts of Christ's life, death and teaching and also by means of the operation of the *Logos* in each human being and in creation. This is why he spent so many hours labouring to purify the Gospel text.

The Christian church for Erasmus was not necessarily the Church of Rome or Wittenberg or, indeed, anywhere else. His view of the true church of Christ is, perhaps, best elaborated in his letter to Paul Volz, which was written as the preface to the second edition of the *Enchiridion* in 1518.[121] This depiction of a true church or *ecclesia* shows how Erasmus' concept of the *Logos* or spirit of Christ worked in practice. In this letter he envisioned a Christian society or *ecclesia* as one that had Christ at its centre with three concentric circles running around it. The first circle was the domain of 'those who are nearest Christ - priests, bishops, cardinals, popes, and those whose business is to follow the Lamb wherever he may lead them.'[122] The second circle contained 'lay princes who with their armies and their laws serve Christ after their fashion'.[123] In the third circle are the common people, 'as the most earthy portion of this world, but not so earthy that they are not members of Christ's body just the same.[124] It is clear that Erasmus here was speaking allegorically. While this ideal state was a closed one, it was not, however, static. There was an organic progression taking place in it. At its centre Christ was like an everlasting fire who 'draws the order of priests close to him and as it were kindles them and purifies them from all earthly contagion'.[125] These in turn draw the next circle of princes to themselves.[126] The princes and rulers have a duty to those in the third circle to provide justice and peace.[127] He wrote that 'even in these there is a subdued image, a shadow, rather, of divine justice'.[128] However he said that it ought to 'shine forth much more distinctly and visibly and in greater purity, in the character and the legislation of priests. A reflection is one thing in polished steel and another in the glass of a mirror.'[129] In the third circle were the common people 'the most earthy part of this world'.[130] They, nevertheless, belonged to the body of Christ. The notion of a progressive dynamic was again evident when Erasmus described how in this body he who was at one time the foot could become the eye.[131] He argued that the members of the system would strive towards Christ each according to his or her own strength. He then drew an analogy between this system and the four elements. He likened the members of each circle to the different elements. Of these he said that Fire occupied the highest place and that, little by little, it 'sweeps all things into itself and transforms them so far as it may to its own nature. Water it evaporates and turns into air, and air it rarefies and transforms into itself.'[132] Thus in the Erasmian Christian system each of the elements of society would play its part in the continual progression of all towards the central target which was Christ. The spirit of Christ itself, like fire, had the power to transform all other entities into itself. The true Church, for him, was not about rules or ceremonies; its function was nothing less than the transformation of all the human earthly material elements of the human being into Christ.[133] In 1515 he wrote to Beatus Rhenanus that his name in Greek, *Makares,* or the blessed ones, was a title the ancient Greeks had ascribed to the Gods; 'Not of course that the honour of such a distinguished name belongs to any mortal, unless he is so engrafted in Christ that he is already as it were transfigured and made one with him, and so deserves to be given a share in his immortality and in that splendid name'.[134] Erasmus believed that it was possible for human beings to achieve Christ. This is much stronger than to say that they can become Christians. They can actually become Christ: the embodiment of the divine traits of truth and wisdom.

The difficulties posed for orthodoxy by Erasmus' particular emphasis of the human incorporation of Christ did not go unnoticed. Edward Lee, the English Franciscan, questioned a remark in *The Praise of Folly* about Plato's notion of holy madness where Erasmus had written that it was an experience, a foretaste, of future blessedness 'by which we shall be absorbed into God and shall live in future more in him than in ourselves'.[135] Erasmus defended this and asserted that he had said that

> the soul was absorbed by God because it is wholly rapt into him by love, and the soul exists more truly where it loves than where it gives life. For it is rapt in such a way that it does not disappear but is made perfect'.[136]

It was not surprising that Edward Lee took exception to this because it implied that humans in the process of perfecting their souls became part of God. At very least this was an extremely radical interpretation of the doctrine of the mystical body of Christ but taken at face value it would have been outright heresy to imply that an ordinary person could become God. What Lee was probably accusing Erasmus of was the kind of heterodox mysticism found in Meister Eckhardt and Tauler. This was no mere slip of the pen for Erasmus; It was a vital part of his *philosophia Christi* and he also explicitly espoused this idea in his annotation on the second chapter of Philippians in which he claimed that Christ as man, rather than as God, could be equal to God.[137]

For Erasmus, Christ was the way, the truth and the life. This rich concept was the spirit of God through which all truth and wisdom were made manifest to humanity. He believed that the truth of human existence was that although each human being was born into a condition of 'sin' they could nevertheless struggle to achieve a higher state. Christ by his teaching and through the symbolic example of his life was the most perfect teacher of the way of perfection. The eternal *Logos* and the specific manifestation of Christ in Jesus both ultimately functioned to enlighten us. Erasmus believed that if we achieved perfection we would then share in the nature and name of Christ. Thus Christ, for Erasmus, was in fact the essence of the spirit of perfection.

Chapter 2

Erasmus' Concept of the Human Being

The second foundation stone of Erasmus' view of the process of human perfection was his concept of the human being. Humanity, for him, was the centre of the divine creation, the entire purpose of which was to serve the process of human perfection. Human nature was both the basic raw material, and the starting point, of the process. Human perfection was achieved by a process of internal struggle that was built into our nature in such a way that it was, in fact, inseparable from it. We were actually designed for perfection. Thus, it was theoretically possible for each human being to partake of the process of perfection by simply coming to know him or herself in the most profound way. This was how we could access the divine *Logos.* In practice, however, Erasmus thought that this process was very difficult and that we, therefore, needed all the help we could get to reach this understanding. That was the function of Christ's incarnation as the man Jesus and the record of his teaching in Scripture. It was also the purpose of all of Erasmus' own writings.

The influence of Plato on Erasmus' concept of human nature is always discernable and this has consequences for his version of Christianity. He was a firm fan of Plato but he, nevertheless, believed that Christianity was *the* philosophy: the *philosophy of Christ* and that as such it had no need of any human philosophy as a bulwark to its theology. All human philosophical systems were, at best, a pale imitation of the pure truth of the Christian philosophy. His use of the term *philosophy of Christ,* which was a rather obscure patristic term, may also have been a humanist allusion to Ficino's *Theologia Platonica.* So, just as Ficino called

Plato's philosophy a theology, Erasmus called Christian theology a philosophy. Ficino thought that 'lawful philosophy is no different from true religion, and lawful religion is exactly the same as true philosophy'.[1] While Erasmus agreed with this he may have been gently chiding Ficino for emphasizing Plato rather than Christ. In fact they were both, in their different ways, uniting Christianity and Platonism. The starting point for both of them was human nature. Philosophy and religion, which they both saw as being the same thing, could only be verified in human experience.

The *Enchiridion* is the richest source for Erasmus' views on human nature and, although it was one of his earliest published works, dating from 1501, his description in it of the components and function of human nature remained unchanged throughout his life. It is telling that in 1518, when he had become very famous due to the success of his New Testament and several other writings, he reissued his *Enchiridion* but with no revisions or additions to the original text.[2] His aim in writing the *Enchiridion* was to give us a deeper understanding of our true nature. In the *Enchiridion* he first outlined a dual, and then a more elaborate triple, division of the human psyche.[3] Like Christ, each individual human was also a composite being. In the dual model Erasmus envisaged human nature as being composed of two basic elements: matter and spirit, or, body and soul.[4] He believed that these two elements were locked in mortal combat, but that, ultimately, this dissension concealed an underlying unity. He said 'such is their confused turmoil and strife that they seem to be distinct from one another, although they are one'.[5] The turmoil resulted from the two elements being pulled in opposite directions. In typically Platonic terms, he explained that:

> since the body is itself visible, it takes pleasure in things visible. Since it is mortal, it pursues temporal things; since it is heavy, it sinks downward. The soul, on the other hand, remembering its heavenly origin, strives upwards with all its might and struggles against its earthly burden. It despises those things that are seen, for it knows that they are transitory; it seeks those that are true and eternal. Being immortal, it loves things immortal; being heavenly, it loves that which is heavenly.[6]

This polarization was not by any means the natural condition of the elements. Erasmus believed that the discord had been produced by sin, which for him meant, above all, missing the target.[7] He said that

> it was not the fabled Prometheus who implanted this discord by mixing a particle from every living thing in our minds, nor was it instilled into us by our primitive nature, but sin corrupted that which had been well put together, sowing the poison of dissension between two harmonious entities.[8]

This is reminiscent of Plato's description of the disharmony that resulted from a state of injustice in which the elements of the psyche were dissenting among themselves.[9] Erasmus, like Plato, thought it was possible to overcome the state in which the elements of the human psyche were at war. This would result in the creation of a true, perfected human being in whom the disparate elements had been merged into a harmonious unity.[10] The perfected person was one who had hit the mark or achieved his or her true aim. Erasmus believed that this unity had existed at some previous time. He harked back either to a golden age or, arguably, a prior state, in which 'previously the mind commanded the body without any trouble, and the body obeyed the mind freely and willingly'.[11] Again there is a Platonic echo here of the theory that we come from the realm of the divine and can dimly remember it.[12] Erasmus was aware that this idea could be heretical when applied to the Christian soul because it potentially implied reincarnation but he nevertheless had a clear affection for it. He also referred to it in his work on letter-writing. There, he recommended that in order to support the concept of a divine element in the mind of the human being the reader should quote Plato's 'conception of souls descending to earth whose knowledge here is nothing but a dreamlike memory of what they once saw free from their bodies in the presence of God'.[13] What appealed to Erasmus in this idea was the notion that we could access and recognize the divine truth for ourselves however hazy our view of it might be.

The pursuit of perfection was no easy matter, however because it is clear, particularly from the *Enchiridion*, that Erasmus believed the ideal, harmonious order of spirit and flesh was usually reversed on earth. He argued that in the earthly realm 'the passions of the body strive to have dominion over reason, and reason is forced to accede to the wishes of the body'.[14] Then using an overtly Platonic example to explain this dissension he wrote:

> that is why the heart of man is not inaptly compared to a turbulent republic, which, since it is made up of different kinds of men, is subject to frequent upheavals and conflicts because of discordant interests, unless supreme power is vested in one man, who will ordain nothing that is not for the best welfare of the state.[15]

This is an allusion to Plato's *Republic*.[16] Erasmus went on to utilize this Platonic comparison of the human being as a microcosm of the macrocosmic state in order to expand on his view of the true nature of the distinct elements of human nature. He explained that the ruler, or king, in us is reason and that the 'king himself should obey none but the law, and the law corresponds to the idea of the good'.[17] Next to the king come 'certain physical but not brutish emotions, like filial respect for one's parents, love for one's brothers and sisters, kindness towards friends, compassion for the afflicted, fear of disgrace, desire for a good reputation, and similar qualities'.[18] Then come

> those passions of the soul that are further removed from the dictates of reason and are debased to the lowliness of beasts, consider these to be like the lowest dregs of the masses. Of this kind are lust, debauchery, envy, and similar disorders of the mind.[19]

Like Plato, Erasmus' description of the human psyche has obvious echoes of his description of the perfect society.[20] In the perfected individual all the elements are subject ultimately to the idea of the Good. In Erasmus' perfect Christian society or *ecclesia* all elements are subject to Christ. The one reflects and corresponds to the other. The rule of Christ and the rule of the idea of the Good are the same rule. In one image the terms are Christian while in the other they are Platonic. For Erasmus all truth was the truth of Christ and, among the ancients, Plato came closest to the *philosophy of Christ*.

Having outlined his view of the dual nature of the human being, Erasmus went on to elaborate on this by presenting his concept of the threefold division of human being.[21] The tripartite concept of the human being had been condemned by the ninth-century council of Constantinople and by most of the Church Fathers. Moreover, the medieval Fourth Lateran Council had also upheld a dual division of human nature. Thus, Erasmus clearly believed this was an important point because he was willing to risk censure by proposing it. The heretical tripartite division was a Platonic concept that had also been propounded by the early church father, Origen, some of whose views had been declared heretical. Erasmus was careful to argue that in proposing a tripartite division of the human being he was not only following the partly heterodox Origen but also the completely orthodox St Paul. Moreover, he also attempted to protect himself by arguing that Plato's anthropology was, in fact, the same as St Paul's although they had used different words to describe the elements of the psyche.[22] His declared reason for portraying the tripartite human being was that it would render the reader 'even more enlightened and self-aware' than the dual concept of human nature had.[23] The three parts were the flesh, the spirit and between them the soul. He declared that he agreed with Origen's view that the body or the flesh is the 'lowest part of us, in which, through the fault of our first parents, the cunning serpent has inscribed the law of sin, and by which we are incited to base actions and once vanquished, joined to the devil.'[24] The spirit was that part

> by which we reproduce a likeness of the divine nature, in which the supreme maker has engraved with his finger, that is, his Spirit, the eternal law of goodness, drawn from the archetype of his own mind, by which we are glued to God and are made one with him.[25]

Then he proposed the third part: the soul. He believed that the soul was that part which lay in the middle between the other two and was 'capable of sensations and natural movements'.[26] The soul was of vital importance to the process of salvation. It was there that the struggle for perfection took place. He described this struggle thus:

> as in a republic rent by factions, the soul cannot but attach itself to one of the two sides; solicited on this side and on that, it is free to incline to whichever direction it wishes. If it renounces the flesh and goes over to the side of the spirit, it will itself become spiritual, but if it abandons itself to the cupidities of the flesh, it will degenerate into the body.[27]

Erasmus saw the inner workings of the human psyche as a duality of spirit and flesh, which, in truly Platonic terms, were fused together in the soul. This created a dynamic involving three forces, which were positive, negative and neutral: the spirit being positive, the body was negative and the soul was perceived as the area of neutrality. He wrote:

> the spirit makes us gods, the flesh makes us brute animals, the soul constitutes us as human beings. The spirit makes us religious, the flesh irreligious, the soul neither the one nor the other. The spirit seeks heavenly things, the flesh seeks pleasure, the soul what is necessary. The spirit elevates us to heaven, the flesh drags us down to hell, the soul has no charge imputed to it. Whatever is carnal is base, whatever is spiritual is perfect, whatever belongs to the soul as life-giving element is in between and indifferent.[28]

Given the arguable heterodoxy of this tripartite division of the human being and its dynamic, Erasmus insisted on elaborating it because he believed that it, rather than the dual division, was the deeper reality of the human psyche. The dual division was easier for us to understand and was adequate at a certain level of development but more profound self-knowledge required consciousness of a triple inner division. The fundamental law of human nature for Erasmus was this continuum of positive, negative and neutral forces. Crucially, this was not a fixed system: it was dynamic. The body and the spirit were fixed elements but they exercised a pull in opposite directions. The soul was the neutral area where free choice operated. It could unite with the flesh or with the spirit and so be changed into whichever it chose. It could not, however, remain neutral. There was some kind of necessity for it to transform upwards or downwards. It was the area of transformation and this was the dynamic of perfection. The soul was also the area where consciousness resided. Erasmus suggested that the other two parts could only be expressed through the soul. They were given individual human expression and brought into consciousness when the soul adhered to them. The brute was made manifest, or the divine was made manifest in the area of the soul. Thus perfection involved increased consciousness of the divine realm of the unseen realities as the grip of the material world on the soul was lessened.

The perfecting transformation of the human being by means of the dynamic struggle between spirit and flesh was an onerous one and Erasmus thought it unlikely that anyone could reach a state of perfect equilibrium, in which the higher part permanently ruled the brutish part, while still living on earth. He wrote: 'we are not so perfect as never to admit any sin (I cannot say whether or not this is granted to any mortal in his lifetime)'.[29] As we have seen, even Christ, according to Erasmus' interpretation of the agony in Gethsemane, had to struggle with the effects of human weakness right up to the time of his death.[30] Only someone who was willing to take on relentless and almost crippling toil could approach perfection. In typically syncretistic mode he several times interpreted the myth of the labours of Hercules as being an allegory for this process. When writing in the *Enchiridion* about the struggles of St Paul he compared them to those of Hercules and said that

> when all other vices have been subdued, the sole vice of vainglory is still lurking even in the midst of virtue, like the hydra that attacked Hercules, an indestructible monster that reproduces itself from its own wounds, which at the very end, after enduring every toil, we can barely defeat.[31]

In a spirit of hope, however, he then quoted the maxim: "relentless labour masters all".[32] He also wrote quite a lengthy exposition of the Herculean myth in his *Adages* where he argued that Hercules' labours were of two kinds.[33] First, there were those exertions required by a great task and, secondly, those that 'bring very great blessings to other people, but almost no return to the man who undertakes them, except a little reputation and a great deal of ill-will'.[34] Erasmus was here explicitly identifying his own work of compiling adages as belonging to the second category. In this work, as in all of his other literary output, his purpose was the same: he wanted to contribute to the knowledge necessary for the perfection of humankind. His description of the type of sacrifices this work demanded invokes the question of what possessed him to take on this task.[35] He acknowledged that anyone who was not a 'real Hercules in mind, able to do and suffer anything for the sake of serving others' would not be willing to undertake it. Moreover, he clearly saw this work as being part of the process of his own perfection. He said that it was proof of a 'lofty and unconquerable mind' if, despite the onerousness of the task and the envy of others, a person strove nonetheless for immortal fame:

> to think what you can do for others no matter how great the cost to yourself, and to reckon it the finest and greatest reward of virtue if you can promote the greatest happiness of the greatest number,

> imitating in that respect, as far as any mortal can, the immortal deity.[36]

He believed that this kind of gruelling toil was a necessary part of the struggle. Quoting Cicero he said that '*aerumna*' or afflictions 'is the very gloomy name which our forefathers gave to labours from which there was no escaping, even in the case of a god'.[37] He asserted in the *Enchiridion* that the path to salvation, which entailed these labours, was a narrow one over which few people walked but that Christ himself had walked it. For him the labours of Hercules were, in fact, analogous to the suffering and crucifixion of Christ. In his work on writing letters Erasmus demonstrated that he saw the same struggle depicted allegorically in both the Iliad and the Odyssey. He said that the difficulties encountered by Ulysses in the Odyssey and the Iliad were Homer's way of allegorizing the struggle for perfection.[38] He argued that in these works Homer's purpose was to show us that 'the path to virtue is difficult and lies through the hardest toil'.[39] He then linked this back to Hercules and went on to say that the stories about Hercules had the same purpose. 'Hercules, after enduring so many labours, suffered his body to be consumed by fire and was carried off into the company of the gods.'[40] This meant that 'immortality was only the lot of those who had spent their whole life in honourable labours and unquenchable ardour for virtue, and had waged war tirelessly upon the monstrous apparitions of all vices'.[41] We, in imitation of Christ, had to strive to the limit of our powers and beyond, in order to overcome temptation and achieve perfection by means of an internal personal struggle. Then, having achieved an initial level of knowledge, there was an onus on us to participate in the divine work of helping our fellow human beings. There is a suggestion here that the work of being of service to others is the milieu in which we are tested and forged anew.

In the *Enchiridion* Erasmus described the struggle against temptation in some detail. He compared this process, in which the soul was torn apart by passions, to Virgil's description of Proteus who 'in wondrous transformation ...becomes Fire and hideous beast and flowing stream until he returns to his original form'.[42] Throughout this blind and all-encompassing struggle we had to hold fast to the soul even if we could not control it. Indeed, Erasmus suggested that holding on was all we were capable of at this point. He quoted Virgil again 'the more new forms and shapes you see him take, the more draw tight the tautened bonds'.[43] He then reinforced his point by an allegorical interpretation of the story of Jacob from the Old Testament. He urged the reader to be like Jacob and 'press on steadfastly in this nocturnal struggle until the dawn of divine help will shine upon you, and say "I shall not let you go until you give me your blessing"'.[44] If we struggled relentlessly in the dark we would, of necessity, be rewarded with an immediate angelic blessing. He argued that 'after conquering temptation man is always given a surplus of divine grace so that he will be much more fortified for the next attack of the enemy'.[45] He illustrated this by explaining that having struggled, Jacob was struck in the thighbone and began to limp on one leg, which meant that the passion of the flesh had so died out in him that he was now supported by the right leg, or the spirit.[46] Moreover, he was then re-named Israel, which Erasmus, after the fashion of Jerome, said meant 'taste and see how sweet is the Lord'.[47]

For Erasmus, overcoming a temptation was accomplished by understanding and experiencing the truth or reality of one's own nature. A person who had done this was one who had managed to hold on while his or her soul changed tumultuously into phantasms until the peace and calm of the only truth, that is the spiritual truth, dawned on them. What the individual in question held on to was consciousness of their true self despite the ravages of passion. By knowing that they were not a single entity they could at least try not to identify with their brute part. As a practical exercise in this method of experiencing the truth Erasmus suggested to the reader that in order to overcome the passion of anger it would be useful to 'make it a point, when you are mentally sound yourself, to look at the face of a man in a fit of anger, or when you are the victim of anger, look at yourself in the mirror'.[48] He concluded that the image such a person would see would hardly be human at all.[49] What he was advocating was that when an individual was in a state of reason they should observe in another person what it was like to be in a state where base passions were in control. In doing this, the observer would realize that at that time the impassioned person was hardly human because they had given themselves over to their brutish side alone. Erasmus also thought that by watching oneself it was possible to separate consciousness from unconscious reaction and observe through the eyes of reason the brutishness of one's own anger. For him the true human being was one who had made a conscious decision in his or her soul to subjugate the flesh to the spirit. Erasmus believed that in order to overcome base instincts, it was not good enough simply to try to keep control of one's passions as the church advocated, but instead, it was necessary to observe oneself and others when they were out of the control of reason. He believed quite simply that an attempt at self-control without self-consciousness would not work. He was careful to emphasize that we must hold on in the dark and in the most violent circumstances to the idea of truth, or reality, or the spirit and that in this way the storm would necessarily be weathered and the victim would be strengthened on account of it. This was the function of faith for Erasmus. If a person was not shaken by the phantasms of the passions then, when they had receded, he or she could see them for what they were and this consciousness would render them less powerful in the future. This was how grace worked in practice. Thus, rather than assuming that a person could control their passions by some immediate exercising of will, Erasmus observed and understood that this was not always possible. This did not in any way negate his belief in the freedom of the will but he did understand how little freedom we have in fact. The free choosing of the good was an absolutely necessary prerequisite for its achievement. He argued that anyone who was seized by the madness of anger, who could not repress it but who nevertheless admitted that they were not sane at that moment was well on the way to sanity.[50] If a person took the first step they, like Jacob, would be given angelic help, which would remind them to walk on the right path in the future. Erasmus' morality was never a question of 'thou shalt not' but rather it was ' thou shalt be conscious'. In this way, crucially, sin and even the flesh itself became an occasion of perfection.

This concept of the mechanism of perfection meant Erasmus believed that ignorance of the true nature of existence and, particularly, of one's own being was the first and principle obstacle to human perfection. In the *Enchiridion*, where he outlined his general rules of true Christianity, the first of these was against the 'evil of ignorance'.[51] He thought that the majority of people lived in a state in which 'a cloud of ignorance ... obscures the judgment of reason'.[52] He argued that there were several reasons for this:

> First, the pure light of the divine countenance, which the creator had instilled in us, was partially obscured by the sin of our first parents. Then faulty upbringing, evil companionship, perverse desires, the darkness of vice, and the habit of sin have so covered it over with mildew that only the barest traces of the laws divinely engraved in us are visible.[53]

Attempting to overcome this human blindness was the first stage in perfection.[54] The second stage in the process was overcoming the dictates of the flesh because they 'influenced the passions in such a way that even if we recognize what is best, we love the very opposite'.[55] The third stage was defeating weakness which he believed 'causes us to give in to weariness or temptation and thus abandon virtue once we have acquired it'.[56] Clearly, these three stages relate to the three different parts of the human being as Erasmus envisaged them: the spirit the flesh and the soul. The first, blindness, relates to the spiritual part that knows the law of goodness. The second is related to the flesh that obscures our view of reality. The third relates to the soul in which will resides. Thus, in order to attain perfection each part of the human being had to be free to operate properly within its own sphere and not interfere with the working of the other parts because each human element had its own role in perfection. The perfected human being would, therefore, be one in which all of the elements operated in a kind of equilibrium. In a later section of the *Enchiridion*, Erasmus, while elaborating on St Paul's description of the mystical body of Christ, described this harmonious condition thus:

> God has so harmonized the parts of the body that he gave greater dignity to that which was inferior so that there would not be discord in the body but that the members would have equal care for one another...You are the body of Christ and members each in a different fashion.[57]

When this is applied to the individual human being it explains the apparently stronger pull exerted by the fleshly element. Erasmus believed that because this element was, in fact, inferior to the others God had consciously created it stronger in order that equilibrium would be possible.[58] Again this shows the importance for him of the dynamic of struggle or conflict in the perfection process because if the superior spiritual element were stronger in the human being then it would easily overcome the flesh without the necessity for struggle.

The strength of the flesh together with the element of free will, of course, meant that perfection was not necessarily assured. One had to choose the Good and struggle always to keep it because without struggle the soul would incline towards the fleshly element, which, like gravity, would pull it downwards. Our reason, which allows us access to the innate idea of the Good, is the countervailing force to this degeneration. Consciousness of the self was the essential requirement for the attainment of wisdom and this in turn would lead to perfection. He said: 'the beginning of wisdom is to know oneself'.[59] Wisdom, for Erasmus, was also interchangeable with the concept of Christ because he believed that Christ was not only the author of wisdom but that he actually was 'wisdom itself'.[60] Thus, in order to achieve Christ, we had first to come to know ourselves. Erasmus dedicated a whole section of his *Adages* to this maxim.[61] He introduced this section by asserting that the exhortation to 'know thyself' was 'the most famous of all utterances of wise men'.[62] He related this saying to the adage *In Se Decendere*: 'To Venture Down into Oneself'. He explained that 'to venture down into oneself is for a man to contemplate his own faults'. This was a reference 'to those cavernous recesses of the human heart, which Momus thought should have been supplied with windows'.[63] The onerous nature of this task meant that people were very reluctant to participate in it. He found evidence for this in the saying of Persius that 'none, none dare venture down into themselves. They watch the wallet hanging on the back of him that walks before.'[64] Despite this, however, Erasmus believed that each human being had to overcome this reticence because the process of self-knowledge ultimately contained the remedy for 'the source of all life's troubles'.[65] This was his main aim in writing the *Enchiridion.* It was his way of trying to enable his fellow humans to achieve this self-knowledge. In its opening pages he addressed the reader thus:

> since you have entered into war with yourself, and since your greatest hope of victory lies in knowing yourself as fully as possible, I shall set before you a kind of likeness of yourself, as in a painting, so that you may have a clear knowledge of what you are skin-deep.[66]

He warned the reader that it was foolish to imagine they already possessed this knowledge. He said:

> let no one rashly lay claim to possessing such wisdom that he is sufficiently known to himself. I doubt whether anyone has an accurate knowledge of his own body, and are we to think that anyone at all will be conscious of his own state of mind?[67]

Here he made it clear that he was referring to a very profound state of consciousness of the self. Again, in his *Adages,* Erasmus highlighted the fact that when Laertius was asked what was the most difficult thing for a person to do; he replied that it was to know oneself.[68] Plato, too, acknowledged the importance of this maxim and Erasmus recounted the prominence he had given it when he had said it was inscribed on the front doors of the famous temple at Delphi.[69] Here too, Erasmus' emphasis was on the difficulty of the task. He quoted the *Phaedrus* in which even the divine Plato said of himself: 'I cannot yet achieve the self-knowledge of the Delphian inscription'.[70] Nonetheless, Erasmus believed that 'the only road to happiness is first to know yourself and then not to act in anything according to the passions but in all things according to the judgment of reason'.[71]

Blindness and ignorance were not just an individual problem for Erasmus; he believed that they also existed on a grand-scale. The central message of his satirical masterpiece, the *Praise of Folly,* is that the entire world is blind to the truth and that consequently true Christianity, which of necessity embodies the truth, is therefore in opposition to the world. Thus, what is perceived as folly by the world is, in fact, often the highest reality and, conversely, worldly wisdom is in fact folly. The most profound example of this for Erasmus was the crucifixion of Christ, which to worldly eyes was an act of supreme folly, but in truth it was an expression of the highest wisdom. One of his main sources for this notion was, of course, St Paul.[72] In the *Enchiridion,* he paraphrased Paul and said 'there is no greater stupidity than earthly wisdom, which one must unlearn if he truly wishes to be wise'.[73] He found precisely the same notion in the writings of the ancients most notably in Plato's myth of the cave.[74] In this famous section of the *Republic,* Plato allegorised ordinary unenlightened existence when he depicted imprisoned and deluded cave dwellers who believed that the shadows cast on their wall, of events happening in the world outside the cave, were the only reality. Erasmus interpreted this in several of his writings as meaning that the world was blind to the truth.[75] In juxtaposition to worldly wisdom, the true philosopher, for Erasmus, was one who loved the things that the common herd ridiculed.[76] His role was to wake people from their state of ignorance and denial in order that they could then begin to seek the Good. Erasmus approved of the saying of Socrates that 'virtue is simply the knowledge of what is to be sought after and what avoided'.[77] He said that this is not to say that Socrates 'did not see the distinction between the knowledge and the love of good'.[78] There is, however, a strong suggestion that the former would necessarily lead to the latter. Erasmus explained that in his discussion with Protagoras, Socrates 'proves that knowledge has so great an importance in all virtue that sins arise solely from false opinions'.[79] He thought that if we could understand the true nature of reality as expressed in Scripture then we would also understand that it was in our best interests to live in accordance with the precepts of Christ. For him, there was no need for blind belief. True religious belief was dependent on, and a consequence of, proper understanding. In his *Paraphrase on Mark* he argued that 'he who does not believe does not understand'. Consequently, proper understanding, which starts with self-knowledge, was essential. This was why Erasmus took such a great interest in the education of children. He argued:

> it should be the chief care of Christians that from the cradle onwards, amidst the blandishments of nurses and the kisses of parents, under the tutelage of their teachers children should imbibe convictions worthy of Christ, because nothing sinks more deeply into the mind or adheres to it more tenaciously than that which is instilled in it in early years.[80].

Nevertheless he believed that it was never too late to engage in this practice. He said:

> There is no time of life when this rule should no be put in to practice so that all vulgar errors may be pulled out of the mind by the roots and salutary opinions be put in their place and so reinforced that nothing will be able to dislodge them.[81]

Thus, just as he believed that wisdom and Christ were

interchangeable, so too he thought that wisdom and virtue were synonymous. He wrote: 'the purest virtue, perfect in every respect, is called wisdom' by both Stoics and Christians.[82] The perfected human being, therefore, would be a person who had achieved a state of perfect knowledge and understanding of all things: a true philosopher.

The starting point was, of course, the self. In the *Enchiridion* he argued that his description of the human being should be used as a guide to understanding the invisible ineffable mysteries and even the celestial realm. He wrote; 'perfect piety is the attempt to progress always from visible things, which are usually imperfect or indifferent, to invisible, *according to the division of man discussed earlier'*.[83] In short, we can understand our higher spiritual nature by observing our material nature and through observation of our total being we can, in turn, understand the higher mysteries, which are reflected in it. Erasmus, in true Renaissance fashion, placed great emphasis on this idea that the human being is a microcosm reflecting the macrocosm of the universe. He believed that ignorance of the pre-eminence of the invisible eternal reality was a serious evil. He wrote: 'this precept is most pertinent to our discussion since it is through neglect or ignorance of it that most Christians are superstitious rather than pious, and except for the name of Christ differ hardly at all from superstitious pagans'.[84] Erasmus followed this statement with a passage that set out the precise nature of his concept that visible reality was merely a reflection of the higher metaphysical true reality. He then moved from his concept of the human being, as a reflection of both the visible and the invisible worlds, to its corollary, in which the entire visible world was a diagram of the human psyche and thus an aid to the knowledge necessary for perfection. He described it thus:

> Let us imagine, therefore, two worlds, the one merely intelligible, the other visible. The intelligible, which may also be called the angelic, is the one in which God dwells with the blessed spirits, while the visible world comprises the celestial spheres and all that is contained therein. Then there is man, who constitutes, as it were, a third world, participating in the other two, in the visible world through the body, and in the invisible through the soul.[85]

This corresponds to the Erasmian tri-partite division of the human being.[86] The body corresponds to the visible world, the spirit to the angelic or divine, and the soul, which Erasmus believed to be that element that makes us human, lying between the two, corresponds to humankind in the macrocosmic image. The significance of this version of reality, for Erasmus, was that it afforded us the opportunity to understand the higher truth of our existence and purpose. He insisted that we should not identify with the physical world but should 'relate by a fitting comparison everything that occurs to the senses either to the angelic world or, in more practical terms, to morals and to that part of man that corresponds to the angelic'.[87] He gave some examples of this and explained that

> what the visible sun is here in the visible world the divine mind is in the intelligible world and in that part of you related to it, namely, the spirit. What the moon is here is in that world the assembly of angels and blessed spirits, which they call the church triumphant, and in you is the spirit. Whatever influence the upper world has over the earth, which lies beneath it. God exercises this same influence over your soul.[88]

Erasmus argued that by using the visible world and our visible part to learn about the invisible realm 'whatever offers itself to the senses will become for you an occasion for the practice of piety'.[89] Again, he was clearly alluding to the Platonic cave myth when he said 'be so convinced of the existence of invisible things that those things that are seen become but mere shadows, which present to the eye only a faint image of invisible realities'.[90] This was the method by which we could follow the sage and attain true self-knowledge. Erasmus said 'whatever we perceive in the body must be understood to exist also in the soul'.[91] Clearly, he believed that perception began in the physical realm and only then moved on to the more real spiritual world. There is a great emphasis on personal verification of truth in this method. He put it thus:

> The road to the spiritual and perfect life consists in gradually accustoming ourselves to be weaned from those things that do not really exist but appear partly to be what they are not, such as base pleasure or worldly honour, and are partly in a state of flux, hastening to return to nothing, and let ourselves be carried away to things that are real, eternal, unchangeable, and authentic.[92]

This has distinct echoes of his definition of true philosophy in which he agreed with Plato that 'philosophy is nothing but a meditation on death' and that it 'withdraws the mind from the physical and coarse things to those that are eternal and intelligible'.[93] This then is the method of perfection contained in highest example of true philosophy for him, which, of course, was the *philosophy of Christ*. The method of perfection entailed a broadening consciousness of the self and the world and all of its values and honours because dawning consciousness would show these to be unreal ephemera. The perfected individual would then edge closer and closer to union with the divine spirit of God. Erasmus was not prescribing a set of beliefs that the reader was obliged to accept, but rather, a method by which the reader could come to experience and know the Truth.

Erasmus believed that this state of wisdom or religious perfection was, in fact, a state of true humanity. This is where his humanism and his Christianity meet. As a committed Christian, he believed that the purpose of our life was to struggle for perfection in the religious sense; as a humanist, he believed that we have to struggle to reach a state of full humanity. For him the state of religious perfection and the condition of full humanity are one and the same. The goal of perfection is the same goal in both instances and the struggle is the same struggle. We are not simply born into a state of true or perfect humanity. This is something that can only be achieved by dint of very onerous struggle. In the introduction to *De Pueris Instituendis* he expressed it clearly thus: 'man certainly is not born, but made man. Primitive man, living a lawless, unschooled, promiscuous life in the woods, was not human, but rather a wild animal. It is reason which defines our humanity.'[94] To drive home his point he then quoted Diogenes who, while walking through a crowded place one day, said; "I am looking for a man". Erasmus explained that Diogenes was 'aware, of course, of the crowd around him, but to him it was nothing more than a herd of animals, not a gathering of human beings'.[95] He went on to say:

> it is beyond argument that a man who has never been instructed in philosophy or in any branch of learning is a creature quite inferior to the brute animals. Animals only follow their natural instincts; but man, unless he has experienced the influence of learning and philosophy, is at the mercy of impulses that are worse than those of a wild beast.[96]

We are born with the potential to become, at one extreme, something wonderful: a fully developed human being, or, at the other extreme, something horrific: a degenerate being capable of great evil. In order to become fully and perfectly human, the right kind of education was essential. He said: 'birth does not create a man, but only something capable of having man's nature. What is born is the raw material, so to speak, education gives it shape'.[97] This education was not the usual formal training of ordinary school. He argued that the best possible educational program should include not only 'learning' but also 'philosophy'. By this, of course he meant the *philosophy of Christ.* He did not believe that this was some mysterious and unintelligible religion accessible only to highly trained theologians. Instead he believed it was a way of showing the true nature of existence to all of us. Moreover, because he thought this truth was also innate in us he believed that it would therefore have a special resonance within the human psyche. In the *Paraclesis,* where he first explicitly defined the term *philosophy of Christ,* he said: 'this philosophy easily penetrates into the minds of all, an action in especial accord with human nature'.[98] He went on specifically to equate the process of Christian perfection with the perfection of human nature when he asked 'what else is the *philosophy of Christ,* which he himself calls a rebirth, than the restoration of human nature originally well formed?'[99] In his *Paraphrase on Romans* he said that there is no one of any race who is without the law of God.[100] We all have the truth within ourselves. The human being, therefore, is elevated to the central position in the all-important process of perfection. Thus the works of people in the past who were striving for the goal of perfection and who had access to the truth by virtue of their own humanity became very important instruments for Erasmus. He believed that the best classical writings supported and enhanced Scriptural studies.

Erasmus's greatest contribution to the humanist and, more importantly, the Christian traditions was precisely this fusion of human and Christian. The universality of this quest was based on the fact that he believed that all human nature was designed in such a way that people were naturally driven into the struggle for perfection unless thwarted by the distractions of the world or the flesh. His basis for this was essentially Epicurean. He believed that we were designed to seek happiness above all and that the things that engendered ultimate happiness were also those that led to perfection.[101] Thus if only we could see clearly what would lead to happiness then this basic drive would also ensure that the goal of perfection was pursued. He presented the reasoning for this in the *Enchiridion* where he argued that if we were to ignore the illusions of the flesh it would be clear that 'the way of Christ is not only the only one that leads to happiness, but even without considering the reward it is the most advantageous one to follow'.[102] He thought that since mortal life was full of sorrow and strife anyway and there was no way of avoiding it, it was therefore better to accept this and engage in the struggle for the highest goal of perfection. He argued that we are designed in such a way that there is no real lasting happiness or peace outside of the struggle for perfection: 'no pleasure is lacking when there is a tranquil conscience. But no misery is absent when an unhappy conscience torments us. These must be regarded as matters of absolute certitude.'[103] In short, he believed that the intrinsic design of the human psyche tends towards the struggle for perfection because what makes us happy, in the ultimate sense of the term, also makes us good. This led him to the belief that people who lived prior to Christ had also struggled for, and indeed achieved, a measure of perfection.

He thought that, in particular, Plato and his followers in their notions of the idea of the Good and the struggle for virtue were very close to the *philosophy of Christ.* He argued that

> although they did not have certain knowledge of God and were not inspired by the hope of attaining the kingdom of heaven or moved by God's spirit, nonetheless, they thought intently about the nature of virtue with whatever strength their mortal minds possessed, and delved deeply and subtly into so many things, and showed forth in their deeds many examples of virtuous accomplishments, (or, if you prefer, the appearance of virtuous accomplishments).[104]

The complexity of this statement is testimony to the fact that Erasmus had to take great care when he expressed his view that some of the ancients had achieved a state of virtue. The question of the salvation of pagans was a thorny one for the Renaissance scholar and there was no orthodox way of solving it. Erasmus' view of human nature and the process of perfection led him to hold views that would not have had the approval of the Church. While he did not intend to harm the authority of the Church in any way, his views in this matter, as we have seen, tended to minimize the role of the Church in the process of salvation. Erasmus clearly believed that people before Christ had achieved perfection. He thought that Socrates, for instance, had achieved such a state and that as a proof of this he exhibited virtue in his way of life. He said that Socrates was 'not only the wisest of philosophers but also the most incorruptible man of all time'.[105] What he valued in Socrates was that he had 'brought down philosophy from the contemplation of natural phenomena into the midst of human life' and diverted all study 'to the consideration of morals'.[106] Erasmus was never very interested in the study of natural phenomena, or what we would call science. His chosen study was the human being and how the truth of Christ could be incorporated and operate through each of us. His most famous syncretic statement appeared in his colloquy *The Godly Feast* in which Socrates is effectively canonized.[107] Cicero, too, is singled out for the highest praise in the same work. He wrote to his friend Jacob de Voecht that he found himself thinking as he read Cicero,

> what justice, what purity, what sincerity, what truth in his rules for living! All is in harmony with nature'...'How many lessons he teaches, and how like a saint - almost a deity! - on how we should do good to all men even without reward, on the maintenance of friendship, on the immortality of the soul.[108]

Erasmus found a scriptural source for this in St Paul. In his own *Paraphrase on Romans* he argued that God approved the meritorious actions of non-Christians, even those who had never heard of the Law of Moses:

> for when the races foreign to the law of Moses do of their own accord under the guidance of nature the things which are ordered by the law even though they are instructed by no prescription of the Mosaic law, they themselves are a law unto themselves because they express the substance of the law, engraved not on tablets but on their own minds. Whatever among them is usually done before a tribunal of justice is done in their hearts; your conscience gives testimony for or against you, and your thoughts contending with one another, alternately accuse and defend you.[109]

This idea is also apparent in his treatise on the education of children where he said that three things were needed for the perfection of human happiness: these were 'nature, method, and practice'.[110] He defined nature as 'man's innate capacity and inclination for the good'.[111] The method was to engage in a process of proper education. By practice, he meant 'the exercise of a disposition which has been implanted by nature and moulded by method'.[112] In sum, he said that 'nature is realized only through method, and practice, unless it is guided by the principles of method, is open to numerous errors and pitfalls'.[113] Since, for Erasmus, the perfection of human nature was also Christian perfection, at all stages in the process Christ is essential. The learning he referred to was, of course, the truth of Christ and the practice was living a virtuous life according to the principles of Christ. For him, the New Testament was the essential and best guide to the truth. Its effectiveness, however, was absolutely dependent on the effort an individual made to understand its precepts and, more importantly, practice them. When he produced his new edition of the Gospels in 1516, he called it the *Novum Instrumentum*. Like his *Enchiridion* the title portrays the fact that he saw it as an instrument or tool rather than simply a record of religious significance.[114] His purpose in writing was always to provide whatever help he could to the aspiring Christian who wanted to effect a transformation of his or her nature.

In relation to this of transformation, there was an important difference between Erasmus and his two most influential sources: Platonic philosophy and Christian Scripture. Like the Platonists and orthodox Christians, he certainly believed that the spirit was superior to the flesh and that therefore the flesh should be subjected to the higher power of spirit. Unlike them, however, he thought the flesh was nevertheless crucial in the process of perfection.[115] The clearest exposition of this view is again to be found in the *Enchiridion* where it is interwoven seamlessly with a more orthodox Christian Platonism. In this work he quoted the arguments of the Stoics and Peripatetics to highlight what he called two 'slightly different views' on the function of the flesh in perfection.[116] Having described 'the diversity of the passions' which, for him, were expressions of the flesh he said:

> the Stoics believe that when you have used as guides those passions that are awakened most directly by the senses and have arrived at

> the point of being able to judge and discriminate what is to be sought after and what avoided, then they should be abandoned altogether. From then on not only are they useless for the attaining of wisdom, but even detrimental. For this reason they wish that the perfect wise man should be free of such promptings as if they were diseases of the mind.[117]

On the other hand, he explained that

> the Peripatetics teach that the passions are not to be eradicated, but subdued. They consider them to be of some use, imparted to us by nature as incentives and inducements to virtue, such as anger as an incentive to courage, or envy to industry and so with the rest.[118]

What he was showing here is that while both of these schools thought the passions played an important role in the struggle for perfection they differed on the whether the passions could ever be annihilated and if true perfection could be achieved in this life. As we have seen, Erasmus inclined towards the view that we could not actually achieve a state of ultimate perfection on earth. He also touched on this point again a few pages on in the *Enchiridion*. Having interpreted the biblical account of Abraham and Sara allegorically as meaning that Abraham had reached a state of equilibrium with his flesh as represented by Sara he exclaimed: 'O blessed old age of those in whom the earthly man is already so dead that it presents no trouble to the spirit'.[119] He went on to qualify this, nevertheless, and wrote: 'I for my part should not venture to assert that such perfect concord in all matters can be granted to a man in this life. *Perhaps it would not even be advantageous*'.[120] What Erasmus thought was that a permanent state of equilibrium was not attainable on earth and moreover that the flesh actually played an important part in the human struggle for perfection until death. This is clear also in his *Praise of Folly*, where he questioned the validity of the Stoic desire for the eradication of all passions, and he made Folly say that 'these emotions not only act as guides to those hastening towards the haven of wisdom, but also wherever virtue is put into practice they are always present to act like spurs and goads as incentives to good deeds'.[121] He then underlined the point by criticizing the 'double-dyed' Stoic, Seneca, who, he said, striped the wise person of every emotion and 'leaves nothing at all of the man, and has to "fabricate" in his place a new sort of god who never was and never will be in existence anywhere'.[122] Erasmus believed that while it was possible to progress towards perfection on earth, this was not a state that coincided with the Stoic state of wisdom.[123]The Erasmian state of perfection on earth was was one in which the flesh had been subdued but, crucially, not annihilated. The tension between flesh and spirit continued until death but in this perfect state the higher principle always ruled behaviour. Ultimate perfection, in which the flesh was permanently subdued, was only possible after death when we would come face to face with the Deity.

In defence of his emphasis on the importance of the flesh to his concept of the human being, Erasmus went as far as to take issue with the words of Christ himself, as reported in the *Gospel of John*. According to this account Christ had said: 'the flesh is of no profit, it is the spirit that gives life'.[124] Erasmus questioned this and argued: 'I would have had scruples to say: "It is of no profit", it would have been sufficient to say: "it is of some profit, but the spirit is much more profitable". But Truth itself said: "It is of no profit".'[125] Clearly, Erasmus had qualms about the pronouncement of 'Truth', or Christ, here. He then showed why he took issue with the reported words of Christ himself when he went on to argue: 'The flesh is useful in this sense, that it leads our weakness to the spirit by degrees'.[126] Erasmus knew how unacceptable it was to contradict Christ in this way but the point was too important to him to pass over in silence. He compensated for this, however, by going on to elaborate in great detail on the Pauline emphasis of the spirit and the rejection of the flesh.[127] The subtlety of his own belief in the usefulness of the flesh was partly obscured by his eloquent arguments in favour of the orthodox position of the spirit as the goal of perfection. In truth, however, none of these arguments were incompatible with his own emphasis on the flesh and the attentive reader could still gain a real understanding of his position while he managed to preserve the appearance of orthodoxy. There can be no doubt that he held a very sincere belief in the absolute superiority of the spirit *vis a vis* the flesh and so he could agree with most of what St Paul and the Church had to say on the matter. In the case of Plato, Erasmus was on surer ground in expressing his disapproval of the philosopher's disregard for the body. The Platonic belief that the body was the tomb of the soul and only a kind of shadow was heretical.[128] In his work on letter-writing, Erasmus expressed his disagreement with Plato, the philosopher he held to be first in virtue and wisdom among non-Christians, on the usefulness of the flesh. He complained that Plato refused to accept that 'the body forms part of man's nature, that it is the instrument, habitation, or vehicle of the soul, and that the soul is the whole of what we call man'.[129] In *The Godly Feast* he goes even further when he has his character Eusebius say that our bodies are our 'partners'.[130] Then, casting a clear barb at the Platonic and Pauline notions, he said he preferred 'partners' to instruments or dwellings or tombs.[131] This issue was of such importance for Erasmus that he was willing to disagree with both Christ and Plato about it. While he could not, and would not, question the authority of Christ overtly, he manifestly did not agree with the dictum. Perhaps this was because his own experience contradicted it.

The reliance on individual experience as an instrument of judgment was an important feature of Erasmus' thought. It is crucial to his concept of the human being. His views on this subject were rarely expressed overtly but were nevertheless often apparent. They were outlined, if somewhat obliquely, in his exposition of the phrase, 'double diapason', in the *Adages*.[132] This was the name given to the harmony produced by striking the first and last notes of two consecutive octaves. He argued that the double diapason was the limit of harmony despite the fact that contemporary musicians 'do not hesitate to extend the limits of harmony to the twentieth note of the gamut'.[133] He quoted Ambrogio Leone of Nola as an authority for his argument. Leone had asserted that nature fixed the limit at the double diapason 'by arranging it that the human voice should not reach beyond the fifteenth interval'.[134] Erasmus continued by arguing that as far as reason is concerned there could be a 'thousandth diapason' but that this was not acceptable because

> the physical senses have their own limits prescribed for them by nature, and if they transgress these, they gradually become misty and wandering, and can no longer judge with certainty as they used to do, but through a cloud, as they say, or in a dream.[135]

He concluded, therefore, that 'it was not fitting that principles of art should be drawn from an uncertainty of judgement'.[136] Erasmus believed that, in art, human judgement could not be relied on if its conclusions could not be verified by means of the senses. As with art, so also in the process of human perfection, he believed personal verification using the senses, or the body, was the only real way of knowing something. This was a second, and vital, function of the body in the process of perfection. What he hated most about the scholastic theologians of his day was their endless abstract reasoning, which, if it was not rooted in some kind of reality or experience, was, at times, nothing more than a dangerous kind of false imagination.[137] In *The Praise of Folly* he described them as having been engaged in 'quibbles..about concepts, formalities, quiddities, ecceities, which no one could possibly perceive unless like Lynceus he could see through blackest darkness things which don't exist'.[138] He contrasted this with the simple message preached by the Apostles who had personal experience of Christ and had been moved by his spirit.

In conformity with this principle Erasmus was against endless speculation into unknowable things. He subscribed to the dictum, which he ascribed to Socrates: 'the things that are above us are nothing to us'.[139] He said this was 'a remark of Socrates which discourages us from restless enquiry into heavenly things and the secrets of nature.'[140] In *The Praise of Folly*, Folly laments the passing of the Golden Age of innocence when it was thought to be 'sacrilege for mortal man to attempt to acquire knowledge outside his allotted portion'.[141] This concept is also apparent in his exposition of the adage 'you move what should not be moved'.[142] He wrote, of this, that Plato recorded it in the *Laws* 'where he brings forward a law that he calls the statute of Jove, god of boundaries, about not altering bounds or frontiers'.[143] He added to this the epigram 'not Death himself grasps what may not be moved'.[144] On the other hand, of course, Erasmus believed fervently in the power of reason and the importance for us of attaining true knowledge and wisdom. He believed that we should try with all of our strength and talent to understand the things that are accessible to human experience and the powers of reasoning. This, for Erasmus, was the tension we were required to live within. We had to strive constantly for knowledge while not going past the bounds of our capabilities where our judgment would become hazy and useless. This is one possible interpretation of Erasmus' complex and richly allegorical personal device which was an image of the upper torso of a youth with flying hair embedded in a block of stone with the motto *cedo nulli* which later became *concedo nulli.* The motto and the block represent the god Terminus, god of boundaries, while the torso represented Iuventas or Youth. It is a perfect depiction of the unity of opposites within which the human being is compelled to live on earth. The optimism, energy and innocence of youth embedded in the dead, limited, reality of stone is a perfect depiction of the Erasmian notion that we must ever strive to reach the limits of our capabilities while at the same time always living within those limits.[145]

The precise nature of the importance that Erasmus placed on the role of the body in human perfection was an important distinguishing factor of his thought. He insisted on this despite the fact that the leaders, in his estimation, of the two highest branches of philosophy had denied it. Erasmus believed that the soul was housed by the body, was expressed through the body and was served by the body. In this, of course, he was not in serious disagreement with Christ or Plato. He believed, in conformity with Christian and Platonic principles, that the true, or perfected, or ideal human being would recognize that the body was indeed a tomb and the spirit was all-important.[146] Where he differed was in describing the means to achieve their common goal. His concern was the practical interpretation of the innate and revealed *philosophy of Christ* in order to help those who were toiling on the road to perfection. People already knew that they should abhor the flesh and cling to the spirit but they did not know *how* to achieve this. Erasmus' overriding aim was always to describe a *method* of perfection rather than the goal or state of perfection itself. This led him to emphasize the role of the flesh in perfection

This process was dependent on the most important function of the flesh, which, for Erasmus, was its power of temptation. He believed that we were so designed that we actually needed to be tempted in the flesh in order to perfect the spirit. He wrote that the three evils of human nature: blindness, the flesh and weakness, acted in us as a 'safeguard of humility and as raw material and a fertile terrain for virtue'.[147] The flesh acted both as a spur to virtue and also as a safeguard against the very dangerous sin of pride by reminding us of our weakness. Moreover, since any perfection reached on earth was not permanent and could at any time be lost, even the perfect needed the weakness of the flesh in order to remain in a state of earthly perfection. He said that 'at times temptations are not only not dangerous for those who are perfect but are even necessary for the preservation of virtue'.[148] He acknowledged that it was a 'strange kind of remedy' but it was nonetheless true that 'strength is made perfect in weakness'.[149] Even St Paul was tempted by pride lest he should become proud, and 'in order that he be unwavering in Christ, he is forced to be weak in himself'.[150] Erasmus interpreted the Pauline concept of strength through weakness as meaning that without the weakness of the flesh we would have no means of achieving perfection.[151] Every time we fell to the pull of the flesh and managed to look at ourselves on the ground with the eyes of reason we learned a vital lesson about our true state. This lesson served to weaken the hold of the flesh over us. Only ignorance or denial of the power of the flesh was really dangerous and not the actual fall itself. He advised the reader of the *Enchiridion* that

> if the storms of temptation descend upon you more frequently and more violently, do not immediately begin to be dissatisfied with yourself as if you were not dear to your God or pleasing in his sight, or as if you were lacking in piety or any less perfect. On the contrary give thanks that he is training you as a future heir, chastising you as a dear son, putting you to the test as a friend. It is the greatest proof that a man has been rejected by divine mercy when he is assailed by no temptations.[152]

Erasmus valued St Paul highly and he interpreted the tribulations of the saint's life and the human weakness he described in his Epistles as being a symbol of how he had 'carried the treasures of heavenly revelation in a vessel of clay to show that such transcendent power came from God and not from himself'.[153] This is also the lot of all people according to Erasmus. Even the perfect individual is tied to their body and as long as they live they will carry the treasures of heaven in a vessel of clay. He elaborated on this when he described the pre-perfect and perfect states of the human being in allegorical form. He said that in the Bible woman or 'Eve' represented the carnal passions 'whose glance the clever serpent attracts daily. When she has been corrupted, she proceeds to tempt her spouse to participate with her in evil.'[154] This is the state of the ordinary human being before they have reached perfection. Then he described the perfect state. He wrote:

> but what do you read about the new woman, the one who is

> obedient to her husband? "I shall create enmity between you" (obviously the serpent) "and the woman, and between your seed and her seed. She will crush your head, and you will strike insidiously at her heel."[155]

Then Erasmus united this Old Testament account with the New Testament, thereby showing the timelessness of the message, He said:

> the serpent has been thrown down on its belly; the death of Christ has broken the force of his attack. All he can do is lie in wait to strike blows at her heel from ambush. But by the power of faith the woman has been turned into a female warrior and with great heroism crushes his poisonous head. Grace has been increased; the tyranny of the flesh has been diminished.'[156]

Erasmus attributed the demise of the serpent to Christ. For him, the spirit of Christ is timeless as are the myths of the Old and New Testaments. He believed that the Old Testament, in particular, should be interpreted allegorically.[157] In this allegory Eve, or our carnal part, becomes the warrior and hero participating in the death of Christ by dying to the world. Perfection is achieved by means of the heroic deeds of the body.[158] The spirit is already perfect but the body must be transformed by means of the soul adhering to the spirit. It then plays its part heroically in the struggle for personal salvation and, ultimately, for the salvation of others.

This transformation of the flesh occurs when the human soul clings to the sprit. Erasmus believed that on account of the soul, that is the area in which conscious choice occurs, the human being could even reach a higher state than the angelic one. He said: 'with regard to the soul we have such a capacity for divinity that we can soar past the minds of the angels and become one with God'.[159] Human beings, on account of their souls, could achieve a state in which their spiritual and fleshly elements were fused into an harmonious unity. When we incorporate Christ then 'there is neither male nor female but a wholly new creature'.[160] This state would be achieved by choosing to elevate the spirit over the flesh. Erasmus went as far as to suggest that because angels are born spirit and do not have to struggle they are a slightly lower form of entity than a human being who has had to struggle with the flesh in order to overcome it and achieve a spiritual transformation. God and humans have souls but angels are pure spirits. Pure spirit was somehow slightly less than the perfected union of spirit and matter. Although Erasmus did not expand on this, the superiority cannot have resided in the material element of the human being itself since matter was inferior to spirit. The superiority must therefore have resided in the area of conscious choice that was created by the existence of the two opposites in the human being. The freedom to choose between spirit and matter, God and the world, good and evil, was a necessary part of the human struggle. Angels being pure spirit could not engage in the struggle between spirit and matter.[161] The dialectic of the struggle produced a higher form of entity than an angel. It is as if the resulting transformation was a creative act and therefore divine. We had the capability, through struggle, to transform ourselves into a new and more perfect type of human being.[162] This is why the notion of free will was crucial for him. Without it his entire system would have collapsed.

Erasmus had a further distinctive view on the nature of matter; he believed that in the end spirit and matter, despite their apparent disparity, were in fact one.[163] This, perhaps, stemmed from his belief that God was, in essence, spiritual.[164] Since, however, he was the creator and architect of the natural world, matter actually came from him. So matter was in some way formed from spirit. Thus, if we succeeded in unifying spirit and matter in ourselves, we would then share in God's nature, become one with him and rise above the angels who had not had to take part in this struggle. The dynamic of the struggle was therefore of great value and the flesh, or matter, being vital in this process was also invaluable. In *The Praise of Folly* he described the ultimate state of perfection, which was only achievable after death in the next life. He wrote: 'the spirit will be the stronger, and will conquer and absorb the body, and this it will do the more easily for having previously in life purged and weakened the body in preparation for this transformation'.[165] He went on to say 'this perfect happiness can only be experienced when the soul has recovered its former body and been granted immortality'.[166] Thus even in heaven the body would have a role in the life of the perfected human being. While this is consistent with the orthodox doctrine of the resurrection of the body, it is nevertheless different, in that the heavenly absorption of the body by the spirit in Erasmus' thought is a natural consequence of his belief in the effectiveness of the conflict between these two entities. The conflict produced the means of perfection by facilitating consciousness of the true nature of reality. In this struggle to overcome the impulses of the flesh, the soul was purified. This purification or perfection came about by the uniting of the two disparate parts into an harmonious whole. Erasmus, under the obvious influence of an unorthodox Neoplatonism, ultimately believed that the perfected soul was then absorbed into the Supreme mind. He said that having absorbed the body ' the spirit will itself be absorbed by the supreme Mind, which is more powerful than its infinite parts'.[167]

Despite the fact that Erasmus was seen during the eighteenth-century and later as having aspired to the spirit of Rationalism, his system was nevertheless one that contained mysteries that were difficult to grasp. He himself was very much aware of this problem of communicating the full truth. He believed that perfection was a state achieved in stages and that the mystery would therefore unfold by degrees. He said: 'piety like other things has its infancy, it has its periods of growth, it has its full and vigorous adult strength'.[168] He thought that if we directed our minds toward the spiritual then

> the Lord will draw nigh in his turn to the one who draws nigh to him, and if you will attempt to the limit of your powers to rise out of your moral darkness and the tumult of the senses, he will obligingly come forth to meet you from his inaccessible light and that unimagined silence, in which not only all the tumult of the senses, but also the forms of all intelligible things fall silent.[169]

We could only do a certain amount to achieve our own perfection but, if we did, then God would do the rest. We had to work in the dark seeing only shadowy reflections of the light of truth. As we strove towards the spiritual, we would become more spiritual and, by virtue of this, we would then attract the spiritual to ourselves and in turn become more attracted to it. This attracting principle of transformation is the same one as Erasmus outlined in his description of the Christocentric society, or true Church, where he said that Christ, the centre, would draw all things to himself so that they would be transfigured in him. Like fire he converts all things to himself.[170] Erasmus conceived of love in the Platonic sense as being the same energetic attractive force that facilitates transformation. He said:

> my brother, do not progress slowly by dint of reluctant effort, but by moderate exercise arrive at quick and vigorous adulthood in Christ. Embrace zealously this rule, not to be willing to crawl along the ground with unclean animals, but supported on those wings whose growth Plato thinks are induced in our minds by the heat of love and shoot out anew, raise yourself as on the steps of Jacob's ladder from the body to the spirit, from the visible to the invisible, from the letter to the mystery, from sensible things to the intelligible things, from composite things to simple things.[171]

Thus, although Erasmus placed a special value on the fleshly or worldly nature of the human being in the work of perfection, the whole point of the process was the transformation of the human soul into a more spiritual and superior entity. This could only be achieved because part of our nature was already spiritual. This, too, was a vital part of his concept of the human being. Erasmus believed we were born with a divine element that, with work, could become the dominant factor in our actions.

His belief in this divine element of the human psyche was, in many ways, quite orthodox, in that, he thought we contained a soul that was godlike and eternal. In the treatise, *De Contemptu Mundi,* he argued that on account of our souls we 'approach to some extent that divine and eternal nature'.[172] For him, the soul was 'heavenly, light, divine, immortal, lasting, lucid and noble'.[173] His views on the way in which the human being could be transformed into a more spiritual being were, however, more complex than this. He believed that a person who had transformed their original nature to a state in which their spiritual element was dominant merited the title 'Son of God', and that it was 'the highest nobility to be both a son and heir of God, a brother and co-heir of Christ'.[174] In short we could reach a state of perfection in which we shared in the divinity of Christ as a true son or daughter of God. While it is perfectly orthodox to say that we are all God's children, Erasmus, in his view of the way in which we can incorporate Christ, comes very close to saying that we really become a type of Christ also. Pushed too far this would, of course, be blasphemy and he carefully avoided this but there is a sense in which the goal of human perfection, for him, is really the goal of achieving Christhood. Erasmus referred to this state particularly throughout his scriptural writings and it is St Paul above all who is his primary source. In his

Paraphrase on Romans he said: 'all those who are impelled by the spirit of God are sons of God'.[175] This happened when a person incorporated Christ. 'When we are one with Christ we are no longer servants but sons and call him Father'.[176] This process began with the true baptism: 'we are grafted to the body of Christ through baptism and in a way are transformed into him'.[177] This was the beginning of our proper inheritance. Having been thus transformed we would then be

> heirs indeed of God, from whom as the source all things flow; and as co-heirs with Christ, incorporated into his body, we have begun to have the same Father as Christ, through whom we have attained the right of a common inheritance.[178]

We would attain this common inheritance in the same way that Christ himself had. Here, again we see a very close correlation between Christ and the perfected human being who had to travel towards Christhood

> on the same road by which Christ himself reached it....Christ attained possession of the good by bearing evil, he came to power through obedience, he came to glory through dishonour, he attained immortality by death. We must therefore suffer with him so that we may enjoy these gifts with him, we must obey so that we may reign with him, we must bear the insults of the world so that we may be fortified with him, we must die with him for a time so that we may live with him forever. This is the law by which one gains this inheritance.[179]

It was God's law and his plan for us that through one son he 'would produce many sons for himself, among whom Jesus Christ would be the head and leader and, as it were, the first born, sharing his own rights also with others'.[180] In his *Paraphrase on John,* Erasmus elaborated on this further when he declared that

> whatever persons, of whatever nation and whatever rank, accepted this word, to them in return he brought such honour that, once implanted in Christ by faith and baptism, and once having proclaimed his name, they themselves also became children of God, so that what Christ was by nature, they became through adoption', they became 'children of God, brothers of Jesus Christ, and heirs with him of the heavenly kingdom.[181]

Erasmus and the Process of Human Perfection

In Erasmus' dual version of the anatomy of the total human being it was the mind or soul that contained the divine element. In his work on letter writing he said:

> the mind of man, which has a heavenly origin, should not degenerate from its kind. And as it is natural for fire to make its way upwards, drawn to its origin by an inborn force, so the inborn nature of man, though immersed in these corporeal vapours, still cannot forget its beginnings.[182]

Once again Erasmus used the image of fire attracting and transforming as the mechanism of perfection. He believed that a vestige of the divine law remained in the human mind on account of its divine origin and that it was because of this that we were attracted to God. In the *Antibarbari,* Erasmus commented on the appropriateness of the verb *traho,* which Christ used when he said that having ascended to heaven he would then draw all creation to himself.[183] This mechanism of attraction is also found in Plato's concept that the philosopher attains 'knowledge of the true nature of every essence by a sympathetic and kindred power in the soul, and by that power drawing near and mingling and becoming incorporate with very being'.[184] Like Plato, Erasmus believed that love was the attracting force which was necessary for the perfection of being and that we are only attracted to things we can recognize by means of an inherent sympathy with them. He said that God fashioned Adam out of clay but 'breathed into this mud image a tiny bit of celestial breath through which we might resemble more closely our parent God himself and because of the similarity in nature might recognize him more easily'.[185] In this way the divine spark in humanity helped to dispel the darkness of the world. In the *Enchiridion* he said; 'as a consequence of the divine law that is engraved in him, our king (reason) can be overthrown, but he cannot be corrupted without protesting and seeking redress'.[186] Thus while the world contrived to obscure the divine law inscribed on the human mind, we, nevertheless, had the means at our disposal to overcome this blindness and achieve consciousness of ourselves and our position in the universe, primarily, on account of the strength of our reason. Our reason was the tool we had been given by God in order that we might overcome the corruption of the world. It was not itself the divine law but it was the instrument that allowed us to recognize the divine law. This law was the guiding principle of all creation and Erasmus equated this with the *Logos* and therefore with Christ in the universal sense of the term. The Erasmian notion that the means of perfection lay in being conscious of the tension or dialogue between the disparate elements in the human being is mirrored in his concept of the *Logos* as a creative dialogue. When an individual entered into this conscious struggle they embodied the *Logos* of Christ, or the divine dialogue, which, for Erasmus, was the one true law of creation that operated eternally throughout the universe.[187]

In addition to this rationally accessible, innate, divine law, Erasmus also believed that we shared in divinity by another means. This was on account of our spiritual nature itself. By means of his or her personal spirit each individual participated in the universal Holy Spirit. In the *Querela Pacis,* he depicted the Holy Spirit as the force that bound all people together. He called it a 'fiery spirit' and asked: 'what else can it be but love? Nothing is so beneficial to all as fire, and fire is kindled from fire without diminishment'.[188] We could have access to this force if we chose to cling to the spirit within us. Thus Erasmus envisaged the divine spirit in the human being as being akin to fire that, in turn, he thought represented love or that force which bound us to each other in mutual harmony. This harmony or peace was, for him, 'the source of all human happiness'.[189] Christ was the embodiment of this force. When, in turn, an individual embodied Christ he or she could also dispense the force for the good of all people. In this sense Erasmian Christianity is expressed in terms of mutual love. Love of neighbour was the expression of divinity in us. This was not, of course, that emotion which humankind usually called love. Erasmus was contemptuous of that and said it was usually so flawed and selfish that it was, in fact, often a form of hatred.[190] The love he spoke of was that which sublimated the good of the self to the good of the rest of humanity. This was not a recipe for some kind of self-annihilation. It was the creation of a true self rather then annihilation of the self. The divine quality could not be expressed until a person had first conquered their lower instincts and this was a process of the integration of the separate parts of human nature in such a way that a true harmony, which embodied the spirit of Christ, was achieved. He declared: 'man is a battlefield within himself: reason is at war with the passions and these are in conflict with each other'.[191] This state of war is overcome by adhering to the spirit of Christ. He argued that 'whenever the spirit of Christ is present, there one's own nature gives way to the nature of the creator'.[192] This was the state in which a human being could truly love. The fundamental law of Christ, for Erasmus, was love. The spirit, which was the divine part of the human being, was a force of love and our mind, which contained a vestige of the divine law, was an important instrument in achieving this goal of love. Love is a cohesive, harmonious, uniting force and Erasmus believed that the dialectic produced by the union of spirit and flesh was the means of perfection. Thus the *Logos* was a dialectic of love or integration and harmony.[193] In the *Enchiridion,* when Erasmus was discussing the two parts of the human being, he said that the condition of most ordinary people was one in which reason was a slave to the passions and that, in total ignorance of reality, these people called this state one of peace. He wrote of this mistaken appellation:

> this is that hapless peace which Christ, the author of true peace, who made the two one, came to destroy by stirring up salutary warfare between father and son, husband and wife, and between those things which a base accord has badly joined together.[194]

In short, the dialectic of salvation, according to the example of Christ, was a struggle between the two factions in the human being, which, if it were pursued in the correct way, would result in a true harmonious unity in which the passions were subjected to an informed reason and the spirit of Christ.[195]

Indeed Erasmus thought that the whole mission of Christ was to bring about just such a situation of perfect peace in each human being and, ultimately, in the whole of creation. The attracting force of love produced this condition of peace or harmony. He asked 'what induced the Son of God to come to earth if not his wish to reconcile the world with the Father, to bind men together with mutual and indestructible love, and, finally, to make man his own friend?'[196] Clearly he believed that this union was something extraordinary. He said that at the Last Supper Christ asked his disciples to do something for him that was 'no ordinary thing'.[197] He asked them to look after his flock and 'keep them through thy name, that they may be one as we are'.[198] Erasmus argued that Christ was speaking here of a special type of unity. This was not simply that they should be of one mind but that they should be 'united in the most perfect and inexpressible way'.[199] What Erasmus understood this to mean was that they would be transformed into Christ and so they would all share in the divine nature. For him, the whole of human nature was designed to move towards this point of union with Christ and thus to union with others who had also achieved this state. Perfection was a process of union and of love. Therefore, while he was one of the most severe and influential critics of what he perceived as the degenerate state of church practices, he was horrified when it became clear that there was going to be a split in the Christian church. Faction and disunity were such fundamental opposites to his belief-system that he could never conceive of good emerging from them. The fundamental law of Christianity, which he said, was 'love one another' was absolutely central to his esoteric beliefs.[200] For him the whole point of the central sacrament of the Eucharist was that it ratified 'a new kind of concord which should never be broken'.[201] Thus the assertion of many of his contemporaries, and many historians since, that Erasmus was a conservative Christian or even a coward, which are primarily based on his unwillingness to join the reformers, fails to take account of the true basis for this seemingly conservative action. Actions were never as important to Erasmus as intentions and so he must be judged on his own terms.

The centrality of divine love to the perfection process was not a simple tenet of blind faith for him, but rather faith informed by the rational analysis of observable experience. He believed that this was apparent from the evidence of Nature and could be assessed by the power of reason.[202]. He argued that observation of Nature showed that the celestial bodies and the elements exist in a state of peace and concord.[203] Similarly, he believed that observation of human beings themselves disclosed this law of harmony. He said:

> what can be so dissimilar as body and soul? Yet the closeness of the tie with which Nature has bound them together is indeed revealed when they are torn apart. Just as life is nothing other than the union of the body and soul, so health is the harmony between all the parts of the body.[204]

He observed that Nature had given the human being an essentially peace-loving disposition:

> which is inclined towards goodwill between him and his fellows, so that he delights in being loved for himself and takes pleasure in being of service to others - so long as he has not been corrupted by base desires, as if by Circe's potions and degenerated from man to beast.[205]

He also argued that it was evident that people needed each other in order to survive and prosper.[206] He said of peace that everything points the way to it; 'first natural instinct and what we might call the human principle itself, then the Prince and author of all human happiness, Christ'.[207] Finally, he believed that this principle of unity and love was also apparent on a cosmic scale in Christ. In him the best example of the perfection of the whole of creation, by means of the union of the opposites of spiritual and material principles, was exposed to us. The important processes of the Incarnation and Redemption were premised on this union. The universality of the principle meant that God had to participate in human weakness in order to save us.

> For the Son of God and God himself sent himself down to our lowliness just to raise us by faith to his own loftiness. He took upon himself the shame of our mortality just to make us sharers in his divine glory. He chose to be born bodily flesh of flesh just so that we might be reborn spiritually of God. He came down to earth just to carry us up into heaven.[208]

The corollary of this, for Erasmus was that if God became a human being then humans could become God. He argued that

> it is not surprising if a human being is somehow reshaped to share in the divine nature, when the divine word humbled himself for this reason to put on our flesh, that is, a mortal body, from a virgin, joining in himself two quite dissimilar things, God and human. What is frailer than human flesh, or more despised? What is mightier than God, or more sublime? Do not wonder that these could be joined; it is God who did it. And do not lack faith that humankind can become children of God when he so loved us that for our sake he chose to become a son of man.[209]

This is the central mystery of Christianity for Erasmus. He said:

'these are the mysteries of God the Father, these the secret purposes of the divine mind, whereby it seemed good to him to make God into a man, and to make mankind in a fashion into gods'.[210]

In the *Adages* when he was arguing in favour of a divine element in us Erasmus quoted Gregory of Nazianzus as having said that 'by imitating the mercy of God you will become God to the sufferer, for man has nothing so divine as kindness'.[211] The significance of Gregory of Nazianzus was that he had written against the Christological heresy of Apollinarius who, in his concern to maintain the divinity of Christ, had diminished his humanity. Erasmus' beliefs meant that, on the one hand, he emphasized the humanity of Christ, while on the other hand, he emphasized the divinity of the human being. In both cases he went further than was currently orthodox and consequently he was accused of both Arianism and Pelagianism. By using Gregory of Nazianzus, who was a defender of the human element in Christ, as a source for the divine element in the human being there is a sense in which Erasmus is linking these two concepts in a seemingly orthodox way. The extremism of his concepts of Christ and the human being however, meant that they were far more similar entities than orthodoxy allowed. By emphasizing our divinity and Christ's humanity there is a sense in which the historical Jesus and the perfected human being are not very different entities. Jesus is the son of God, but so is the perfect human being. Jesus is Christ, so also is the perfect human being who only reaches the perfect state when he or she embodies Christ. Erasmus' belief in the complete embodiment of Christ in the perfect human being was very close to the doctrine of the Incarnation of Christ. Nevertheless, throughout his corpus Erasmus wrote in a perfectly orthodox way about the central tenets of Christianity, such as the Redemption, the Incarnation and the Resurrection. When we analyse everything he said on these subjects, however, it is apparent that there are layers of meaning in these seemingly straightforward statements. Because of his belief that Christianity was a state achieved gradually and by degrees he was always very careful not to tear down a belief which was useful to the salvific process without putting something in its place.[212] He would therefore leave the basic tenet intact while also adding an extra dimension of meaning to it so that the reader could take whichever level he or she could accept from it. In this way, Erasmus was all things to all people. His religion was an esoteric one; it was a condition of the inner human being rather than the outer one. The struggle for perfection took place inside each individual, and the world simply acted as an occasion of sin or a means of temptation. Outward expressions of religion were therefore relatively unimportant to him and thus he condoned whatever ceremonies were deemed necessary for those who needed them. Real truth and knowledge were only accessible to those who engaged in this inner struggle. While he believed it was not possible to communicate the truth directly, his writings are nevertheless always lucid and rational and so the metaphysical side of his thought is often neglected.

The fact that he did not join the reformers, despite his own, often severe, criticisms of the church is also explicable in the light of his view of the human being. His emphasis on inner transformation and his consequent belief that reform of state, society or church had to start in the individual heart meant that he thought institutions could play an important part in aiding or hindering the process of perfection but ultimately they could not achieve it. Each person was both responsible for, and instrumental in, their own destiny. The individual was the essential unit of operation. Erasmus' creed was not corporate; for him the function of any institution was always to aid individuals and never the furtherance of its own existence.[213] While he certainly hoped that the church would facilitate the process of individual transformation, he would not sacrifice the peace or harmony, which was an expression of divine love for him, to the cause of reforming a church that could only play a peripheral part in the process of perfection. Although he always respected the traditions of the Roman Church, he did also hold a more ambiguous view of what the true church was. He believed it was a spiritual gathering consisting of true Christians and that many people who were nominally baptized were not, in fact, worthy of the name Christian.[214] The true church was a community, above all, in which peace and love were central. He wrote:

> what else rings through all Paul's letters, but peace, gentleness, and love? What does John say, over and over again, but "love one another"? And Peter? What else do all true Christian writers say? How comes it that there is such a commotion of wars among the sons of peace? Is it a mere fable, when Christ says "I am the vine, ye are the branches? Who ever saw branch fight with branch? The

> expression Paul used more than once, is it meaningless? - that the church is nothing if not one body with many members, joined to one head, which is Christ? Who ever saw the eye fight with the hand, or the belly with the foot? In this universe, composed of such different elements, there is a harmony. In the body of a living creature, there is peace between one member and another; each part has its own gifts, and uses them not for itself but for all the others. If anything happens to one, the whole body comes to its help. Are we to suppose that the natural bond uniting the parts of a perishable body is more powerful than the bond of the spirit in the mystic and immortal body?[215]

Erasmus believed that this *concordia* was the fundamental distinguishing factor of Christianity and thus faction and disunity among Christians were unthinkable for him because if there was discord then, *ipso facto,* there was no Christianity.[216]

The second reason why he did not join the reformers is also intimately connected to his concept of the human being. His view of the role of the individual in the transforming process of perfection was absolutely contrary to the new protestant emphasis on salvation through faith alone. The concept of *sola fide* meant that we were powerless in relation to our own salvation. There was nothing arbitrary therefore, about him choosing free will as the topic of dispute with Luther. This was the true kernel of his divergence from the new creed. He agreed with many of the other proposed reforms, particularly the emphasis on Scripture and the drive towards a purified text, but the stumbling block of *sola fide* was too great for him. He had one further reason for rejecting the reformers: this was their dogmatic approach to Christian beliefs. Erasmus was not a dogmatist. He never laid down dogmatic beliefs. Both of the main parties in the reformation dispute were dogmatic. His religious philosophy was individualistic and fluid. He believed there should be as few tenets of faith as possible. In the letter, which served as the preface to his edition of St Hilary, he said that the peace and concord of the church could not be preserved unless 'we define as few matters as possible and leave each individual's judgment free on many questions'.[217] He did not believe that you could impose faith on anyone. He outlined in the same letter how the church had degenerated since patristic times; he said that now

> we force men by intimidation to believe what they do not believe, to love what they do not love, and to understand what they do not understand. Compulsion is incompatible with sincerity, and nothing is pleasing to Christ unless it is voluntary.[218]

While he accepted that faith was a God-given gift he also thought that, in practice, belief originated in experience and moreover, since the process of transformation was one in which the individual played an active part, the idea that it could be forced on anyone made no sense to him.

Erasmus' concept of the human being was also at odds with the prevailing Augustinian view. This led him to take issue with the traditional dogma of original sin on the one hand, and with the reformer's concept of the enslavement of the will, on the other. Both of these doctrines are ultimately rooted in Augustine's concept of human nature. Erasmus appreciated the importance of Augustine's writings for contemporary theology but he, nevertheless, did not give him the foremost position among the Fathers. While he accepted that the Doctor of Grace was 'one of the great doctors' he nevertheless thought that he was not the equal of 'any of the Greeks'.[219] In 1518 he acknowledged, in a letter to Eck, that despite the 'schoolmen's' adulation of Augustine he himself learnt 'more of Christian philosophy from a single page of Origen than from ten of Augustine'.[220] Augustine's anti-Pelagianism, which resulted in an extreme view of the human will, was the basis of Erasmus' rejection of his primacy in theological studies. The inherent predestinarian tendencies of Augustine's writings were incompatible with the crucial Erasmian view of the freedom of the human will.[221] Erasmus directly challenged Augustine's interpretation of Romans 5:12, which was the scriptural text used to underpin the concept of original sin. He claimed that he did this on philological grounds, and while there was some merit in his argument, it is clear nevertheless that his own views on original sin are epitomized in his interpretation of this verse.[222] In his New Testament version of Romans 5:12, which describes how sin came into the world when Adam sinned, he changed the Vulgate reading 'in whom all have sinned', to 'inasmuch as all have sinned'. This had the effect of weakening the doctrine that we inherit original sin as a personal state from Adam. He was severely criticized for this change because of the importance of the verse.[223] While he took great pains to defend his reading of the Greek and pointed out that some of the Fathers had interpreted the passage in a similar way he was, nevertheless, well aware that he was demolishing a pillar of the scriptural basis for the church's version of original sin. Moreover, one of the authorities he cited in his defence was the 'learned man' whom he referred to as 'whoever he was whose scholia on all the Epistles of Paul bear the name of Jerome' [224] This work has now been identified as a commentary by Pelagius with interpolations.[225] While we do not know if Erasmus suspected this, we do know that he was aware the author was not Jerome. It is significant, nevertheless, that he was, in fact, using the authority of a supposed patristic commentator, who was in fact Pelagius, as an authority in his defence against the charge of Pelagianism.[226] While he insisted that he did not deny the existence of original sin, it is clear that his understanding of its exact nature did, in fact, differ from the accepted Augustinian doctrine. His version stressed that our nature was not inherently sinful as a result of Adam's sin. This invoked severe criticism from the theological establishment and in 1529 he was forced to defend his position against the accusations of the Louvain theologian Titlemans.[227] Throughout his defence he referred to the mechanism of transmission of original sin as that of imitation. Thus while he accepted that the sin of Adam had led to his descendants being weakened by his sin he thought that the way in which this operated, in practice, was that Adam had introduced sin into the human race and then his descendants had imitated his weakness down through the ages.[228] Erasmus admitted that we had a propensity to sin but said 'I think [this propensity] proceeds from example rather than from nature'.[229] He argued that in *Romans* 5:12 St Paul was 'talking about the sins that individuals have committed in imitation of Adam'.[230] When he paraphrased *Romans* he wrote:

> it was provided by the wonderful and secret plan of God that the way by which our well-being was restored would correspond to the way in which we had suffered ruin. Accordingly, through Adam alone, who first transgressed the law of God, sin crept into the world, and sin dragged along death as its companion inasmuch as sin is the poison of the soul. And so it happened that the evil originated by the first of the race spread through all posterity since no one fails to imitate the example of the first parent.[231]

Again, here, Erasmus interpreted Adam's sin as an evil example that has been imitated ever since. In his treatise on the education of children he affirmed his belief in original sin and then said:

> while this is indisputably man's condition, however, we cannot deny that the greater portion of this evil stems from corrupting relationships and a misguided education, especially as they affect our earliest and most impressionable years.[232]

The significance of his position on original sin was that it contradicted the Augustinian model, which stated that we were naturally inclined to evil and incapable of earning our own salvation.[233] While Erasmus never denied God his part in our perfection and always agreed that without divine grace we were powerless, it was, nevertheless, fundamental to his thought that each individual had a vital part to play in his or her own perfection. He could not therefore subscribe to a fully Augustinian view of human nature and original sin. This, then, was the issue on which he publicly broke with Luther in 1524. As early as December 1522 the pope, Adrian VI, had exhorted Erasmus to take up cudgels against Luther.[234] In his letter the pope left him little choice in the matter even to the point of implying that if Erasmus did not defend the church he would, *ipso facto*, be deemed an enemy of the church. Despite this order from the head of Christendom, however, Erasmus clearly did not want to take sides in the dispute but when he did finally and reluctantly enter the fray it was Luther's thoroughly Augustinian denial of our capacity to participate in perfection that he chose to challenge.[235] As early as 1522 the Lutherans had shown an awareness of this disagreement between themselves and Erasmus. They had been critical of his paraphrase of *Romans* 9 because they thought he allotted too much to the freedom of the will in it.[236] Erasmus acknowledged that as a result of his stance 'Luther's party in their public utterances tear me to pieces as a Pelagian, because they think I give more weight than they do to free will'. The truth was that his view of the operation of the human will differed from both the reformers and the traditional church.[237] He defended himself against both sides in 1523 when he laid out his own views on free will in a letter. He said that he had tried to steer between

> the peril of Scylla, persuading us to put our trust in good works, which I admit is the greatest threat to religion. On the other side I

> could see Charybdis, a monster yet more terrible, by whom not a few of them are now held fast, saying, "Let us do as we please; for whether we torment ourselves or please ourselves, what God has decided is sure to happen."[238]

As a consequence of this he said that he thought it best to allot a small amount to free will. In truth he would certainly have preferred to leave such a thorny question un-defined. In the same year he argued that philosophers had been debating about *fato* long before Christ,

> and from them there have descended to us these insoluble problems about foreknowledge, about predestination by God, about human free-will, about contingency of future events, in which I think it the best course not to spend too much anxious time, since this is an abyss no man can get to the bottom of.[239]

By 1524, however, circumstances had dictated that this doctrine should occupy centre-stage. It was of such great import to him that he could no longer keep a scholarly distance and instead he had to engage in the debate with Luther.[240]

In this debate Erasmus' views are firmly in the camp of Renaissance humanism. He was a man of the Renaissance. His views were fully formed before the advent of Luther and he did not change his mind on any of the fundamentals of his Christianity after the advent of the Reformation. His humanism, which was absolutely central to his interpretation of the *philosophy of Christ*, comes particularly from the milieu of the Ficinian revival of Plato. The historian, Jacob Burckhardt, put forward the theory that one of the most important facets of the Renaissance was the rediscovery of man and his central position in the universe.[241] This, he claimed, resulted in the elevation of the individual and meant that individual experience and judgment became fundamentally important. Even the most eminent opponent of the general Burckhardt thesis, Kristeller, has agreed that in the field of humanist literature 'abstract generalization gave way to personal opinion and individual experience'.[242] The debate about the Renaissance has raged for centuries and need not be rehearsed here in detail but it was central to Erasmus' brand of humanism and so it is necessary to examine its essential character in order to fully understand the Erasmian Christian philosophy.[243]

Erasmus and the Process of Human Perfection

What was actually new in the Renaissance world of thought was the increased interest, influence and availability of the works of Plato. It has been established that there was a Platonic and Neoplatonic movement of sorts in the middle-ages, based on the translations of several texts of Plato and Proclus, and on Boethius and other Latin Platonists and, above all, on St Augustine and the extremely widespread texts which circulated under the name of Dionysius the Areopagite. This movement, however, never became a mainstream force; the Aristotelian-based scholasticismbas ruled supreme.[244] In the Renaissance, Platonism became a force to be reckoned with in Europe west of Greece for the first time in over a thousand years.[245] It had an influence that was not limited to the field of philosophy in the modern sense of the term. The central concept of this Platonic humanism and the driving force of the Renaissance stems from Plato's concept of the human being and, more particularly, the notion that we contain within ourselves an image of the Divine or the Good. The present world is not the true reality it is merely a shadow of reality. The human being as the microcosm reflects the macrocosm of the universe and, perhaps more importantly, he or she reflects God. Thus we contain within ourselves the seeds of all knowledge: an ideal against which we can verify truth. Above all, the Platonic human being had the possibility of perfecting himself or herself by means of proper education in philosophy because this would lead to knowledge of the unseen reality. This is expressed very succinctly in Plato's myth of the cave in the *Republic*,[246] which was an important recurring theme in Erasmus' work. Burckhardt, who has not really been superseded in this understanding, thought that the central achievement of the Renaissance was 'the discerning and bringing to light' of 'the full, whole nature of man'.[247] In the final sentence of his famous work, Burckhardt acknowledged that the blossoming of this concept during the Renaissance is the sole reason why this period must be called 'the leader of modern ages'.[248] Human beings became the centre of their own universe and the *prima materia* of their own perfection. By definition, this Platonic concept would not produce a single fixed philosophical system since it elevated individual experience. It would, and of course did, produce a flowering of individual creativity in all spheres of artistic and intellectual endeavour. Crucially, people who adhered to this concept were freed from the shackles of traditional authority. They could express their own individual genius in the comforting knowledge that it reflected the divine mind. This is precisely consistent with Plato's own desire that his philosophy should not become dogma.[249] The religious expression of this concept was that we could determine our own path of perfection. In the very early days of the church this fusion of Platonism and Christianity had produced the Gnostic tendency among others. The better-established church of the Renaissance would not brook such heresy. All of the Platonic humanists were Christians and most of them were anxious to show that the two viewpoints were totally compatible.

In the writings of Erasmus we see a high point of the fusion of Platonic Humanism and Christianity. The philological efforts of the humanists in scriptural matters can be seen as an important expression of the newfound confidence in individual discernment. Prior to this time the Vulgate had acquired an almost sacred authority in itself. Thus, changing a Vulgate reading was considered by many as being tantamount to blasphemy and it certainly was a revolutionary act. It is clear from an early letter of Erasmus to Christopher Fisher that he was well aware of this.[250] The humanists, however, were prepared to risk censure in their efforts to achieve a true reading of Scripture. They worked outside of the established theological tradition using new methods of textual criticism which, in most cases, they developed as they worked. In essence, then, they were putting their own individual judgment above that of centuries of church tradition, although, of necessity, they strenuously denied this. The spell of unquestioned authority had been broken. This new view of human nature and its capacities was applied to many spheres of human endeavour and was the central underlying achievement of the Renaissance. For the humanists, the pronouncements of authority were acceptable and deemed correct only if individual judgment assessed them to be so. The new humanist educational programme, the *studia humanitatis*, in sharp contrast to the medieval liberal arts, was designed to educate people to think for themselves and pass on this new intellectual freedom to others. Its emphasis on eloquence was inspired by the desire to communicate. In the *Ciceronianus* Erasmus was scathing in his criticism of those humanists who misunderstood this vital point. For him, antiquity was to be valued not for itself but because the ancients had perfected methods of communication and ideals of moral virtue.

If attempts to understand humanism concentrate on the manifestations of the concept without reference to the central idea itself then confusion necessarily results. The problem here is that some renowned humanists did not overtly state their support for this concept but they nevertheless tacitly developed and promoted it in their work. Martin Luther, for instance, was in favour of the humanist approach to the text of Scripture but his concept of justification by faith alone, in which faith is a freely-granted gift from God and not something we can merit ourselves may appear to be in opposition to the elevation of the individual. Luther, however, reached his theology of salvation by means of a personal soul-searching that was brought on in part by the fact that the message of the medieval church did not satisfy the longings of his own heart. He went on from this to develop his own theology based on a personal reading of Scripture. Thus the method of achieving his theology was imbued with the notion that individual discernment was paramount. He trusted his own judgment above that of the medieval church. In that, he exhibited a thoroughly humanist belief in the importance of individual experience. This also applies to the numerous other protestant reformers such as Melanchthon and Calvin who championed humanist educational, literary, and philological aims but did not believe in the primacy of the individual's role in the process of perfection. Conversely, Erasmus, whose writings are permeated with the concept that the human being had a vital role to play in perfection, did not reject the church's authority.

This argument about the centrality of the Platonic vision of the human being in humanist thought has been rejected by Kristeller, one of the foremost experts on Renaissance ideas. He claimed that humanism was primarily an educational system which aimed to produce a particular culture and that it must be differentiated from Renaissance Platonism. He said that 'humanist culture as such was neutral with regard to certain theological or even philosophical doctrines, and each humanist was free to formulate his opinions according to his own convictions and inclinations'.[251] He correctly pointed out that 'we find humanist scholars and men of letters, as well as men reared in the humanist culture, among the Catholics, Protestants and heretics of the sixteenth century'.[252] He has also identified humanists who were

Aristotelians as well as those who espoused Platonic doctrines. Kristeller's viewpoint is that of a philosopher. As such, he could see clearly that there was no distinct philosophical system that could be called humanism. He therefore concluded that humanism was an educational, cultural phenomenon rather than something that was based on an idea or set of ideas. He noted that 'most of the works of humanists have nothing to do with philosophy'[253] and that the themes of humanist treatises 'are neither profound nor rigorous, if measured according to criteria of ancient, modern or even medieval philosophy'.[254] He then went on to say that 'the conclusions are often ambiguous, and even the various theses of Petrarch, Bruni or Valla do not constitute systematic thought or a collection of doctrines which could generally be accepted by the other humanists'.[255] He believed that they shared 'general attitudes characterized by the cultural ideal which was based upon the study of Latin and Greek classics'.[256] For him the defining principle of humanism was its relationship with the educational programme contained in the *studia humanitatis*.[257] He believed that its direct contribution to the history of thought came through the writings on moral philosophy which were part of this programme. The indirect contribution was through scholars whom he considers were not humanists but who had a humanist education and manifested this in their own 'rich and complex thought'.[258] He held that Renaissance Platonism was quite distinct from humanism. He said: 'it is imperative to consider and treat Renaissance Platonism as a movement unto itself, as distinct from Aristotelianism and humanism'.[259] In Kristeller's terms some Platonists had humanist elements in their thought and some did not. Thus he believed that there was no necessary connection between the two. Indeed there were humanists who were Aristotelians such as Pomponazzi. There were even Aristotelians who espoused Platonic doctrines and Platonists who espoused Aristotelian ones.[260] Kristeller's thesis is very difficult to dispute within its own terms. It is cogently argued and based on meticulous scholarship. There is a problem with it however, in that while he acknowledged that humanism was 'the intellectual movement which in many respects is the most characteristic of the Renaissance',[261] his thesis does not adequately explain how this educational cultural phenomenon could have produced such an enormous effect in all the intellectual and creative fields of the time if its parameters were simply educational and cultural. Moreover, and crucially, the flowering of Renaissance creativity was achieved before the educational system was fully operational or widely accepted.

If we define humanism by its educational, philological and cultural manifestations alone, we do not explain the impulse underlying these manifestations. This impulse was Platonic. Often humanists did not express, and sometimes perhaps they did not even know, the Platonic origin of this impulse. Kristeller accepts that the humanists were free to adhere to whichever philosophical or religious impulse they judged to be correct. This freedom to choose whatever is discerned to be best is an essential part of the underlying impulse in the diverse movement that we still correctly see as a unity. Burckhardt's notion is the underlying impulse. Kristeller himself admits that

> every thinker who is called Platonic represents his own synthesis of Platonic, extraneous and original elements, which must all be carefully examined; it is quite possible to find two thinkers who are correctly identified as Platonic or Platonising, but who share no common doctrine.[262]

Platonism of its essence inspires an individual response. Platonic philosophy is not, or should not be, dogmatic. The great Socrates was only sure of one thing and that was that he knew nothing. Plato, himself, never finally elaborated his famous theory of Forms in any dogmatic sense. The flowering of the individual creative impulse, which characterized the Renaissance, was a diverse effect that had a single underlying cause. This was the new prominence that was given to the essentially Platonic vision of the nature of the human being.

Kristeller did not include Pico della Mirandola, whose *Oration on the Dignity of Man* was the most important exposition of this new vision, in the ranks of the humanists. He also excluded Ficino, Pomponazzi and Patrizi, all of whom are normally seen as exemplary humanists.[263] He did, however, accept that there was an element of humanism in the rich and complex thought of each of these men.[264] The difficulty with a definition of humanism, of course, is that there was no such thing as humanism in the Renaissance period. Technically Humanists were teachers of the humanities. There was no concrete movement called humanism with easily identifiable and accepted members who were called humanists. Thus it has been all too easy for historians to define what they believe humanism was and then exclude any figure who does not fit in with their definition. Kristeller's exclusion of Pico, for instance, facilitates the overturn of Burckhardt's notion of the primary importance of the new vision of the human being. Thus the definition of humanism to some extent will always be arbitrary. It was invented to explain a phenomenon but there is no exact description of the components of this phenomenon. We could agree with Kristeller's minimalist definition of humanism but it is deficient in that it does not explain the idea that underlies the *studia humanitatis*. Something did happen in the Renaissance and it was related to the *studia humanitatis* but it was not a result of this programme. It was a result of the rediscovery of a radical new idea: the idea that we have within ourselves the means of achieving our own perfection. The human being is a microcosm that reflects the divine macrocosm, because we contain a spark of divinity. We can thus discern the underlying laws that operate in all spheres or dimensions of existence. This idea was to be found in the newly flourishing Cabbalistic and Hermetic movements of the Renaissance as well and was to be influential in the seventeenth-century rise of science. The new educational program and the occult philosophies had more in common than is immediately apparent. They were all instruments being used by people who wanted to perfect their own nature.

Kristeller said that 'the diversity of opinions that have been expressed during the last hundred years or so about the Renaissance and its historical significance is so vast that in facing it we are likely to be overwhelmed by confusion'.[265] He went on to observe that

> the subject envisaged is large indeed, and since a scholar cannot hope to master it all, he will be obliged to generalize from the limited material with which he is acquainted. The best he may claim is that he emphasizes what is most significant or most representative, and in effect, he ends up by stressing what he happens to know best.[266]

In another article he has said that 'the long war' about the Renaissance 'has not been settled by victory; it has merely given way to an armistice imposed by exhaustion and boredom'.[267] We must not be defeated by exhaustion and boredom. These states can be caused by too much attention to detail and not enough analysis of which detail is significant and which is not. The typical Renaissance scholar had wide-ranging interests rather than a narrow specialization. Thus the modern specialist has to overcome the urge to make him or her conform to modern norms. Erasmus, in his underlying Platonism, his insistence on the destructive nature of dogma, his belief in the superiority of classical mores, his cultivation of humanist educational practices and, above all in his exaltation of the dignity of the human being, embodied the true spirit of humanism. This underlying impulse pervades his writings and conditioned his interpretation of the *philosophy of Christ.* He expressed this in the *Enchiridion* when he wrote, in the mode of Pico, of the 'dignity of man'.[268] He said:

> man is a noble animal, for whose sake alone God fashioned this marvellous contrivance of the world; he is the fellow-citizen of the angels, son of God, heir of immortality, member of Christ, member of the church; our bodies are temples of the Holy Spirit; our minds are both the images and shrines of divinity.[269]

This wholly optimistic vision of human potential is crucial to an understanding of Erasmus' view of the process of human perfection.

Chapter 3

The Godly Feast

The Erasmian method of perfection, then, involved a process of emulating Christ in a very profound way so that one incorporated Christ into one's very being. This process was, of its essence, an individualistic and private one. It raises the question, therefore, of what role Erasmus saw for the traditional church in the process of human perfection. Erasmus' view of the church was complex. Throughout his life he always accepted the authority of the Church of Rome and clearly believed that it played an extremely important role in the sanctification of Christians. Nevertheless, in line with his belief in the superiority of the unseen spiritual realm over the visible material world, he believed that in addition to the visible church there was a more spiritual, true church or *Ecclesia*. This was very different from the visible church. It was a spiritual and invisible community of those Christians who had progressed on the path to perfection and were seeking their own perfection in an internal and, for Erasmus, more truly Christian way. This was not, in any way, a separate institution because it was not separate from the Church of Rome nor, indeed, was it an institution at all. It was a spiritual phenomenon. The best exposition of the Erasmian concept of the true *Ecclesia* is to be found in his colloquy called *The Godly Feast*. There we see a group of lay Christians engaged in their own quest for perfection using their own individual discernment and abilities to penetrate the mystery. In true Erasmian form, this message in the colloquy is also only visible if you search beneath the surface to its real meaning. Christian orthodoxy held that the means of salvation, including the knowledge required for this, was conferred on Christians by the institutional church. The Erasmian system with its emphasis on the incorporation of Christ meant that it was of the utmost importance to come to know Christ. In the traditional church the source for knowledge of Christ was, of course, primarily Scripture. Erasmus concurred with this but he also believed that there were two other sources for this knowledge: First, the divine creation, and secondly, human nature itself. In each of these sources he thought that the full nature of the mystery lay hidden deep below the immediately apparent surface.

In *the Godly Feast*, Erasmus depicted some like-minded friends meeting for a meal at the country villa of the host, Eusebius. Before and after dining they toured the house and gardens. During the meal itself they discussed some Scriptural passages. In accordance with all Erasmian writings the conversation and the whole tone of the piece is Christian. On the surface, the work is a description of the ideal way of conducting a truly Christian meal. Eusebius declares that the practice of reading extracts from Scripture at a meal is highly desirable because 'by means of it we avoid foolish yarns and enjoy profitable conversation'.[1] He goes on to say that he disagrees 'emphatically with those who think a dinner party isn't fun unless it overflows with silly, bawdy stories and rings with dirty songs'.[2] The title of the piece, however, evokes a comparison with the Christian Eucharist and Erasmus makes this quite explicit when he makes Eusebius declare that for Christians a meal was 'an allegory of that sacred last supper which the Lord Jesus had with his disciples'.[3] This sense of the sacredness of the meal is also evident in the ritual cleansing or purification that the participants engage in before and after eating. Erasmus always emphasized the sacrament of the Eucharist as being the most important, aspect of the sacrifice of the mass. Together with Baptism it was central to his concept of Christianity. He believed that the real value of the Eucharist lay in its secret meaning. This was that it symbolized the true process of Christianization that occurred in the psyche or the soul. He said that the sacrifice of the Mass, in this spiritual sense, really means that we are 'one spirit with the spirit of Christ, one body with the body of Christ, a living member of the church'.[4] Thus, for him, the gathering of a group of spiritual Christians to celebrate the true Eucharist is an expression of the true *ecclesia* or church. In his *Paraphrase on Mark,* which he wrote a year after the *Godly Feast*, Erasmus explicitly interpreted a banquet as a symbolic representation of a 'type of the church'.[5] His views on the visible institutional church of his day were highly critical. He certainly did not believe that the hierarchy of the church was the best exemplar of the Christian spirit. There are many criticisms of the contemporary hierarchy scattered throughout his writings but perhaps one of the harshest was spoken, albeit satirically, by his character, Folly, who said

> As if indeed the deadliest enemies of the Church were not these impious pontiffs who allow Christ to be forgotten through their silence, fetter him with their mercenary laws, misrepresent him with their forced interpretations of his teaching, and slay him with their noxious way of life.[6]

This criticism did not, however, lead Erasmus to want to eradicate the formal role of the church in everyday life. He held steadfastly to the belief that the church was very necessary to those who were infants in Christ and that it continued to be useful even after a certain level of Christianity had been achieved. He was adamant that to disrupt or destroy the unity of the Christian family would be a fatal mistake. This is expressed clearly in his *Paraphrase on Mark* when he wrote:

> Old suits old and new suits new. If you mingle them, you do not only labour in vain but also make worse men out of those whom you are trying to improve. For it is better to continue in the old superstition than to take away fear of sinning and thereby invite men to sin freely when you attempt to lead them to spiritual freedom.[7]

As we have seen, Erasmus thought that Christ had revealed the true meaning of the Eucharist to very few people.[8] He believed that it represented the process of perfection, in that, the consumption of the body and blood of Christ symbolized the state of perfection that we can achieve by means of the incorporation of Christ into our being through a process of dying to the world and rising again to live in a new way in relation to the *Logos*.[9] He wrote often of this process to his friends. In 1506 he told Richard Foxe that

> Christianity itself is only that true and perfect kind of friendship which consists in dying with Christ, living in Christ, and forming

> one body and one soul with Christ; it is indeed a communion between men, like the communion of limbs in the body, one with another.[10]

He also addressed the topic in two letters that he wrote in 1515. Here he described the process as one in which the Christian was 'transfigured' and made one with Christ.[11] In allegorizing the true meaning of the Christian Eucharist Erasmus approached the 'holy of hollies' of his religious system. The process of incorporating Christ entailed, of necessity, the acquisition of knowledge of the ultimate truth of existence. Christ is our means of knowing God and the divine plan. This is the Erasmian concept of Christ as the eternal and omnipresent *Logos*.[12] In this colloquy the concept is decisively liberated from the narrow confines of dogma. Erasmus, under the protection of fiction, shows us precisely how and where to find the truth of Christ.

Throughout his writings, as we have seen, Erasmus never strayed very far from Plato. In this piece he came very near to deifying the philosopher. The central character, Eusebius, is imbued with the ultimately Platonic notion that it is Nature who teaches us all we know, particularly, about the supreme object of knowledge, which is God, or, as Plato would term it, 'the Good'. Eusebius declares:

> Nature, in my opinion, is not silent but speaks to us everywhere and teaches the observant man many things if she finds him attentive and receptive. What else does the charming countenance of verdant Nature proclaim than that God the creator's wisdom is equal to his goodness?[13]

In his *Paraphrase on John,* Erasmus also expressed this idea. In describing why God created the world, he said that God himself had no need of the created universe but that he had created the world solely to enlighten the human race. 'So that from the wonders of creation and even from itself it might deduce the power, holiness, and goodness of its maker'.[14] The method of knowing the creator is through knowing and reading his creation and this included the apogee of God's creation: the human being. In the *Enchiridion* Erasmus asserted that the sum of all known wisdom was contained in the concept that we should strive to know ourselves. For him the kingdom of heaven was, truly, within us.

This idea rests on the premise that the visible world or the human being is a microcosm that reflects the macrocosm that can be the universe or the divine realm. The idea that the microcosm reflects the macrocosm flourished anew among many of the occult philosophies of Erasmus' time, from Hermeticism to Cabbala. Most of these philosophies were influenced, initially, by Neoplatonism in either its original, or its Renaissance, incarnation. Erasmus did not display much overt sympathy with these recent philosophical developments preferring, as ever, to drink from the source instead. Nevertheless he did, on the authority of Plato, believe in the idea that the created realm is a precise reflection of the heavenly one. In the *Godly Feast* this idea is central and Erasmus uses it first when he depicts the host as the creator of a perfect little villa, which he consciously designed as a reflection of the higher creation, in order to have an example of the wisdom of God nearby. One of the guests, Timothy, hints at this when he enters the villa. He said that he and his companions arrived early 'in order to have time to walk round and see this palace of yours, which we hear is filled with various delights - not a corner that doesn't bear the master's stamp'.[15] The notion that the master's stamp was all-pervading is reminiscent of Erasmus' view of God's role in his creation. In the *Antibarbari*, for instance, he described the same thoroughly pervasive presence of God in Creation. He wrote:

> the great and eternal Disposer, who is wisdom itself establishes all things with consummate skill, differentiates them with perfect rightness, so that each balances another in a marvellous way; nor does he allow anything to move at random in all the immense variety of the world.[16]

The Erasmian concept of the universe was one of a harmonious entity with the divine law or *Logos* underlying everything. The wise individual would meditate on creation in order to uncover and know the divine wisdom and truth. Eusebius replied to Timothy that he would 'see a palace worthy of such a king'.[17] In fact Timothy had not mentioned a 'king' but Erasmus frequently used the metaphor of a 'king', as Plato had, to depict a perfect man whose worldly material impulses and passions were under the control of his reason.[18] In the adage, *Sileni Alcibiadis*, for instance, Erasmus employed the term in this way: he said that a king should be as near as possible someone who resembled God. He should excel in wisdom and be far from all low passions. He should 'be in the commonwealth what the soul is in the body and God is in the universe'.[19] Further on in *The Godly Feast,* Timothy himself explicitly interprets the word king in a scriptural passage as meaning 'the perfect man, who with his bodily passions under control, is governed solely by the power of the Holy Spirit'.[20] Thus, in the colloquy, Eusebius the host represents the perfected human being and as such is a mirror of God himself because such a person shares in the divine nature.

The villa is depicted as a kind of *theatrum mundi* from which the divine truth can be ascertained. Later in the piece, Timothy hints at this when he says 'there is something of the divine about this place, everything shines so'.[21] The idea that things that were touched by divinity would shine is reminiscent of the section of the *Phaedrus* in which Plato described how the soul can recognize images of the higher world in their earthly shadows which are 'seen through a glass dimly'. He then described a 'beatific vision' of beauty 'shining in company with the celestial forms; and coming to earth we find her here too shining in clearness through the clearest aperture of sense'.[22] Erasmus also expounded on this idea in his paraphrase of the first chapter of John's gospel, in which the *Logos* is portrayed as the true light whose source is God. Erasmus comments on this that 'everything that shines in heaven and earth borrows its brightness' from this source.[23] Surrounding the garden are galleries with frescoes of plants, trees, birds, quadrupeds, lakes, rivers, seas and fish: in other words an image of the totality of the natural world.[24] This represents a self-contained and integrated system of knowledge: Perfectly designed in order to instruct those who visit it and to create the right atmosphere for the acquisition of knowledge.[25] Everything serves this purpose; there is no waste and nothing is superfluous. It is a perfectly functioning whole. Its importance is clear from the fact that Erasmus described it in great detail. If it were not significant then the detail would have been simply tedious and extreme. It is neither, and the reader is drawn into the cohesiveness of the description. It is a microcosm of the natural world from which the seeker of wisdom can learn the true nature of God. One of the clearest expressions of this notion in Erasmus' writings is in his *Paraphrase on the Acts of the Apostles* in which he wrote that

> God cannot be grasped by human intellect because it is weighted down by the body' but reason can 'infer one thing from another - the invisible from the visible, the universal from the particular, the eternal from the temporal, the things that are grasped only by the intellect from the things perceived by the senses; and he has set human beings in the midst of the theatre of the world so that from the created things which they see with their eyes, touch with their hands, experience through use, they might trace out and search for the creator. Like the blind who discover by feel what they cannot see, so human beings through reflection upon the marvellous creation of the universe might arrive at some knowledge of God, whom truly to know is utmost felicity.[26]

This is primarily why he believed that 'earth, water, air, the very celestial bodies and finally even the angels themselves, were created especially to serve the requirements of men'.[27] In his *Paraphrase on John* he again argued that although the nature of God surpasses human intelligence

> even so traces of divine power, wisdom, and goodness cast a dim glow in the created universe. As a result parallels drawn from the things that we do in some fashion grasp with our senses and intelligence guide us towards a vague and shadowy knowledge of the incomprehensible, so that somehow we gaze on them as through a dream and mist.[28]

This belief that all truth was hidden and had, therefore, to be mined from the depths is the key to Erasmus' reading of Scripture. He thought that sticking to the dead letter of Scripture was useless and even, in some instances, potentially dangerous; It was always necessary instead to penetrate to its hidden spirit. This was the only method of perceiving the true wisdom of God outlined in it. The factual historical information contained in Scripture, particularly the Old Testament, was, at best, of limited importance when taken at face value. In a letter in 1518 to Helias Marcqus, an Old Testament expert, he argued that the correct title of the book of the Maccabees should be 'on the Sovereign Rule of Reason', and that 'the message of the narrative is that reason can produce any effect in human beings, once it has mastered their desires'.[29] In the *Complaint of Peace* he confirmed his preference for the psychological allegorical approach to the Old Testament when he argued that the 'bloody slaughters which fill the pages of the

Hebrew Scriptures' should be interpreted 'not as the mangling of human bodies but as the tearing of wicked inclinations out of the heart'.[30] Truth, for Erasmus, was hidden, eternal and spiritual. Therefore literature could only approach truth allegorically. In relation to the Old Testament, he warned the readers of his *Enchiridion* thus:

> if you read unallegorically of the infants struggling within the womb, the right of primogeniture sold for a mess of pottage, the fraudulent seizing of a father's blessing ahead of time, David's slaying of Goliath with a sling, and the shaving off of Samson's locks, then it is of no more importance than if you read the fiction of poets. What difference is there whether you read the Book of Kings or the Book of Judges or Livy's history; if in none of them you perceive the allegory? The latter book contains many things that could amend morals, but in the Bible there are some things that are even absurd at first glance and if understood only superficially can be prejudicial to morals.[31]

In the colloquy the allegory begins when the guests enter the villa by means of a courtyard. This is guarded by an image of St Peter who is depicted as giving a prescription for salvation in the three classical languages and from three different sources. In Latin he says 'if thou wilt enter into life, keep the commandments', in Greek: 'repent ye, therefore, and be converted', and finally in Hebrew: 'the just shall live by his faith'.[32] Here, Erasmus was presenting the idea that the three main traditions from which Christianity draws its precepts have their own unique and different ways of expressing the same important concept of the method of perfection. In this way the visitor to the villa is alerted to the fact that he or she is being invited in to discover the way or method of perfection and, crucially, is also being told that there are various traditions in which this method can be discovered. St Peter, the doorkeeper, as the keeper of the keys to heaven represents the idea that the guests are entering into the way of salvation. He tells them that the first step in the process is keeping the law. In the Erasmian scheme of perfection the difficulties of opposing the flesh that will be encountered in doing this will lead the aspiring Christian to a deeper understanding of the dichotomy between the worlds of spirit and flesh and ultimately to a knowledge of the unseen reality. At this point the Christian will repent, the Greek word for which is μετανοια, which means a transformation of mind. Thus the deeper knowledge of true reality will lead to a transformation. Finally, the Christian who understands this will live by his or her faith in accordance with this new insight. The guests then progress to the next area of the house, which is a chapel with an image of Christ who is also depicted as speaking three messages. This represents the stage in perfection in which the Christian progresses to a deeper knowledge of Christ. In Latin the figure of Christ says 'I am the way, and the truth, and the life'; in Greek: 'I am Alpha and Omega', and in Hebrew: 'come, ye children, harken unto me; I will teach you the fear of the Lord'.[33] The Christian now gradually comes to understand that Christ is all knowledge and wisdom and that by incorporating Christ the world of unseen reality will open up. In the case of both the Christ image and that of St Peter the Latin quotations are taken from the synoptic gospels; the Greek quotations are respectively taken from the Acts of the Apostles and the Book of Revelation. The Hebrew quotes, as one would imagine, are from the Old Testament. They represent the three orthodox sources of Christian doctrine: the synoptic gospels, the non-synoptic cannon, and the Old Testament

In the colloquy, there follows a description of the three upper galleries in the villa. Eusebius described how on the wall of one of these there was a fresco of the 'entire life of Jesus as related by the four Evangelists, up to the sending forth of the Holy Spirit and the first preaching of the Apostles from Acts'.[34] On the opposite wall are 'corresponding figures and prophecies of the Old Testament, particularly from the Prophets and Psalms'.[35] What is significant about this is that Eusebius declares that the latter 'contain nothing other than the life of Christ and the Apostles, told in a different manner'.[36] It was, of course, completely orthodox to believe that the Old Testament prophets foretold the life of Christ but Erasmus was saying something subtly different here. He did not say that the Old Testament was a foreshadowing of the New but that it was exactly the same message told in a different manner. Erasmus believed this because his concept of Christ included the idea that the eternal *Logos* of Christ operated as a perfecting force throughout all time and both within and without time. This is the underlying reason for the most strikingly unorthodox element of the piece: the very high regard that the participants had for some ancient philosophers and writers. This stretched the bounds of orthodoxy at the time, particularly, when they wanted to include some of the ancients in the company of saints. Eusebius said that although Sacred Scripture was the basic authority in everything,

> I sometimes run across ancient sayings or pagan writings - even the poets' - so purely and reverently and admirably expressed, that I can't help believing their authors' hearts were moved by some divine power. And perhaps the spirit of Christ is more widespread than we understand, and the company of saints includes many not in our calendar.[37]

Eusebius' namesake, the church Father from Caesarea, also believed that there were people who were imbued with the spirit of Christ before the time of Jesus. In his *History of the Church* he wrote:

> although we certainly are a youthful people and this undeniably new name of Christians has only lately become known among all nations, nevertheless our life and mode of conduct, together with our religious principles, have not been recently invented by us, but from almost the beginnings of man were built on the natural concepts of those whom God loved in the distant past.[38]

Erasmus may well have been alluding to this when he named the host in this colloquy. Eusebius' *Preparation for the Gospel* is considered to have been the source for Ficino's syncretism and under his influence the syncretism of later evangelical humanists.[39] Thus the humanists in Erasmus' audience would have understood the significance of the name. Unlike some other humanists, Erasmus did not speculate in any philosophical or theological way on the salvation of pagans. It would have been impossible for him to avoid censure if he had made this view more explicit. Nevertheless, his concept of the *Logos* of Christ as an entity that God 'brought forth.. in two ways: once in time, but forever outside all time'[40] was the basis for his belief that people before the coming of Jesus Christ were capable of knowing the way of Christian perfection. The guests at *The Godly Feast* display sympathy with this notion when they discuss several passages from secular classical writings as well as scriptural passages. Here we see the Erasmian belief in the usefulness of these ancient writings in the perfection process because they breathed the spirit of Christ. The guests Nephalius and Uranius demonstrate this by comparing what

Socrates said in the *Phaedo* about the body being a prison with what was to be found in the writings of St Peter and St Paul on the same subject.[41] A discussion then ensued about the proper spirit in which to die and the consensus was that Socrates expressed a far more Christian spirit in this process than most so-called Christians. Another guest, Chrysoglottus, then said:

> I think I've never read anything in pagan writers more proper to a true Christian than what Socrates spoke to Crito ...before drinking the hemlock: "Whether God will approve of my works", he said, "I know not; certainly I have tried hard to please him. Yet I have good hope that he will accept my efforts.[42]

Chrysoglottus interpreted this passage as meaning that although Socrates was suitably diffident about his own deeds, 'yet by reason of his earnest desire to obey the divine will, he conceived a strong hope that God in his goodness would accept them, because he had endeavoured to live righteously'.[43] Nephalius then heaped praise on Socrates saying: 'an admirable spirit, surely, in one who had not known Christ and the Sacred Scriptures. And so, when I read such things of such men, I can hardly help exclaiming, "Saint Socrates, pray for us"'. Chrysoglottus joined in with this sentiment and added: 'as for me, there are many times when I do not hesitate to hope confidently that the souls of Virgil and Horace are sanctified'.[44]

While Erasmus, as always when he was expressing a potentially heterodox view, used slightly ambiguous language here it is nevertheless very clear in the context of the entire piece and his writings in general that he believed the true spirit of Christ and thus of perfection was to be found in some of the ancients and their writings. As we have seen, he believed Cicero too was truly virtuous and that what he wrote was worthy of a saint or even a deity.[45] He also expressed his views on the spiritual achievements of the ancients in the *Antibarbari*. This work is the major source for his belief in the value of pagan writing to the perfection process of Christianity. In it he said that 'the pagans perfected systems of knowledge according to the divine plan, not for us to scorn them, but for our use'.[46] All the good studies of the pagan world had been 'prepared by Christ for his society', he had supplied the intellect and the zest for inquiry and 'it was through him alone that they found what they sought'.[47] The principal character in that piece,

Batt, goes as far as to say that he would, in fact, allow the secular learning of the ancients to be called Christian.[48] Moreover, he also says: 'if we wished to indulge in guesswork, I could easily prove that the great men among the pagans are saved, or else no one is'.[49] Plutarch, too, belonged to this level of saintly ancient. The year after writing *The Godly Feast* Erasmus wrote to Johann von Botzheim and told him that he had been translating several works of Plutarch: 'these exercises I enjoyed all the more because they contributed substantially to the building of character no less than to the learning of Greek; for I have read nothing outside Scripture with such a high moral tone'.[50] Erasmus found a source for this view throughout Scripture but it was in his exposition of St Paul's epistle to the Romans that he found it most clearly expressed. In this work, he paraphrased Paul as saying that many human beings before Christ had sinned with impunity but that God had now revealed his anger against all of them even those who were exempt from the law of Moses. 'For they have not applied the truth *however they have come to know it* to pious and holy living'.[51] Thus even people who knew nothing of the Law of Moses were not exempt from God's judgment because as human beings they had access to this law in themselves and in creation. Again here, he expressed the view that one of the ways of discerning the divine truth was in the creation. He said that besides revealing his truth to us through the prophets and in Scripture God has also 'certainly revealed it in the miracle of this whole structure of the world. For even though God himself is invisible, nevertheless by the intellect he is seen in this world so marvellously created and so wonderfully administered.' He concluded that from the workmanship of the world

> is seen the power of the creator, a power which neither knows any beginning nor will have any end. In fact, the creation demonstrates his very divinity by which he was always in himself complete even before the founding of the world, so that they have no pretext for their own impiety.[52]

Erasmus also found evidence in the same epistle to the Romans for his belief in the other means at our disposal for discerning the truth. This was his view that all human beings had an innate knowledge of the *philosophy of Christ*. He paraphrased St Paul thus:

> God cherishes and approves meritorious action even if there should be no law, and he turns away from those even more who, although they have the law, do not obey it. There is no one, however, who is entirely without the law. For when the races foreign to the law of Moses do of their own accord under the guidance of nature the things which are ordered by the law even though they are instructed by no prescription of the Mosaic law, they themselves are a law unto themselves, because they express the substance of the law, engraved not on tablets but on their own minds.[53]

This knowledge is what Erasmus later in *The Godly Feast* refers to as the 'Master'.[54] He then elaborated on the concept in his *Paraphrase on Romans* and said: 'whatever among them is usually done before a tribunal of justice is done in their hearts; your conscience gives testimony for or against you, and your thoughts contending with one another, alternately accuse and defend you.' He believed in an innate sense of right and wrong in us which could not really be ignored but the more perfect a person became the more fully they would recognize this 'Master'. While this is certainly a description of moral conscience, it is also far more. It is an innate knowledge of the method of perfection. For Erasmus, morality in the usual sense of agreed norms of just behaviour was of little consequence: what was right was whatever aided perfection and what was wrong was whatever hindered it. This interior voice was a guide to the method of perfection.

The principal theological difficulty with the Erasmian version of the existence of the spirit of Christ before the time of Jesus lies in the doctrine of the Redemption. If everyone could have been perfected by a personal insight into the truth of Christ before the saviour was born then this would lessen the importance of the redemptive function of Jesus. Erasmus never engaged in this kind of theological speculation. He thought that it was quite useless for us to speculate on the higher mysteries and he was perfectly happy to accept church teachings on these matters. Whenever he touched on the doctrine of Redemption he always spoke in an orthodox way about it. He never denied, and clearly believed, that Christ redeemed fallen humanity by his passion and death. If, however, his views on the precise mechanism of this act of Redemption were different from the accepted orthodoxy he never expressed them. This doctrine was so central to the Catholic religion that he would have sacrificed his position of influence and even possibly his life if he had denied or amended it in any way. He saw no value at all in martyrdom. He believed that it was perfectly acceptable, if not essential, to hide one's real beliefs if expressing them might be detrimental to the task of saving humanity. In the *Enchiridion* he urged his readers to conceal their true feelings and instead be 'all things to all men, so that you may win everyone to the side of Christ, as far as it is possible, without giving offence to piety'. He also exhorted the Christian to 'adapt' himself or herself 'to everyone exteriorly, provided that interiorly your resolution remains unshaken'.[55] The enigmatic Erasmus followed his own advice. His humanism led him to this belief in the idea of the innate perfectibility of the human being.[56] The Erasmian programme of perfection relies on an intimate knowledge of the self. We must know ourselves in the deepest possible way before we can ever hope to engage in the war of perfection. Pre-Christian humans could engage in this same process and find Christ. This is the beginning of wisdom that we have to mine from Scripture and of which, crucially, the ancients were also aware because they shared our humanity.[57] He believed that the whole struggle for perfection depended on this self-knowing because the process of perfection contained in the *philosophy of Christ* was simply the restoration of imperfect human beings to a state of true human nature.[58] Thus the Erasmian programme of perfection did not emphasize the concept of grace imparted to fallen humanity by God on account of the Redemption of Christ. Erasmus was, nevertheless, truly Christian in his philosophy because he believed that the spirit of Christ was the only, and proper, goal for us. He believed that the heavenly philosophy had never in the past been transmitted to humankind in a more efficacious way than by the historical Jesus but there is an element in his thinking that is purely humanistic. He believed that the human mind contains the divine spark or image of Christ and that if we access this by a process of self-knowledge we will then discern for ourselves the way or method of perfection, which is the *philosophy of Christ.* [59]

This ideal state of perfection was one in which the material bodily urges were directed towards the spirit. As we have seen Erasmus did not believe that a state in which the spirit would permanently conquer the flesh was achievable in this life. In his *Paraphrase on Romans* he clarified this when he asserted that

> although we have received a pledge of our salvation from Christ, nevertheless he did not grant us full salvation here, but wanted us to wait for it in the age to come. In truth, our perfect salvation is dependent on future events of which we have received a certain hope.[60]

The 'certain hope' was made manifest to us through the life of Christ and also by searching the innermost depths of our own hearts to find the spirit of Christ. As we have seen, while he thought that the struggle between flesh and spirit went on until death even in the case of Christ himself, he did, nevertheless, believe that it was possible to achieve a level of perfection that resulted in the hegemony of the spirit in this struggle[61]. That is to say that the struggle continued but the spirit was always strong enough to conquer the urges of the flesh. When a person achieved this he or she would have achieved a harmonious unity in their psyche. They would have enshrined Christ as their goal in all things and at all times. In the *Enchiridion,* in order to depict this state, he quoted the saying 'let your eye be single, and your whole body will be filled with light'.[62] In the famous letter to Paul Volz, when advocating a simplification of the Christian message, Erasmus again used the metaphor of the eye to depict unity and singleness of purpose: he said that to avoid confusion we need 'the single eye filled with light of which the Gospel speaks'.[63] His clearest exposition of the symbol of the eye is in the adage 'One ought to be born a king or a fool'.[64] Here he outlined how the Egyptians used an image of a single eye and a sceptre to depict a prince, because the eye represented the highest wisdom. Thus the eye in Christian terms is Christ the *Logos*. The spirit by means of which we are given the true sight that allows us to see things as they really are. In the same adage Erasmus defined true wisdom as consisting 'not only in the knowledge of truth, but in the love and eager striving for what is good'.[65] Again here, the ultimate state of wisdom was not simply a static one, but one that involved active participation in the search to achieve goodness. Christianity was not an intellectual exercise, for Erasmus, It involved a rich, diverse and, above all, individual process of transformation and was not, therefore, amenable to dogmatic stipulations or outside coercion

In the piece the villa represented the totality of the visible creation, from which we could ascertain the higher spiritual reality but Erasmus also used the characters themselves to symbolize aspects of true spiritual Christianity. The names of the four guests and what he called their 'shadows', together with Eusebius, the host, represent these aspects. The 'lover of God', Theophilus is balanced by his shadow Eulalius who is 'sweet spoken' or eloquent. He would, therefore, allow Theophilus to express his divine love in a comprehensible and acceptable form. Conversely the 'golden-tongued' Chrysoglottus has Theodidactus with his 'godly teaching' skill as his shadow. The latter would provide the former with the requisite knowledge for his sweet speeches. In both of these duos the very important attributes of love and knowledge are combined with the necessary skill for their transmission. Erasmus believed that in order to achieve the goal of Christ it was necessary to acquire knowledge of all aspects of this goal but he also believed that it was absolutely crucial to love it. It was this attractive force alone that had the power of transformation. Thus these four characters contain the elements that were essential for the achievement of perfection. The character Timothy represents the friend of St Paul who helped to set up and administer the early church. He is hailed as the elder of the group and as such he represents the community of the first Pauline Christians. He also alerts the attentive reader to the concept of syncretism contained in the piece. He is a syncretic figure because in his *Paraphrase on Acts* Erasmus pointed out that Timothy, who was the chosen messenger of Paul, was the product of a mixed marriage: his mother was a Jewish convert to Christianity and his father was a pagan.[66] He has as his shadow the 'moderate and discrete' Sophronius. The reflection of this couple is the duo of the young Hellenist Uranius and his 'moderate and calm' shadow Nephalius. The shadows in both cases are moderating, uniting forces while their partners represent the sources of Christian wisdom. In the Erasmian system pre-eminence is given to the synoptic writings and the writings of St Paul, of course, but Erasmus was always at pains to point out that a reading of the classics, especially Greek philosophy, was the ideal training for a proper interpretation of the New Testament.[67] Each character has a shadow who is moderate, signifying that the sources of wisdom should be treated with discretion and discernment and never used in a fanatical or extreme way. The host, Eusebius, represents the Christian duty of service and generosity to humanity. Eusebius provided the venue and the food for everyone. He also directed the more important mental food, or conversation. At the end of the piece he had to rush off on Christian work in the service of others.[68] In the ultimate sense being properly of service to others was work that could only be done by a true perfected human being. Only such an enlightened person would have the understanding necessary to know precisely what kind of help an aspiring Christian would require. His or her intentions, objectives, and understanding would all have to be the correct ones. He or she would not be led by selfish passion or worldly ambition and would have acquired true wisdom by dint of Herculean labours. Thus they would be capable, through having reached this state of objectivity and true wisdom, of knowing accurately what help another individual needed. The Greek name Eusebius means godly or pious. Thus the godly man provided an appropriately godly feast for his friends.

The fact that each guest has a 'shadow' is consistent with the Erasmian theme of the dichotomy of the spirit and the flesh, or the spirit and the law, which pervades the entire piece. It is an allusion to the fact that the present world of the senses is merely a shadow of true reality and that we have to cultivate a spiritual way of looking at it in order to see through it to the hidden reality. The notion of shadows is also reminiscent of the Platonic cave myth that Erasmus used in *The Praise of Folly* to demonstrate this dichotomy. He used it to show that humankind's perception of reality was in fact a miasma.[69] In the *Enchiridion* he advised his reader to 'be so convinced of the existence of invisible things that those things that are seen become but mere shadows, which present to the eye only a faint image of invisible realities'.[70] Theophilus says that God rejected the Jews 'not because they observed the rites of the Law but because, foolishly puffed up by keeping them, they would neglect what God especially requires of us. They embraced the shadows and neglected the substance.'[71] Erasmus, of course, Christianized this platonic view that only the spiritual realm was real and that the material world was but an inferior temporal shadow of this true eternal and unchanging reality. He believed that God was spiritual in essence and that since we were of God and made in his likeness that our true nature was thus spiritual. The folly of the world was that people did not understand this and thought the only reality was that which was accessible to the physical senses.

This was a prime reason for Erasmus' rejection of

Aristotle. He believed the latter taught that if a thing cannot be measured and weighed and repeated in experiments then it is not real. It struck Erasmus as ironic, but very human, that a religion which was obviously concerned mainly with the metaphysical realm would take Aristotelian philosophy as its main intellectual bulwark. This was precisely what the medieval scholastics had done. In the 1515 edition of the *Adages* he said that the church had reached the point where 'the whole of Aristotle was accepted as an integral part of theology and accepted in such a way that his authority was almost as sacred as that of Christ'.[72] He went on to complain that

> from him we have learnt that human felicity cannot be complete without worldly goods - physical or financial. From him we have learnt that a state cannot flourish where all things are held in common. We try to combine all his doctrines with the teaching of Christ, which is like mixing water and fire.[73]

Here we have much more than the contemporary anti-scholastic humanist rejection of Aristotle as inimical to Plato in philosophical terms. Erasmus viewed Aristotle as a representative of the blindness of the world in his glorification of dialectic whereas he viewed Plato as the champion of the wisdom of the true unseen reality.[74] He believed that the human condition was such that we could not easily understand this. This was a condition that humanity had reached because of an initial blindness which is 'a cloud of ignorance that obscures the judgment of reason'.[75] This blindness 'makes us incapable of distinguishing in our choice of things, so that we pursue the worst instead of the best, and choose the less profitable over what should be preferred to it'.[76] The only way we could perceive the truth was indirectly by means of metaphor, allegory and image because truth or true reality was spiritual. Erasmus believed this quite literally and not in some mysterious way. He thought that the method of perceiving the truth was necessarily indirect and that the 'divine spirit has its own peculiar language and modes of speech'.[77]

In *The Godly Feast* the shadow, Sophronius, interprets a piece of Scripture in this deeper and indirect way. Before he does this, however, he expresses reservations about his ability. He says 'if you'll take in good part whatever I say, I'll try my best to tell you how the matter looks to me. How else could a shadow shed light on darkness?'[78] Eusebius replies to this: 'shadows have their own light, one more suitable to our eyes'.[79] Here we see the precise nature of the value Erasmus placed on the physical realm. Shadows are useful to us because we have the ability to read them. Thus he made a shadow delve into the hidden meaning of the scriptural passage to show us the truth. In a later part of the dialogue Theophilus employed a similar, if rather unusual, method to solve a problem under discussion. He said: 'my mind is dreaming and is bringing forth something, I know not what. If you order me to, I'll set it before you, whatever it is, and you'll be the interpreters or midwives'.[80] The problem in question had been expressed in terms of a mathematical equation. On the face of it then, it is all the more strange, that it should have been solved by a method as indirect as dreaming. It is, however, another example of the Erasmian concept of the appropriateness of the indirect approach to the truth of Christ. The enigma that lies at the heart of his own corpus was deliberately constructed, but not for spurious reasons. He believed that wisdom and perfection were achieved when a Christian incorporated the gospel message and lived it. Experience, reflection and introspection were essential to its assimilation.

In the Erasmian world-view then, the body is shadow and the spirit is the true reality. As we have seen, however, Erasmus placed a very high value on the body.[81] It was only by means of the struggle between the body and the spirit that perfection could be achieved. Thus the shadows who represent the world of the flesh in this piece perform the very important function of balancing reality. Eusebius expresses this idea when he declares that our bodies are the 'partners of our minds'. He went on to say that he preferred the word '*partners* to *instruments* or *dwellings* or *tombs*'.[82] This is significant because here Erasmus made Eusebius consciously reject St Paul, who, as Uranius told the group a little later, called the body 'a tabernacle', which was a type of dwelling.[83] Erasmus, speaking in his own voice, in the *Enchiridion* did the same thing.[84] There he was willing to question the reported words of Christ himself because they did not fit in with his interpretation the role of the body in the perfection process.

The exaltation of the role of the individual Christian in this process was next explored in *The Godly Feast* when the guests, who were all laymen, engaged in some biblical exegesis. In conformity with the spirit of a Christian meal, Eusebius suggests that they should read and interpret three verses of the book of Proverbs as they eat. This was a text favoured by Erasmus because of its association with Solomon whom he believed was a prefiguration of Christ.[85] Eusebius then prays that Christ should also attend the feast and 'mingle with all our food and drink, so that everything may taste of him, but most of all may he penetrate our hearts!'[86] Here we are alerted to the fact that a central function of the feast was the incorporation of Christ into the hearts of the guests. In order to create the right atmosphere for the reception of Christ into their midst Eusebius then asked his servant to read some scriptural verses which the guests in turn would interpret. Erasmus had perhaps signalled this exercise earlier when, in describing the villa, he had depicted various water-features including a stream, ponds, and a fountain. In the *Enchiridion,* when he was advocating the allegorical approach to the interpretation of Scripture, he said that water was often used as a symbol for 'knowledge of the divine law'.[87] He went on to say that there was frequent mention

> in the sacred writings of wells, springs and rivers with this meaning, by which we are to understand that the diligent inquiry into the mystical writings is commended to us. What is the meaning of the water hidden in the veins of the earth but that the mystery is veiled by the letter? What is the meaning of water gushing forth in cascades but that the mystery is unveiled and explained? And when this mystery is spread abroad far and wide for the edification of the listener, what is to prevent us from calling it a river?[88]

The verses chosen were as follows:

> the king's heart is in the hand of the Lord, as the rivers of water: he turneth it whithersoever he will. Every way of a man is right in his own eyes: but the Lord pondereth the hearts. To do justice and judgment is more acceptable to the Lord than sacrifice.[89]

Erasmus was well aware that his depiction of laymen interpreting Scripture was potentially controversial. It was a rather audacious act given the context of religious upheaval in 1522. While he certainly did not want to fan the flames of dissent, the notion of everyone being capable of being a theologian and an interpreter of Scripture is central to his belief system. He had explicitly expressed the notion in 1516 in the *Paraclesis* where he said that he disagreed 'very much with those who are unwilling that Holy Scripture, translated into the vulgar tongue, be read by the uneducated, as if Christ taught such intricate doctrines that they could scarcely be understood by very few theologians'.[90] He then argued that a true theologian is anyone who

> teaches not by skill with intricate syllogisms but by a disposition of the mind, by the very expression and the eyes, by his very life that riches should be disdained, that the Christian should not put his trust in the supports of this world but must rely entirely on heaven, that a wrong should not be avenged, that a good should be wished for those wishing ill, that we should deserve well of those deserving ill. That all good men should be loved and cherished equally as members of the same body, that the evil should be tolerated if they cannot be corrected, that those who are stripped of their goods, those who are turned away from possessions, those who mourn are blessed and should not be deplored and that death should even be desired by the devout, since it is nothing other than a passage to immortality. And if anyone under the inspiration of the spirit of Christ preaches this kind of doctrine, inculcates it, exhorts, incites, and encourages men to it, he indeed is truly a theologian, even if he should be a common labourer or weaver. And if anyone exemplifies this doctrine in his life itself, he is in fact a great doctor.[91]

As always, here we see Erasmus' belief that the important thing is transformation and not learning or worldly office. If someone is capable of living the *philosophy of Christ*, then they have reached the pinnacle of human and Christian endeavour.

There were, at the time of composition of this colloquy, groups of laymen with humanist leanings established in many of the imperial cities calling themselves sodalities, who met regularly to discuss Scripture. These groups were beginning to be very influential in the reception of the Reformation in their respective cities. In the colloquy, Eusebius questions whether it is permissible for simple laypeople to discuss theological topics but Timothy in true Erasmian fashion answers that 'it would be permissible even for sailors, in my opinion, provided there is no rash attempt at formal definition'.[92] Erasmus, here, was in danger of undermining the fundamental authority of the church to interpret and disseminate Scripture. Indeed the council of Trent subsequently strictly forbade this kind of lay activity. Timothy continued:

'perhaps Christ, who promised to be present wherever two men are gathered together in his name, will help us, since we are so many'.[93]

In a truly Erasmian spirit Eusebius began the examination of the first scriptural passage by saying he would lay aside the various conjectures of the traditional commentators and seek the moral sense himself. Essentially, he interprets the passage as meaning that the king's passions are the will, and sometimes the instrument, of God so that there is no point in opposing them. Timothy then searches out the deeper meaning of the verse. He interprets the verse as being a description of the state of perfection. As we have seen, he interprets '"king" as 'the perfect man who, with his bodily passions under control, is governed solely by the power of the Holy Spirit'.[94] He goes on to explain that this man does not need external constraints on his behaviour. This clearly includes the laws of the church, although Timothy does not say this explicitly. What he does say is that

> to compel such a man to conform to human laws is perhaps inappropriate. Instead he should be left to his Master, by whose spirit he is led; he is not to be judged by those circumstances through which the weakness of feeble men is drawn, in one way or another, to true godliness. But if he does anything unrighteously, we ought to say with Paul: "God hath received him; to his own master he standeth or falleth." Likewise: "He that is spiritual judgeth all things, yet he himself is judged of no man." Therefore nobody may prescribe to such men, but the Lord who set the bounds to sea and rivers has the heart of the king in his hand and directs it whithersoever he wills. What need is there to prescribe to him who voluntarily does more than human laws require? Or what foolhardiness would it be to bind by human regulations the man who (as is evident by certain signs) is governed by the inspiration of the Holy Spirit?[95]

Here, again we can see that Erasmus' view of true morality is not at all the conventional one. The perfect human being does not have to obey the letter of church laws because he or she embodies the divine spirit and can do no wrong. Perfection cannot be achieved by any amount of outward conformity to worldly laws or the man-made laws of the church. In his *Paraphrase on Mark,* Erasmus pointed out that this type of outward conformity to the laws of Moses was not what Christ wanted. He said:

> He who does his duty for fear of punishment cannot be joyful; but the sons, who have drunk from the spirit of liberty and realize that they are the bridegroom's love and care, are not disturbed by anxiety, fearing that they might be sinning against laws that are prescribed for a time for men of a servile disposition, such as ablutions, Sabbaths, choice of foods, clothing, feast days, and sacrifices. They trust in the power and goodness of the bridegroom who, without any of these things, can confer perfect justice.[96]

This is echoed later in the colloquy by Chrysoglottus when he comments on the emphasis that the majority of Christians place on outward participation in ceremonies. He says that for most Christians these ceremonies are the 'alpha and omega of life'.[97] He describes how a child is first baptized then

> soon he's anointed again, at length he learns to confess, takes communion, becomes accustomed to resting on holy days, to hearing divine service, to fasting at times, to abstaining from meat, And if he does these things, he's considered a Christian beyond question. He marries - and receives another sacrament. He takes orders - and is once more anointed and consecrated; his clothes are changed, prayers said. All these I approve of, but doing them from custom rather than from conviction I don't approve of. The notion that nothing else is need for Christianity I reject absolutely, since a large part of mankind, while trusting to these things, loses no time in making money by hook or by crook and becoming enslaved to anger, lust, malice, flattery, until at last they come to death's door. Here again ceremonies are ready. Confession is made over and over; extreme unction added; the Eucharist administered; sacred candles, a crucifix, holy water are at hand; indulgences produced; a papal brief displayed or brought on the spot for the dying man; a lavish funeral ordered; once again a solemn contract is made one man shouts in the dying person's ear - sometimes in fact, pesters him to an earlier death if (as frequently happens) he's too loud or well liquored.[98]

Then Chrysoglottus says that although some of these ceremonies, which are sanctioned by the church, are acceptable, 'there are other, more interior means of helping us to depart from this life with cheerfulness and Christian trust'.[99] This amounts to a fairly damning indictment of most of the common religious practices of his day and yet he holds back and modifies somewhat his very extreme condemnation by saying that some of these practices are acceptable. It was this apparent ambiguity that led most of the reformers to reject Erasmus as a weak and vacillating man.[100] They misunderstood him because his views were too subtle and considered for the revolutionary times he lived in. In many ways, however, his views were even more radical than the reformers. His notion of an interior church and the interior method of perfection went far beyond the views of Luther or Zwingli but his belief that Christianity was only reached by degrees and that therefore those who were in the early stages of the process needed the guidance of the church meant that he was violently opposed to bringing the church into disrepute because it would be very detrimental for the majority of Christians who needed it.

Erasmus' views on ceremonies were quite clear if definitely unorthodox. In his *Paraphrase on Mark* he brought the scorn of the Paris theologians down upon himself with his interpretation of the incident in which the disciples and Jesus picked corn to eat on the Sabbath. He paraphrased Jesus thus: 'I do not give them rules of this kind' - eat, abstain, work, dress and such like - 'lest they remain weak forever if they have once learned under my direction to trust corporeal things'.[101] When Jesus was tackled by the Pharisees, Erasmus depicted him replying: 'the man who, free from the tumult of evil passions, violates the Sabbath from a desire to help his neighbour violates it in a pious fashion'.[102] He continued, 'those who adhere to the Son of Man, who is master of all law, and teaches us to observe spiritually the regulations which have been prefigured by those carnal laws, are free from such Judaic ceremonies'.[103] All of this has echoes in St Paul although Erasmus had his own way of interpreting it and in the colloquy this is highlighted by Eulalius who reads a passage from St Paul's letter to the Corinthians: 'All things are lawful unto me, but all things are not expedient: all things are lawful for me, but I will not be brought under the power of any'.[104] In his examination of this verse Eulalius employs the typically humanist procedure of placing it in its context by looking at the whole letter. He then concludes that despite Jewish food regulations St Paul believed it was 'permissible ... to eat anything one liked, and "unto the pure all things are pure" '.[105] The Erasmian view of ceremonies, however, had another vital element in it. In the colloquy Eulalius went on to add a proviso that the exercise of freedom by the true Christian from ceremonial law was not necessarily always expedient:

> that all things were permissible was a matter of gospel liberty; but charity everywhere regards what contributes to the salvation of our neighbour and on that account frequently abstains from what is permitted, preferring to yield to the welfare of a neighbour rather than exercise its liberty.[106]

Eulalius clarified this further with reference to the views of the church Father, Ambrose. He said that he believed that when St Paul wrote 'I will not be brought under the power of any', he meant:

> though for the sake of my neighbour's salvation and the advancement of the Gospel I abstain sometimes from foods used in sacrifices, or forbidden by the Mosaic law, yet my mind is free, knowing I may eat whatever I please to satisfy my mere bodily needs.[107]

What Erasmus is saying through his character Eulalius is that the observance of traditional ritual is not an essential prerequisite for perfection. Indeed the person who has progressed on the path of true Christianity has no need whatsoever of such rites but they have a duty to their weaker fellow Christians to avoid undermining a rite that could function to increase their purity. While this was always Erasmus' view of the purpose of church ritual it was particularly important for him to point this out in 1522 when the Reformation was exploding onto the European stage. Erasmus was, of course, walking a tightrope with this view. He was in real danger of totally undermining the sacramental system of the church. In an age of increasingly virulent polemic and entrenchment of dogma this was a serious problem. He dealt with this problem by always paying due deference to church doctrine and rites while criticizing what he perceived to be the wrong interpretation of their function at the same time. He genuinely wanted reformation rather than re-formation and schism.

Having extolled the interior liberty of the true Christian *vis a vis* official religious observance the guests then went on to castigate the lavishness and profligacy of the church. Eusebius led the charge:

> those who build or adorn monasteries or churches at excessive cost, when meanwhile so many of Christ's living temples are in danger of

> starvation, shiver in their nakedness, and are tormented by want of the necessities of life, seem to me almost guilty of a capital crime.[108]

He then went on to give many specific examples of lavish spending. He said:

> when I was in Britain I saw St Thomas' tomb, laden with innumerable precious jewels in addition to other incredible riches. I'd rather have this superfluous wealth spent on the poor than kept for the use of officials who will plunder it all sooner or later.[109]

Moreover he believed that the intentions of the lay benefactors themselves were less than laudable. He thought their benefactions were signs of

> a thirst for glory, not charity. Rich men covet a monument for themselves in churches where formerly there was not room for saints. They take care to have their likenesses carved and painted, with their names and an inscription about their gift added.[110]

While these people are silly and of bad intent, Eusebius' real scorn is poured upon the priests and bishops who ought to know better. He says:

> if I were a priest or a bishop, I would urge upon those thickheaded courtiers or merchants that if they wanted to have their sins forgiven in God's sight, they should spend their money secretly for the support of those who really need it.[111]

Instead of this, these clergymen 'consider money wasted that is scattered thus, piecemeal and secretly, to relieve the immediate needs of the poor, since no memorial of it will survive for posterity!'[112]

Here, Erasmus made explicit what he had been implicitly saying all along in the piece: that the earthly church left much to be desired. In describing the ways in which we can come to know the method of perfection in the *Godly Feast*, he ends up giving his blueprint for the true, spiritual Church of Christ. The truly spiritual Christian did not need worldly institutions and dogma for perfection. It was possible to know Christ by reading God's creation as an allegory of the spiritual reality. Ultimately, each one of us could find the way of perfection by coming to know ourselves truly. In the piece, all outward expressions of the Church are severely criticized and instead we are presented with a group of educated laymen mining the depths of Scripture for themselves. The Erasmian *ecclesia* was a spiritual one in which the person pursuing true Christian progress could participate whether he or she was ordained or not. Christianity was the perfection of human nature itself and so human nature was the raw material for the process. The institutional Church was not at all the true Church containing as it did many wicked people. While it was necessary for the weak in spirit and those in the early stages of perfection the true and more perfect Christian would participate in the real spiritual *ecclesia* wherever he or she found it in order to continue on the path of Christ. Erasmus wrote the colloquy in order to elaborate for his more discerning readers, the true spiritual nature of the method of incorporating Christ in all its splendour and diversity. This was the true meaning of the Eucharistic Christian banquet for him.

Chapter 4

The Ciceronianus

The divine spark in each human being was the seed that could, with hard work, grow and progress until a person had not just incorporated the gospel of Christ, but had in fact reached a state of Christhood. The way in which this could be achieved was through understanding and living the *philosophy of Christ*. In Erasmus' view the best way to achieve this was by imitating Christ because not only did he give us instructions that we could follow, but his very life itself was a paradigm for the process of human perfection. Erasmus' particular view of the precise nature of this *imitatio* reveals how rich and profound the process of incorporating Christ was for him. The best exposition of this view of proper *imitatio* is in his dialogue called the *Ciceronianus*. In it, under the layers of polemic, it is possible to get a deeper understanding of precisely what he believed the true nature of imitation to be. On the surface the *Ciceronianus* is a work in which Erasmus criticized some of his contemporary literary colleagues, mainly Italian writers, who, in his estimation, were doing Cicero a disservice by being too narrowly literal in their imitation of him. As such, it appears that he was simply engaging in the current literary debate and in the course of this critique he outlined his own view of the correct method of imitating Cicero. Underneath this surface layer of meaning, however, there was a deeper and, for Erasmus, a far more important purpose: This was the elaboration of the true method of imitation as applied to the all-important imitation of Christ.

He set the parameters of the piece in the dedicatory letter that served as its preface. First, he established that, for him, the object of 'good letters' was to 'proclaim the glory of Christ our

Lord and God with all the richness, brilliance and magnificence that Cicero displayed in speaking of things pagan'.[1] Here, from the beginning, he alerts the reader to the fact that everything he writes is for the purpose of expounding on the *philosophy of Christ*. The piece is set out as a kind of Socratic dialogue between the two main characters, Nosoponus and Bulephorus; the latter is aided and abetted by a minor character called Hypologus. Nosoponus is generally thought of as representing the Italian opposition to Erasmus.[2] Bulephorus the 'counsellor' and his supporter the 'responsible' Hypologus are the main exponents of Erasmus' own arguments. Throughout the text Nosoponus defends the extreme Ciceronian cause while Bulephorus attempts to persuade him that he is mistaken in his view of what it means to be a follower of Cicero. Essentially Bulephorus is objecting to the kind of extreme Ciceronianism that only allowed the use of a word if Cicero had actually used it. This literalism had particularly ridiculous results when the Ciceronians wrote about Christian subjects for which there were no proper Ciceronian terms.[3]

Bulephorus argues throughout the piece for a kind of holistic approach to the imitation of Cicero. He said that the Ciceronians were missing the point of Cicero's own eloquence and that they were nit-picking and narrowly literal in their methods.[4] There is a clear parallel here with Erasmus' view of the petty logic of scholasticism as opposed to the more holistic method of the new humanism. Bulephorus takes great pains to emphasize the primary importance of ascertaining the essence of Cicero's message itself rather than settling for a strict adherence, in superficial fashion, to his, undoubtedly, rich style and vocabulary. He argues in favour of the spirit rather than the letter of Cicero's writings. His belief is that it is more important to depict things appropriately using whatever language is best fitted to the task rather than to follow Cicero slavishly.[5] In defence of this he describes how he once heard a Roman orator speaking about the death of Christ in the Ciceronian manner. He contends that it was tedious and irrelevant and concludes that the Roman 'spoke so Romanly that I heard nothing about the death of Christ'.[6] The orator in question had more than one problem on his hands from the Erasmian perspective. First, by limiting himself to using actual words that Cicero had written, he had no proper vocabulary to expound on the Christian themes. Secondly, and more importantly, his very adherence to strict

Ciceronianism itself meant that he was incapable of understanding the primacy, in Christian terms, of the spirit over the law. Erasmus chose to illustrate his point here by using the example of the death of Christ. He believed, as we have seen, that its deeper mystical significance was that we should die to the world as Christ had. The world here included all ephemeral worldly and man-made systems such as logic and the law. These are always inferior to the more permanent divine realm of the spirit. Thus the orator, as someone who insisted on the letter of Ciceronianism, would have been incapable of appreciating the higher spirit of Christianity. He not only lacked the proper vocabulary to expound this mystery but, more importantly, he had no true understanding of it either. Erasmus was highlighting the ridiculousness of the attempt. He then pointed out that Cicero himself had not stuck rigidly to the letter of classical Latin when it failed him in his attempt to communicate something. For instance, when he was elucidating tenets of Greek philosophy, which had no Latin equivalents at the time, he had invented words or changed the meaning of existing ones.[7] This is Erasmus' central argument, which is then expanded and reiterated throughout the piece by Bulephorus until, in the end, Nosoponus finally sees the error of his ways and capitulates.

The work was a treatise against the contemporary Ciceronians, but it was also very much an apology for Cicero himself. Erasmus argued that Cicero was not simply a superlative literary craftsman but, much more crucially, he was a superlative human being. This was why he valued Cicero highly and often praised and quoted him.[8] In a letter to his friend Jacob de Voecht, he said that he found himself thinking as he read Cicero 'what justice, what purity, what sincerity, what truth in his rules for living'.[9] He then sanctified and even deified Tully: 'how many lessons he teaches, and how like a saint - almost a deity! - on how we should do good to all men even without reward, on the maintenance of friendship, on the immortality of souls'.[10] Erasmus was at pains, in the *Ciceronianus*, to show that the true Ciceronian was one who, above all, appreciated the value of Cicero's knowledge and wisdom and not simply his prose style because Cicero himself had used his personal gifts to further the cause of human knowledge and promote right living. Erasmus' essentially humanist viewpoint was that in emulating Cicero each person should use his or her own gifts in the same way as Cicero had. The result of this could never be a slavish imitation of the literary style of Cicero; instead it would necessitate the development of new and appropriate styles. Cicero, above all, was truly Cicero. This is exactly what Erasmus believed a person who had travelled on the way of perfection would also achieve. Not only would they become a truer human being, but they would also become more truly themselves. Thus, ironically, in order to be like Cicero each person would have to endeavour to be truly himself or herself and thus not at all like Cicero.

Erasmus, in his own work, did not believe in literature for literature's sake, everything he wrote was written to further the cause of the *philosophy of Christ*. As such, he was only interested in the Ciceronian debate insofar as it contributed to a better means of communication. Eloquence was desirable only as a means of communication and persuasion and was not of value as an end in itself. Near the end of the *Ciceronianus,* Erasmus drew an overt parallel between the correct method of Christianity and the correct Ciceronian method. Bulephorus says:

> the person who studies Christian philosophy with as much application as Cicero did pagan philosophy; who drinks in the psalms and prophets with as much enthusiasm as he did the poets; who works as hard and as long to understand the commands of the apostles, the rites of the church, the origins, progress, and decline of the Christian world as he laboured to grasp the rights and laws governing the provinces, municipalities, and allied states associated with the city of Rome; who, finally, adapts all he has learned by such studies to suit his present situation, He will have some right to claim the title of Ciceronian.[11]

It is quite clear that such a person would also have the right to claim the title of Christian. Erasmus believed that in the sixteenth-century context a true Ciceronian would be a person who was a true Christian. What was implicit in this was that the higher purpose of all superior writing was to communicate the truth. Erasmus thought that Cicero had used all the writings, and accumulated wisdom, of his age to enlighten his contemporaries and that therefore a true follower of Cicero in the sixteenth-century who had the superior *philosophy of Christ* at his or her disposal would, like Cicero, use all of their talent to communicate it to their contemporaries. As we have seen Erasmus' concept of human nature was such that he believed everyone contained the divine imprint and so could discover it within themselves. This meant that people who lived before Christ had the capacity for perfection. Therefore any truth discovered by anyone in any age could be related to the truth of Christ. Indeed, for Erasmus it *was* the truth of Christ. The *Logos,* or transforming spirit of Christ, was always, and had always been, the instrument of our perfection. The value of Cicero, for Erasmus, was that he was just such a virtuous and saintly pagan. What Cicero had attempted in his work was to reach the essential truth of existence. He had done this with the best material at his disposal. This was what impressed Erasmus most about Cicero: the purity and goodness of his life and the way in which he used his writings to help his contemporaries. Erasmus believed that people who had been exposed to the Christian message had much better material to hand for the pursuit of truth than Cicero had. Nevertheless, it is clear that the Erasmian character Bulephorus believed the achievements of Cicero were in some way comparable to the achievement of true Christianity because any real search for the truth such as the one Cicero was engaged in would ultimately lead to the truth of Christ. Truth of its essence had to be singular; therefore all truth was the same. This humanistic syncretism is apparent throughout Erasmus' writings but he was always careful not to define it too clearly and thereby put his orthodoxy in peril. In this way, for him, a sixteenth century Ciceronian writer who was truly emulating Cicero would be one who was striving to be a true Christian. Thus the ultimate aim of true Ciceronianism and true Christianity were one and the same for Erasmus.

In the piece, then, Erasmus used the discussion of the *imitatio Ciceronis* as a cover for his views on the correct method of pursuing the *imitatio Christi.* The reason he chose to hide his message was because it was a radical concept that was potentially heretical. As such, it could be damaging to those readers of Erasmus who were as yet infants in Christ. It was more efficacious to hide these ideas under a layer of allegory so that those who had progressed on the Christian path could uncover and use them while at the same time the weaker readers would not be scandalized or damaged by them. In his *Paraphrase on Mark* he tells us that Jesus warns 'us that we must not disclose everything to everyone, but that the gospel doctrine must be dispersed only at the appropriate time and according to the understanding of the listeners'.[12]

Erasmus had many spiritual reasons for wanting to present his vision of the correct method of *imitatio Christi* but perhaps the most pressing one was rooted in the more worldly situation he found all around him in 1528. By then the church reform movement had progressed to the point where the various Christian factions were becoming ever more entrenched in their opposition to each other. Erasmus' emphasis of the fluid and individual nature of the transforming *imitatio* served to undermine the warring dogmas. The entire piece is an exercise in resolving opposing viewpoints. Although Bulephorus is scathing in his criticism of his opponents the 'Ciceronian apes' he, nevertheless, modifies his tone considerably when dealing with the extreme Ciceronian Nosoponus.[13] In a truly Christian spirit, the two main protagonists, Nosoponus and Bulephorus, do not ridicule or perceive each other as illogical fanatics. Although Nosoponus is portrayed as an extreme and even farcical character, both he and Bulephorus are described as having a genuine understanding and acceptance of their respective desires to reproduce the best of Cicero. Nosoponus was a character who employed the accepted rather pedantic Ciceronian method of word-lists and grammatical and rhetorical devices copied directly from Cicero. While these traits are inimical to Bulephorus he accepts that Nosoponus' faults are mitigated by his genuine and firm desire to be a true follower of Cicero. They recognize that they have a common aim. Bulephorus speaks of 'our goal'.[14] The debate is never presented as a divisively factional one and here Erasmus was surely pointing the way for the resolution of the divisions that had arisen within contemporary Christianity. He could see clearly that all of the opposing Christians wanted to represent Christ in his entirety but the different emerging denominations disagreed about the best means of achieving this. He believed that in the current conflict, faction could have been avoided if all the participants had concentrated on the unity of their goal, rather than their differences of opinion as to the best method of achieving this end. For Erasmus, the essential spirit of Christianity was unity and harmony. Faction was, by definition, un-Christian, therefore anything or anyone who created faction was anathema to him. In his *Complaint of Peace* he explained that the Greek word for church, *ecclesia*, meant a 'bringing together' and that the fact that this was the chosen term for the Christian people was significant because it implied a common purpose.[15] As early as 1521 he had severe reservations about the methods that Luther was employing in his reforms because he was afraid that the latter would stir up more hatred and cement faction on account of his immoderate polemic. In a letter to Justus Jonas about the Lutheran controversy he said that

> For seeing that truth of itself has a bitter taste for most people, and that it is of itself a subversive thing to uproot what has long been commonly accepted, it would have been wiser to soften a naturally painful subject by the courtesy of one's handling than to pile one cause of hatred on another.[16]

Erasmus was always at pains to emphasize the common humanity of humankind rather than the differences of race or belief or nation. It was part of his Christian humanist manifesto that the process of Christian progress was the same for everyone. He wrote:

> The same laws govern birth, the same necessity brings all to old age and death. All share the same founder of the human race, the same author of their faith; all are redeemed by the same blood, all are initiated by the same rites and sustained by the same sacraments. Whatever benefits come from these stem from the same source and are shared equally amongst all. There is the same church and the same reward offered to all.[17]

There are echoes of this in the *Ciceronianus* when Nosoponus points out to Bulephorus that he would conceal nothing from him because the latter was 'an initiate in the same mysteries'.[18] This phrase is, clearly, more apt as a description of a religious tradition rather than a literary fashion. Harmony was the fundamental distinguishing attribute of Christians. Erasmus pointed out that according to Jesus the single aim or goal of humankind is to 'love one another'.[19] He wanted, above all, to avoid the faction and enmity that would destroy any chance of achieving this goal. He believed that in order to avoid confusion and disharmony it was necessary to recognize and emphasize the fundamental meaning and purpose of *ecclesia* rather than being too dogmatic about the precise parameters of an ideal church organization. In 1528 when Erasmus wrote the *Ciceronianus* the battle-lines were hardening in the split within

Christianity in Europe. His own frame of mind is apparent from a letter he wrote to Hermann von Wied, the archbishop of Cologne, in which he said that the violent divisiveness of certain people was ripping apart the fabric of the state and shattering the harmony of the whole church, and that this was destroying all he had worked so long and hard for.[20] On this level, then, the piece was certainly an Erasmian plea for harmony and reconciliation among the factions. If everyone concentrated on their own individual imitation of Christ then this common goal would negate the need for factions. In the end, Nosoponus was finally convinced of the superiority of Bulephorus' method because the latter, who was in charge of the debate, always kept their unity of purpose in mind.

Throughout the dialogue Bulephorus never values the literary technique of Cicero in itself. It is precisely the glorification of the technique to the detriment of the goal that Bulephorus denounces when he rails against the Ciceronian apes who sacrifice everything for the technique. He accuses them of being more concerned with *how* Cicero did things rather than *what* he did. There is an important parallel here with Erasmus' view of Christ's life work. He believed that it was essential to emulate the essence of Christ's life rather than engage in an outward adherence to Christian rituals and laws. The spirit of Christ was always superior to the letter of Church law. Over and over in his writings Erasmus stated that outward displays of religious fervour were useless unless they were expressions of an inner experience. This is a central theme in both the *Enchiridion* and *The Praise of Folly*. It explains the lack of any blueprint for an ideal form of church institution in his otherwise extensive writings. It also goes a long way towards explaining why, although he supported Luther in the early days, he, nevertheless, opposed him later on. Even the stumbling block of *sola fide* might have been overlooked by Erasmus as something that could have been solved by persuasion, if the Lutheran cause had not resulted in schism. He agreed with Luther's early emphasis on the true goal of Christianity and the need for reform in the Church. The latter, like Erasmus, highlighted the fact that the church had lost sight of this goal and instead had lapsed into emphasizing ritual and dogma. When the Lutheran creed began to be institutionalized as a separate Christian creed, however, Erasmus could not support it any longer. He did not believe that a division of the Christian church would serve any useful function because the defining principle of Christianity was harmony or peace. He thought that the only true reformation would be one that took place in people's hearts. He spent his life writing in order to re-educate the hearts of his fellow-Christians. The process of institutionalizing the Lutheran faith increasingly involved standardizing and laying down rules and strictly defining dogma. Erasmus believed that this would be divisive and would not lead to a true reform.

There was a direct parallel between Erasmus' views on the over dogmatic approach to the Christian message and his views on the Ciceronians. In the colloquy, his mouthpiece, Bulephorus, argues that since Cicero was pagan and did not use Christian terms it would not be possible to represent Christian concepts correctly while adhering rigidly to his vocabulary because the ultimate aim of writing, which was communication, could not be fulfilled. He gave the description, already mentioned, of a Roman orator he had once heard talking about the death of Christ, as an example of how ridiculous this was. He considered that it was not beneficial for a Ciceronian to imitate only the outer surface layer of Cicero's writings He argued that this defective method of imitation had also caused many great men to be misinterpreted. He said that Augustine, Benedict and Francis were all defamed by their 'so-called followers'.[21] Then he drew a direct analogy with Christ. He said that Christ, too, had suffered this fate at the hands of 'those who have nothing of him but his name'.[22] Furthermore, he thought that in the past giants of men had been aware of this. The implication was that it took an extraordinary individual to understand the essence of a great truth presented by a great teacher. The lack of such individuals had resulted in many misunderstandings and misinterpretations of Christ's message. Erasmus believed that it took a person of enormous experience and wisdom to understand the totality of the Christian message. In the light of this difficulty he thought that there should be as little dogma as possible and that the exoteric message of Christianity should be kept simple. In May 1521 he wrote to Justus Jonas that St Paul was 'all things to all men' because he understood the need to minister to his flock on the basis of their particular level of understanding.[23] Christ himself had this gift which Erasmus called *prudentia.* He had accommodated himself to the temperaments of his fellow Jews. Erasmus described how Christ 'said one thing to the multitudes, who are somewhat thick-witted, and another to his disciples; and even so he has to bear with them for a long time while he gradually brings them to understand the celestial philosophy'.[24] Thus the *philosophy of Christ,* in its fullest exposition, was something that had been given to a small group of disciples as a result of personal instruction by Christ over a long period of time. This was the highest degree of Christianity and was, clearly, esoteric. Christ did not dispense this teaching to the masses because they could not yet understand it. He preached the more exoteric elements of his message to 'the multitudes'.[25] So, even people who had been exposed to Jesus himself in person could not reach the higher echelons of Christian knowledge immediately.

The idea that Christ had a secret teaching that he reserved for his immediate disciples has its origin in Scripture. In the *Gospel of Mark,* after Jesus has been preaching to the crowds, it is stated that 'with many such parables he spoke the word to them, as they were able to hear it; he did not speak to them without a parable, but privately to his own disciples he explained everything'.[26] Similarly in the *Gospel of John,* after the account of the doubting Thomas incident, we read that 'Jesus did many other signs in the presence of the disciples which are not written in this book'.[27] Erasmus' particular interpretation of this phenomenon, however, was unusual and has led to some misunderstanding. He has been accused on account of it of being an elitist. He complained that Luther 'in his torrent of pamphlets has poured it all out at once, making everything public and giving even cobblers a share in what is normally handled by scholars as mysteries reserved for the initiated'.[28] While this could be seen to smack of elitism it must be reconciled with his clear desire that everyone should know and read the gospel. In the *Paraclesis* he said that 'Christ wishes his mysteries published as openly as possible'.[29] He went on to say that he wished 'that even the lowliest women' could be enabled to 'read the Gospels and the Pauline Epistles. And I would that they were translated into all languages so that they could be read and understood not only by Scots and Irish but also by Turks and Saracens.'[30] The two views are not mutually exclusive if his belief in the different levels of Christian perfection is taken into account. He wanted everyone to receive the enlightenment of Christianity but he believed that it was only possible to absorb this truth in stages. Consequently, he thought that hurling theological discussions of the more difficult elements of it at people did not work and was potentially detrimental to the process of their perfection. Christ himself had employed parables when talking to large crowds of people but when he was talking in private to his own disciples, whose precise level of understanding was known to him, he had spoken more directly.[31]

In the imitation of Cicero and in the imitation of Christ, then, Erasmus advocated an individual response. Great individuals did not follow a list of rules and regulations. Each one allowed his or her own particular genius free reign. They were creative, innovative and individualistic in their respective fields. If their followers were to imitate them properly, they would each have to use the contents of their innermost being to create their own lives. In his work on preaching called the *Ecclesiastes,* Erasmus expressed this very clearly. Having cited patristic writers who should serve as models for the aspiring preacher, he said that, in imitating these men, the orator should adapt their writings to his or her own capacities and that the ultimate object of imitation was to represent *oneself.* While superficially this could be viewed as a formula for total anarchy in relation to the Christian message; that was the last thing the peace-loving Erasmus wanted. He was well aware of the inherent dangers in such a blueprint and he therefore wanted people to be led gently and carefully to the point where they could be responsible for their own progress. Bulephorus concurred with these reservations in the Ciceronian context, when he declared that

> aspiring to be like Cicero has its dangers....the giants came to a bad end for aspiring to the throne of Jove, and several persons were destroyed by their desire to see the gods face to face. It is a "task with hazard and danger fraught".[32]

The device of elaborating the imitation of Christ under the guise of the imitation of Cicero allowed Erasmus to say what he wanted to without fear of censure and at the same time it ensured that a reader who was unable to understand the deeper meaning of imitating Christ would not have his or her faith distorted or damaged by this argument.

The continuing allegory is discernable in Nosoponus' statement that 'a sacred vocation like this requires a heart not only pure from all sin but free from all care'.[33] For Erasmus, of course, there was only one sacred vocation: that of Christianity and he continually emphasized the need for a pure heart in following its dictates. In the *Paraclesis* he said that the way of Christ was simple and open to anyone but that the main requirements were 'a pious and open mind, possessed above all with a pure and simple faith'.[34] Similarly, in the *Enchiridion,* he said: 'remember that you must approach the sacred Scriptures with washed hands, that is with the greatest purity of mind'.[35] Nosoponus says that because of the need to be free from care he has not married or taken any public or ecclesiastical office.[36] These are exactly the views of Erasmus on his own vocation.[37] They are also the views of St Paul who told the Corinthians:

> I would have you without carefulness. He that is unmarried careth for the things that belong to the Lord, how he may please the Lord: but he that is married careth for the things that are of the world, how he may please his wife.[38]

Nosoponus added to this that 'people who suffer from love, jealousy, ambition, greed for money and other such diseases are wasting their time in aspiring to this honour'.[39] This is what Erasmus also said of the true Christian. In his *Paraphrase on Mark* he gave an allegorical interpretation of the cure of the paralytic and interpreted the bed he lay on as representing all of those carnal desires that hold us back. He said the ordinary human was 'so enervated by excesses, indulgence in pleasure, and desire for fame and money, that he has no strength left in him to raise himself from his sordid cares to the love of heavenly things'.[40]

Nosoponus undertakes very stringent preparations in order to produce writings of the highest Ciceronian quality and while these are in line with the kind of vigilance that Erasmus recommended for the militant Christian, there are, however, other resonances in the description. Nosoponus tells us that he practices his art of writing in

> a shrine of the Muses in the innermost part of the house, with thick walls and double doors and windows, and all the cracks carefully sealed up with plaster and pitch, so that hardly any light or sound can penetrate even by day.[41]

On the surface this is a device to make Nosoponus look ridiculous; however, it is also reminiscent of the hermetic seal employed by alchemists. Moreover, this metaphor is expanded when Nosoponus says that in this sanctuary there is a blazing fire that does not smoke. This calls to mind the intense heat used by alchemists to act on the ingredients they put in the hermetically sealed vessel in order to transmute them into gold. The metaphor is then alluded to overtly when Nosoponus mentions alchemy by name in his description of the mental preparations necessary for the task of writing. He argued that 'a sacred vocation like this requires a heart not only pure from all sin but free from all care, just like the esoteric disciplines of magic, astrology, and so-called alchemy'.[42] Since Erasmus was portraying an extreme Ciceronian in the Nosoponus character there is nothing unusual about his allusion to alchemy. What is unusual is that the Bulephorus character, who represents Erasmus' own views, is also clearly familiar with alchemy and is portrayed as tacitly and explicitly employing some of the same preparations as Nosoponus. Moreover, Erasmus could have used him to teach Nosoponus and the reader a lesson about the dangers of such an art. This lesson, however, is conspicuous by its absence: there is no overt criticism of alchemy in the piece.

Erasmus had no visible interest in the art of alchemy. He was acquainted with two of the most famous alchemists of his day, Henry Cornelius Agrippa and Paracelsus but his primary point of contact with these men was as fellow humanists.[43] In the piece Erasmus used a qualifying adjective with the word alchemy. This suggests that he thought there was some popular confusion about the discipline: that there was so-called alchemy as opposed to a true form of alchemy. In his colloquy called *Alchemy*, which was published prior to the *Ciceronianus* in 1524, he depicted the alchemist as being a rogue and a swindler. This does not automatically mean that he despised alchemy. The colloquies were aimed at a popular audience and were written partly in an attempt to clarify and correct every-day misconceptions and abuses. There is ample evidence that there were many practitioners of the *art* in Erasmus' day who were in fact con-men. Thus he wrote the colloquy in order to warn people against these people. At the end of the piece, however, Erasmus explained that the *alchemist* in question 'understood the *art* about as well as an ass does'.[44] This, again, implies that Erasmus himself had an understanding of the true art of alchemy and that although he despised the popular form he was not so scathing about the esoteric discipline itself. Perhaps Erasmus would have liked to call this esoteric discipline something else in order to differentiate it in the popular mind from the kind of trickery he described in the colloquy. He often distinguished between deep hidden truths and the shadowy popular conception of them. Just as Nosoponus referred to 'so-called alchemy' Bulephorus also ridiculed the 'so-called followers of Francis, Benedict, and Augustine'.[45] Bulephorus was clearly in favour of the true teachings of these saints and similarly Nosoponus was in favour of true alchemy.

Alchemy was the process by which base metals were supposedly transmuted into gold. It was also concerned with the transformation of all base substances into higher ones. There was a spiritual side to alchemy in which the practitioner strove to attain personal perfection by a parallel process of transforming the base matter of his or her own being into more perfect state'.[46] As such, at the very least, it was a very useful metaphor for Erasmus because of the similar nature of his concept of Christian perfection. There was a parallel between this Christian process of transformation and the alchemical one of transmutation. His views on the true nature of the Eucharist, which are outlined in the previous chapter, have much in common with the more esoteric practice of Alchemy. Erasmus said that the true meaning of the Eucharist was something Christ had revealed to very few people. He believed the secret meaning of the Eucharist was that it was a process of the incorporation of Christ into our being which then allowed us to participate in a complete way in the Body of Christ.[47] Jesus transformed the basic material elements of bread and wine into the higher essence, which was Christ. Erasmus believed that Jesus, the pedagogue, was demonstrating in a spiritual and a practical way that the perfection process was one in which our base instincts were transformed into a higher essence of Spirit. Viewed in this way it has very obvious parallels with the more esoteric form of alchemy and Erasmus' more advanced readers would have recognized in Nosoponus' apparently ridiculous actions a deeper and more mysterious allegory of the process of Christianisation.

In this way the alchemical allusions point to the central theme of the piece: the true method of emulation. This, for Erasmus, involved a transformation that affected the very being.

Nosoponus argues that in order to imitate Cicero it was first necessary to absorb him in a holistic way. He says: 'anyone who has absorbed the whole of Cicero cannot express anything but Cicero'.[48] Erasmus' description of how Christians should absorb Christ is very similar. In the *Enchiridion* he wrote:

> if you approach the Scriptures in the correct frame of mind, you will feel that you are inspired, moved, swept away, transfigured in an ineffable manner by the divine power if you approach them with respect, veneration and humility. You will behold the delights of the divine bridegroom; you will behold the opulence of rich King Solomon; you will behold the hidden treasures of eternal wisdom.[49]

Thus, just as the true Ciceronian could reach a state in which he 'cannot express anything but Cicero' by means of absorbing his works, so also, the true Christian would be transformed by a proper digestion of Holy Scripture, into a being who exuded the spirit of Christ. Erasmus pointed out in the *Paraclesis* that in relation to the philosophy of Christ this process of transformation was far more profound and vital than mere understanding. His view was that 'transformation is a more important matter than intellectual comprehension'.[50] Thus, in both the Christian process and the Ciceronian one, Erasmus believed that transformation was all-important. In the *Ciceronianus,* Erasmus expressed the process of transforming a writer into a true Ciceronian in terms of the alchemical process of transmutation. In the underlying allegory, he was also comparing the Christian process to that of alchemy. For Erasmus, the alchemical struggle of the disparate elements of the individual took place in the hermetically sealed vessel of his or her being. The gold or perfection was achieved by the application of intense heat or fire to this vessel. He often used the metaphor of fire to express the force that produced transformation.[51] In his *Paraphrase on Mark* he said that the

> fire of the divine Spirit takes away from and purges the mind of all carnal affections and somehow transforms into God whatever it seizes, so that those who before were concerned with earthly things now disdain them and are carried away to heavenly things.[52]

In his *Paraphrase on Romans* he also used the metaphor of fire when he was elaborating he concept that strength is made perfect through weakness. He wrote:

> Since indeed we have taken up this new example from Christ and received from him an excellent doctrine, namely, that the virtue of endurance is strengthened by bearing evils, we become, by endurance, like gold from the fire, better tested and approved by God and men.

This transforming fire is the spirit of Christ the *Logos*. As we have seen, in his famous depiction of the ideal Christian society Erasmus used the same metaphor of fire to depict how Christ, like an eternal fire, draws in and transforms everyone into himself.[53]

Nosoponus went on, in the *Ciceronianus,* to elaborate on how he prepared for the process of writing in the Ciceronian manner. Again, there is a deeper meaning hidden under the description of his apparently ludicrous preparations. He described how prior to writing he would fast, in order to 'prevent any gross substance from invading the limpid mind, and to make sure no dampness steaming up from the stomach weighs down and nails to the earth the fragment of the divine breath of God'.[54] Given Erasmus' own fastidious disposition and the fact that he was not in favour of asceticism in general, he is here ridiculing the Ciceronians in the guise of Nosoponus. At the deeper level, however, the vision of the divine breath of God being weighted down and nailed to the earth is reminiscent of the recurring image represented by his personal device of the youth with flying hair embedded in stone. This image of spirit encased in matter was indicative of the ordinary condition of the human being for Erasmus.[55] This was the state from which he or she had to progress in order to attain eternal life. Erasmus was using Nosoponus to describe a method of achieving a higher state by overcoming the impulses of the body in order to liberate the spirit. He was describing the proper preparation for truly Christian writing. The person who was engrossed in the material, fleshy world could never write in the true spirit of Christ. In his *Paraphrase on Mark* Erasmus interpreted Jesus' instruction to the apostles not to take anything with them on their mission of evangelisation as meaning that he wanted them to be free 'from all care of those things that often hold the mind back when it goes about some heavenly business'.[56] Nosoponus then went on to say that his next preparation consisted in eating 'ten very small raisins, the Corinthian sort. They are not really food or drink, but yet they are in a way.'[57] Given the Corinthian reference Erasmus may have been referring here to the letters of St Paul to the Corinthians. He valued Paul highly as a major exponent of Christianity.[58] Raisins are dried grapes and as such their contents are condensed and intensified like gems. The first ten chapters of Paul's first letter to the Corinthians reads like a distillation of the *philosophy of Christ*. In them the major Erasmian theme of the folly of the cross being, in fact, true wisdom is to be found.[59] It is here too that the notion of a secret teaching is outlined. Paul says that there are gradations of Christianity and that he has become all things to all people in order that each level of listener may understand him.[60] The chapters are also infused with the Pauline and Erasmian emphasis of the wisdom of the spirit rather than a worldly wisdom based on glorification of the material world of the flesh. There are two further concepts in the first ten chapters of 1 Corinthians that have a particular resonance in the Erasmian view of Christianity. The first of these is the notion that the spirit of Christ existed in the world before the time of the historical Jesus, and, the second is that dissention is inimical to Christians. Chapter ten of the first letter to the Corinthians begins with St Paul affirming that

> all our fathers were baptized unto Moses in the cloud and in the sea; And did all eat the same spiritual meat; And did all drink the same spiritual drink: for they drank of that spiritual Rock that followed them: and that Rock was Christ.[61]

Since St Paul was here alluding to the Israelites of the Old Testament and speaking to Corinthians who were Greek-speaking Gentiles he therefore must have been speaking figuratively when he used the term 'our fathers'. He was referring to the common human ancestry. Yet he declared that they were all baptized and imbued with Christ. It is possible to infer therefore that he was saying that the spirit of Christ existed on earth before the birth of Jesus.

In sum, then the underlying message Erasmus wanted to convey was that in order to write a piece in a truly Christian manner it would be beneficial to read and digest St Paul as part of the preparation process. The first ten chapters of the first letter to the Corinthians were like raisins, in that, they contained condensed and intensified tenets of the *philosophy of Christ*. While it could be argued that because these preparations were outlined in the work by the extreme Ciceronian, Nosoponus, they might not be considered to be the views of Erasmus himself. Again, this is negated by the fact that Erasmus also depicted his own mouthpiece, Bulephorus, approving of this practice. Indeed Bulephorus exhibited unqualified empathy and added that the raisins would 'exude moisture slowly, and stimulate brain and memory'.[62] What this meant was that reading St Paul would create a long-lasting and correct mental attitude in which to write. There is also a possible further alchemical allusion here. The alchemists often used a small portion of real gold along with the base metal in order to produce a larger quantity of gold. Thus, as far as Christian writing was concerned, these raisins or gems of Christian philosophy would act in the same way to produce a larger amount of true philosophy. Nosoponus, then, continued his description of preparations for writing by saying that he also ate three sugared coriander seeds.[63] To which Bulephorus replied 'splendid - that prevents any dampness from the ten raisins flying up to the seat of the mind'.[64] The main scriptural reference for coriander seed is to be found in the Old Testament where manna was said to look like coriander seed.[65] Manna was the food sent by God to sustain the Israelites in the wilderness. In relation to the process of writing, it could be seen to represent a gift from God or divine inspiration. Instead of worldly opinions then, Erasmus advised a Christian writer to consume the condensed tenets of Christian philosophy contained in the writings of St Paul. This should then be supplemented with Divine inspiration in case any worldly interpretation or preoccupation affected the Christian author. He believed that when a Christian wished to write in the spirit of Christ he or she should not merely imitate Paul or the Gospel authors in a literal and slavish way, but they should allow divine inspiration to act on them to produce properly divine writings. Erasmus believed that the ancient venerable authors had done just this. Thus to follow them properly one would have to allow inspiration its proper part. In the *Enchiridion,* Erasmus outlined his understanding of the deeper meaning and spiritual characteristics of manna. He asked: 'what more apt figure than manna could be devised to express the knowledge of the mysteries of the law?'[66] He then answered his own question thus:

> To begin with, since it did not issue from the earth but rained down from heaven, you can observe the distinction between human and divine learning. All sacred Scripture is divinely inspired and has proceeded from God, its author. That it was in tiny particles signifies the lowliness of speech that conceals immense mysteries in almost crude language; that it was white signifies that there is no human learning that is not defiled by some blackness of error, while only the doctrine of Christ is as white as snow, immaculated, and unadulterated, That it was somewhat rough and granular signifies that the mystery is concealed by the letter. If one touches only the surface or the husk, so to speak, of Scripture, what is harder or more unpleasant to the touch? Was it not merely the hard covering of the manna that they touched who exclaimed: "This saying is harsh, and who can listen to it?" Search out the spiritual meaning, and you will find nothing more sweet or succulent. "[67]

In the same work when he was arguing in favour of his preference for the allegorical method of interpreting Scripture he said: 'you must reject the carnal aspect of the Scriptures, especially the Old Testament, and ferret out the spiritual sense. Manna will taste to you like that which you already have on your palate'.[68] Thus the true Christian writer first consumed manna or the spiritual meaning of Scripture before writing and, as like attracts like, that which was consumed and absorbed would facilitate the creation of truly spiritual and divine writing. Erasmus was aware that this kind of approach to Biblical study was potentially dangerous because it relied on the individual discernment of the interpreter. His solution to this was to prescribe a programme of study before such interpretation could be undertaken.[69] During the reformation upheavals some of the radical spiritualist groups claimed to have been inspired by Erasmus. They found his emphasis on the inner spirit and his belief that the outer form of religious observance was not important very attractive. Their radical and often violent departure from the religious norms of the day was just the kind of excess that Erasmus was at pains to avoid. It was for this very reason that, at times, he wrote so obscurely.[70]

Having described the physical preparations which were necessary for the production of Ciceronian writings, Nosoponus then went on to describe his mental preparations. He said that prior to writing he never spoke to anyone in Latin. He explained that 'the riders in a horse-race keep their thoroughbreds from galloping about beforehand so that they come to the serious business vigorous and fresh'.[71] Thus he clearly wanted to keep himself fresh and full of energy for his task. This, however, can also be interpreted in terms of alchemy. It is reminiscent again of the notion of the hermetic seal. Nosoponus used himself as an instrument and kept a lid on his energy in order to refine it and thereby produce the best results. He did not waste the particular kind of energy that went into the speaking of Latin. Instead, he would save it and have it at his command later, when he needed it. He achieved this by sealing it off. Erasmus, himself, was notoriously protective of his privacy and liberty. He consciously lived away from courts and even universities so that he could better work undisturbed. In short, both the physical and mental preparations made by Nosoponus can be interpreted allegorically as belonging to the alchemical tradition. They also show that he had a high degree of insight into the workings of his own psyche. He had clearly observed his psyche as if it operated along strictly mechanical and law-conforming lines. This is precisely the notion of the psyche that Erasmus outlined in the *Enchiridion.* He laid out a clear and complete model of the human being in order to make it easier for the reader to *'know himself'* or herself objectively.[72].

Having described all of his preparations, Nosoponus then proceeded to indicate the exact method of writing in the Ciceronian manner. What he advocated was a holistic approach. He told Bulephorus that it was essential to represent the 'whole of Cicero'. Bulephorus replied by asking him how this can be achieved when 'he didn't reveal himself wholly? And even in the places where he did give us a chance to observe him, he's fragmented and hardly half there'.[73] Again this is like Christ in the gospels. It is clear that we have not got all of his teachings in the Scriptures. In Mark and John, for instance, as we have seen there are references to secret teaching that Jesus gave his apostles in private.[74] In the Ciceronian context Nosoponus' solution to the problem of our lack of the complete works of Cicero was that in attempting to portray the essence of Cicero 'we must do as we are able, when we can't do as we wish'.[75] This was Erasmus' own belief, in a broader sense, in relation to the attempt to be truly Christian. He believed that while very few people ever reached the goal of being truly Christian, this should not prevent us from trying to come as near to the goal as possible. He said that 'to die to sin, to die to carnal desires, to die to the world is an arduous goal, it is a difficult accomplishment' but he then added that even 'if it is not granted to all to arrive at the perfect imitation of the Head, all must nonetheless strive with all their strength to reach it'.[76] Despite the difficulty of the task, however, it was not acceptable to take the easier road of just imitating the ideal in a superficial way. Bulephorus went on to castigate the Ciceronians for concentrating on the details of Ciceronian language instead of working to develop a deep and true understanding of Cicero's thought in its entirety. He argued: 'what a tiny portion of Cicero is offered by those Ciceronian apes who scrape up a few phrases, idioms, figures and rhythmical patterns from here and there and then exhibit just a top surface veneer of Cicero'.[77] Erasmus had criticized the scholastics for similarly concentrating on the details of the theological discipline rather than contributing to a deeper understanding of the philosophy of Christ. In the *Praise of Folly,* in particular, there are clear echoes of this theme being used in the context of scholasticism. Erasmus wrote that the

> subtle refinements of subtleties are made still more subtle by all the different lines of scholastic argument, so that you'd extricate yourself faster from a labyrinth than from the tortuous obscurities of Realists, Nominalists, Thomists, Albertists, Ochamists and Scotists.[78]

Bulephorus then continued his opposition to 'the Ciceronian apes' and argued that 'there are thousands of things we have to speak about often, that Cicero never even dreamed of. But if he were alive now, he would say the same things as we do'.[79] Erasmus was not in a position to say this directly about Christ because to infer that Christ was unaware of anything would have been blasphemous. Bulephorus said, and Nosoponus agreed, that their joint aim was 'to ensure that we ignore the irrelevant chatter of the apes and proceed to imitate Cicero as far as we may, in his entirety and with success'.[80] He then said that this was a dangerous task.[81] Again, this is far more appropriate when applied to Christianity. In the *Enchiridion,* Erasmus, speaking to the reader, had said that the way of salvation is a 'narrow path, on which few mortals walk'.[82] Earlier in the handbook he had also cautioned his readers that the entrance to the abode of wisdom was narrow and that they should be careful not to rashly 'break into the secret room. The doorway is low, make sure that you do not strike your head and be thrown backwards and there is danger in not stooping when you enter'.[83]

The central overt argument of the piece is next presented by Bulephorus who argues that he does not believe

> that a man is speaking in Ciceronian manner, if, being a Christian, he speaks to Christians on a Christian subject in the way that Cicero, being a pagan, once spoke to pagans on non-Christian subjects; but only if he speaks as Cicero would be likely to speak if he were living today as a Christian among Christians, endowed with his original native ability and his oratorical experience, possessed of the same understanding of our concerns that he once had of pagan ones, inspired, finally, with love and loyalty for the Christian world as he was once fired with pride and passion for the city of Rome and the honour of the Roman name.[84]

Towards the end of the *Ciceronianus,* Bulephorus concluded that 'anyone who can be Ciceronian only by being un-Christian is not even Ciceronian'.[85] Then he added his statement that the purpose of studying eloquence was 'to know Christ, to celebrate the glory of Christ. This is the goal of all learning and all eloquence'.[86] Erasmus here closed the circle of his argument. The goal of the Ciceronians was eloquence and according to Erasmus the goal of eloquence was to know and express Christ. The ultimate goal of the true Ciceronian, therefore, was the goal of the true Christian, which was to achieve a state of human perfection. The true Ciceronian in the sixteenth-century context was, of necessity, a true Christian. While it is true to say that most, if not all, of the Ciceronian humanists were Christian; there were some influential churchmen who suspected that a kind of neo-paganism was being stealthily championed by the humanists. Erasmus was here nailing his colours to the mast. He was not interested in literature or any other area of study for its own sake. He was only interested in ultimates; if a discipline did not serve the ultimate goal of human perfection through the spirit of Christ he had no time for it. His respect for many pre-Christian writers including Cicero was only possible because he believed that human beings were so designed that if they wished to achieve the height of accomplishment in any of the higher pursuits of learning it would involve a quest for the truth. Since finding the truth can only be assured if one acquires objectivity, then the quest would begin with the kind of analysis of the personal psyche described in the *Enchiridion*. It follows, in the Erasmian system, that this would then involve warfare of the opposites in the psyche. The seeker would find that no objective truth was possible without first conquering the lower instincts. Erasmus believed that no matter how, or in what era, a person tried to find this truth the result would always be the truth of Christ.[87] Thus if a person, such as Cicero, sought true eloquence he could only achieve it by having something of real worth to communicate. In ultimate terms the only thing that possessed this quality was the truth of Christ. It follows that in order to achieve true eloquence it would first be essential to achieve knowledge of truth. When Bulephorus said that to know Christ and to celebrate the glory of Christ is the goal of all learning and all eloquence, he did not say that it *ought* to be the goal, but that as a matter of fact it *is* thus. He was, moreover, speaking as a true Ciceronian when he said this. The goal of a true Ciceronian was to express Christ.

Nosoponus, having been persuaded by Bulephorus' argument thus far, then asked him how this genuine Ciceronianism could be achieved.[88] In responding, Bulephorus first pointed out that human nature is, superficially at least, diverse: not everyone has the natural gifts of a Cicero.[89] He then expressed the view, however, that everyone

> has his own personal inborn characteristics, and these have such force that it is useless for a person fitted by nature for one style of speaking to strive to achieve a different one. As the Greeks say, no one ever succeeded in battling with the gods.[90]

In an outright attack on the slavish Ciceronians he then argued that 'no one should endeavour to copy Cicero if his natural bent is totally different from Cicero's otherwise he will finish up as some kind of monstrosity, having lost his own natural form and not having acquired anyone else's'.[91] This is the essential point and true message of the piece: to copy Cicero in a pedantic superficial way is an aberration. The true Ciceronian would do exactly as Cicero did and use his or her own personal native talent to achieve eloquence. In the case of Christianity the parallel would be that the true Christian would not slavishly copy Christ in a superficial way but, instead, would use his or her own individual talents to the full to achieve perfection in the true spirit of Christ. It was an individual quest and one that each person had to work out for himself or herself in line with their own individual nature. Again, it would have caused great difficulties for Erasmus had he said this directly. However, in his *De Contemptu Mundi*, he had claimed that the earliest and most ideal form of Christianity had incorporated this ideal. In describing early monasticism he wrote that

> in those times to be a monk meant nothing more than to be a true Christian, and a monastery was nothing else but a congregation of men united in the true teachings of Christ. There was no rule, every man forged ahead of his own account, so that reins were needed rather than spurs.[92]

Bulephorus elaborated on this important individualistic theme by declaring that:

> the natural musician will not be successful as a soldier; the natural soldier will never write satisfactory poetry; the man who is fitted for marriage will never be a good monk; the one who enjoys farming will never get on at court and *vice versa*.[93]

Nosoponus, still displaying his some vestiges of his Ciceronianism, interrupted and replied: 'there is no difficulty which cannot be surmounted by unremitting toil'.[94] This was in line with all of the orthodox Christian teachings and in the Ciceronian context it was also a necessary belief. Bulephorus was not impressed however and said:

> the care of man assists nature where it is already going in the right direction, adjusts it when it is slightly astray, corrects it when faulty; but you will meddle in vain, my dear Nosoponus, with a nature which is totally out of harmony and fitted for something quite different. You can teach a horse to go round in circles and step in time. But it's no good taking an ox to the wrestling school, or expecting a dog to pull a plough, or a buffalo to take part in a horse-race.[95]

Thus Erasmus, through his character Bulephorus, argues that a person cannot go entirely against his or her own true nature. In the orthodox Christian context the view of human nature was that it was enmeshed in sin and that it was therefore necessary to overcome this baseness in order to achieve salvation. Erasmus concurred with this notion that we had to overcome our base instincts in order to see the beauty of Christ but he did not believe that this could be achieved by a distortion of the individual nature. The inner human struggle would result in the fulfilment of each individual's true nature, and, as such, this could only be achieved if the individual used all of his or her natural talents in the struggle. Viewed in this way, any attempt to strangle or manacle natural traits or characteristics would be detrimental to salvation: they were an important element of the process. Erasmus propounded this idea in the *Enchiridion* when he explained how there are certain passions that are 'so similar to virtues that there is a risk of being deceived in distinguishing between them'.[96] He argued that the way to correct these was to turn them towards the nearby virtue. As an example of this he said a person

> who is hot-tempered should curb his feelings, and he will become energetic, self-assured, active, free, and open. Another who is a bit niggardly with a little good sense will become frugal; one who is too flattering will become affable and courteous; one who is inflexible, constant; one who is sombre, stern; one who is foolish, obliging; and similarly with other minor defects of character.[97]

In other words rather than crush the natural instincts of the flesh Erasmus believed that it was necessary instead to try to turn them around and face them in the direction of virtue. This, of course, would entail a different process for each individual depending on the different facets of each individual's character. Despite these differences the goal of perfection was open to all. In Ciceronian terms, Bulephorus expressed a similar notion in relation to the imitation of Cicero when he said that 'it isn't necessary to aim at being identical if one can manage to be equal, or at any rate not far behind, even if different'.[98] He then elaborated by using gems and flowers as an example. He explained that in the case of gems and flowers such as rubies and emeralds, and roses and lilies while they are different in outward appearance, they are, nevertheless, equal in beauty and function.[99]

Bulephorus then added another reason for not copying Cicero slavishly when he repeated his earlier assertion that we do not have a complete knowledge of Cicero: 'He is hardly half there in fact, whether we think of vocabulary, idiom, rhythms, or corpus of writing'.[100] He then said that Cicero exists in his entirety only in himself.[101] Thus he argued that if Nosoponus wanted to express Cicero only in literal Ciceronian terms, then he could not express himself and that would be ridiculous. This leads on to his startling but logical conclusion that

> it may well be that the most Ciceronian person is the one least like Cicero, the person, that is, who expresses himself in the best and most appropriate way, even though he does so in a manner very different from Cicero's - which would hardly be surprising, considering that everything has been completely altered.[102]

Significantly, however, Bulephorus added that we could be like Cicero in one thing; that was that we should 'pursue the "palm of eloquence" along the same paths by which Cicero attained it'.[103] This was the only valid way of imitating Cicero. Imitate the spirit of the man and not the dead letter of his art. To be like Cicero it would be necessary to follow exactly the same path as he had taken by allowing one's own individual form of eloquence to develop as he had, rather than copying him pedantically. In short, while Bulephorus believed that Cicero had achieved the heights of excellence he clearly believed that others could pursue and achieve this goal also, each in his or her own way. In the Christian context, Erasmus also believed that the true imitation of Christ would involve the particular perfection of the individual, each in his or her own way. This would entail a personal deeper and deeper understanding of the mysteries of Christ's life, death and resurrection. In his *Paraphrase on Romans* Erasmus explained what he believed the imitation of Christ entailed. He wrote:

> For since we are grafted to the body of Christ through baptism and in a way are transformed into him, whatever we perceive as having been performed in him who is our head we, who are the members of his body, must either imitate wholly, or hope to do so. Christ is risen, he ascended into heaven, he sits at the right hand of the Father. These things have already been accomplished in Christ; and they are what we must hope for at last, if only we emulate, and, as it were, practise them as far as we can. Consequently, if having received baptism we die to our former sins and wicked desires, and thus represent the death of Christ, as we are able, it is right that henceforth by avoiding shameful things and by engaging continually in pious deeds, we also imitate the resurrection of Christ.[104]

If, then, we translate Bulephorus' comment about following Cicero into the Christian context it is clear that the true Christian would be one who imitated Christ by engaging in the same struggle that he had. Christ died to the world. We had to imitate this, not in a literal way by becoming a martyr but spiritually, by dying to our carnal instincts. The struggle was an internal, individual one. He said that it was 'not a war between one man and another, but a war with oneself, and the enemy battle line springs forth unbidden from our own entrails'.[105] The basic rules for this method of perfection were universal but in individual application they would have to be diverse. In the seventeenth rule of the *Enchiridion* when Erasmus was describing the deeper mysteries of the Cross he said that

> in order to meditate on the mystery of the cross with greater profit it will be necessary that everyone prepare a method for himself, a kind of pious art of warfare, and train himself diligently in it, so that, whenever circumstances demand it he will be ready.[106]

Like the true Ciceronian, true Christians in becoming fully themselves would, of necessity, be the least like Christ superficially. Instead they would each develop their own gifts and confront their own personal demons and defects and would become true human beings in their own way and in their own right. Thus, for instance, the fact that Christ did not marry and lived among tax-collectors and prostitutes would not induce the true Christian to do the same. While most Christians would accept this, Erasmus was pushing the idea further than the norm. To say that the most Ciceronian person was the one *least* like Cicero is a very radical notion when applied to Christ. Erasmus had no desire whatsoever to create the state of religious anarchy that might ensue if this were to become a literal and dogmatic Christian tenet. He was always careful, therefore, to bury it beneath a dense covering of conservative piety. Christianity was a *method* of perfection and not a quick and easy panacea for all spiritual ills. He believed that each person was given a unique set of circumstances, gifts and faults by means of which they could perfect their own particular nature. To copy slavishly someone else who had different attributes and existed in a different environment and era would, of necessity, result in some kind of aberration rather than a perfected human being. While this concept when applied to the imitation of Cicero was feasible it was not acceptable in this radical form in relation to the imitation of Christ. Cicero was an ordinary mortal, albeit one who had extraordinary skills, but essentially made up of the usual bits and pieces. Christ, on the other hand, was the son of God and from this viewpoint it makes no sense that the truest Christian would be one who was least like Christ. Erasmus certainly believed that Christ was the son of God but he also believed that in coming down to earth he had assumed a real human nature. This meant that he engaged in the struggle for perfection just as all human beings do.[107] Erasmus wrote that profiting by his example 'we will win through him in the end, if we fight as he fought'.[108] Thus, in perfect imitation of Christ, the true Christian must be a person of their own times and not a slavish imitator of the first century Jewish Jesus. In order to be most like Christ each Christian must follow their own individual bent in the struggle for perfection. The very way in which Christ taught his message in the Bible elicits this response. The reported teachings of Christ in the Gospels are in the form of parables. These are lessons in the higher truth that lies behind ordinary situations.[109] What Christ was communicating was that we had to make our own effort to uncover the deeper truth of each situation. This involved an individual search for truth. In this way the ordinary commerce of life and each individual human nature are the *prima materia* of perfection.

Bulephorus elaborated further on this when he said that the correct method for the emulation of Cicero was a threefold process that involved practical experience, a real love of the subject and a mental capacity to judge the process. In short, it was necessary to engage one's practical experiential, emotional and mental parts in the process. Nosoponus disagreed with this. He believed simple imitation of Cicero's style was enough. He said that people in the sun go brown and those in a perfumery smell nice. Bulephorus dismissed this and replied that these were just surface effects. He said:

> I would prefer to take internally any fine aromatic substances that are going and get them into my system, so that I don't just scatter a whiff of perfume over the people near me, but am myself thoroughly heated and invigorated, and then, whenever the occasion demands, a voice can be recognized as the produce of a sound, well-nourished personality.[110]

Here again Erasmus in the guise of Bulephorus advocates inner transformation rather than mere superficial change. He believed that it was essential to work on the personality and actually effect a change in it rather than pursuing a surface imitation. He described the nature of the transformation thus:

> all that you have devoured in a long course of varied reading must be thoroughly digested and by the action of thought incorporated into your deepest mental processes, not your memory or word-list. Then your mind, fattened on fodder of all kinds will generate out of its own resources not a speech redolent of this or that flower or leaf or herb, but one redolent of your personality, your sensitivities, your feelings, and the reader will hail not snippets abstracted from Cicero, but the manifestations of a mind packed with every kind of knowledge.[111]

In order to demonstrate how complete this transformation must be Bulephorus then likened it to that of bees making honey. He said they collect material for honey from many bushes. They turn this

> into a liquid in their mouths and inner parts and then reproduce it, transmuted in to their own substance; in it one recognizes not the taste or smell of any flower or shrub the bee has sipped, but a creation of the bee itself, compounded from all the contributory elements.[112]

Bulephorus then pushed the point further and claimed that 'no one who does not understand an art can imitate it, and no one can understand it unless he practices it.'[113] Thus, understanding based in experience is the key to imitation. He explained that he was not trying to deflect Nosoponus from his desire to emulate Cicero provided this desire is 'kept within bounds, provided you emulate Cicero where he is best, provided you try to be as good as your model rather than indistinguishable from him'.[114] He warned Nosoponus against trying too hard because he claimed that this would be disastrous. His final stipulation was that if Nosoponus failed he must not feel that his life was ruined.[115] Bulephorus said that he himself had suffered from this disease in the past but that Doctor *Logos* had cured him.[116] The doctor said to him 'you are suffering from a nasty bout of false shame caused by the fact that you can't take the insult you share with thousands of other men'.[117] This was that he did not merit the title Ciceronian. In the *Enchiridion* Erasmus constantly urges the reader not to give up the battle if he or she falls now and then. He was aware that this is the human predicament. He said: 'weakness causes us to give into weariness or temptation and thus abandon virtue once we have acquired it'.[118] However, he then urged: 'you must persevere in good undertakings, and for that reason weakness must be bolstered so that we do not abandon the path of virtue'.[119] He believed that this attitude of determination was absolutely crucial for success in the process. He said:

> the kingdom of heaven does not fall to the vacillating, but it is glad to suffer violence, and the violent take it by force. While you are hastening to this goal, you must not allow yourself to be detained by the affection of your dear ones or distracted by the enticements of the world or held back by domestic cares, the chain of worldly affairs must be severed if it cannot be untwisted. You must leave Egypt behind in such a way, as never to return in mind to its fleshpots, Sodom must be abandoned with all haste once and for all; it is forbidden to look back.[120]

The sense of false shame in failure, which Bulephorus had been guilty of, was viewed by Erasmus as being very dangerous. He thought it would lead to giving up the fight. It could lead to giving in to a kind of blindness that allowed the person to return to upholding worldly wisdom rather than true Christian values. In relation to this he said worldly wisdom is

> diabolical, and inimical to God, Its end is perdition because pernicious arrogance always follows after it as its attendant; arrogance is then followed by blindness of spirit, blindness by the tyranny of the emotions, and this by a whole harvest of vices and the freedom to commit every manner of sin. This freedom leads to habit, then a fatal dullness of the mind, which produces a complete insensitivity to evil. In this state of torpor the death of the body takes hold of them, followed by the second death.[121]

By this he meant the death of the soul. This greatest of all evils then was a result of a process of degeneration which started with avoidance of the pain of the false shame produced by the failure to recognize one's weaknesses. This resulted in the individual taking the seemingly easier road of self-delusion, which leads by stages to perdition, and in this choice they are supported by the world at large.

Bulephorus explained that he, like Nosoponus, had adhered to the worldly, literal, imitation of Cicero before he had been cured by Doctor *Logos*. Here Erasmus is alerting the reader to the underlying allegory. The spiritual essence of Christ is the *Logos* - the generative reason and creative force of the universe. By incorporating the *Logos* each Christian can avoid the pitfall of literalism. In the *Enchiridion* he encouraged the reader to read those commentators 'who depart as much as possible from the literal sense'.[122] He said that too many modern theologians 'are too willing to stick to the letter and give their attention to sophistic subtleties rather than to the elucidation of the mysteries, as if Paul were not right in saying that our law is spiritual'.[123] Bulephorus declared that Dr *Logos* cured him of his disease of literalism by means of *Logos*. Erasmus was here implying that a person who was imbued with the spirit of Christ would be cured of the blindness of worldly adherence to the letter and would consequently be opened up and capable of seeing the true inner meaning in all things. Christ is the great healer and the *Logos* is Christ. It is by incorporating this universal creative force that we can truly perfect ourselves. This is the ultimate cure for all humanity.

Bulephorus then turned to a discussion of the true purpose of eloquence. He agreed with Quintillion that this was 'the power to stir the emotions'.[124] He said that different people display 'different attitudes towards the various writers, according to whether the moving spirit proves congenial or antipathetic, attracts or repels'.[125] It is a question of being able to inspire and fire the listener or reader with a love of the topic being communicated. Here, again, is the Erasmian notion that true understanding can only be achieved when the emotions as well as the intellect are engaged. Bulephorus went on to say that in the Christian context

> the mysteries of Christ should be handled not only with learning but with religious feeling. It is not enough to regale the mind of the reader with some trivial, temporary delight; one must arouse emotions worthy of God, and that can only happen if you have an intimate grasp of the subject you are treating. You will set no one on fire if you are cold yourself, nor will you inflame your reader with love of things heavenly if you care for them little or not at all. [126]

Similarly, in the *Paraclesis,* Erasmus had expressed the desire for such eloquence. He cited many examples from mythology such as Mercury, Amphion, Orpheus, the Gaul Ogmius, Marsyas, Socrates and Pericles; all of whom he said had this power to move their listeners. The efficacy of eloquence is all. He wished for 'an eloquence which not only captivates the ear with its fleeting delight but which leaves a lasting sting in the minds of its hearers, which grips, which transforms, which sends away a far different listener than it had received'.[127] This was what Bulephorus meant when he said: 'eloquence which does nothing but delight is not eloquence, for eloquence came into existence for quite a different purpose'.[128] The immediate purpose of eloquence was to move the listener but the ultimate goal in all things for Erasmus was Christ. Thus the goal of eloquence to which Erasmus devoted his life was to communicate the spirit of Christ in order to attract as many people as possible to true Christianity.

In summing up, Bulephorus said that Cicero was 'the supreme master of the art of speaking and, for a pagan, a good man. If he had studied the *philosophy of Christ,* he would, I think have been numbered with those who are now honoured as saints for their blameless and spiritual lives.'[129] Elsewhere, Erasmus went further than this. In the preface to his 1523 edition of Cicero's *Tusculan Disputationes* he said that reading Cicero had had a beneficial ethical effect on him. He added that there was in Cicero 'something divine' and that he was among those who hoped that he 'lives peacefully among the heavenly beings'. He then went a lot further than this and said that in terms of morals many of the church Fathers were less blameless than Cicero.[130] Thus, behind what Bulephorus said was the notion that to emulate Cicero was to emulate someone who ultimately attained the perfection and eternal bliss of heaven. It follows that his literary output must therefore have reflected the divine understanding he had attained. This meant that his writings were valuable as an expression of the wisdom of a perfected human being. The goal of human perfection, according to Erasmus, was the same as the goal of the *philosophy of Christ.* This is the fundamental premise of Erasmus' Christian humanism. Religious perfection as expounded by Christ is one and the same thing as the perfection of human nature itself.[131]

Bulephorus added some final elements to his theory on

the imitation of Cicero and said that it was his wish that 'Marcus Tulius should occupy the first and foremost place in the scheme of study, but that there should be others as well'.[132] He went on to say that in his opinion Cicero 'should not be blindly followed, but taken as a pattern and even challenged. Anyone who merely follows treads in someone else's footsteps and obeys rules'.[133] If we continue the allegorical interpretation of the piece and substitute Christ for Cicero here it means that Erasmus thought that while Christ should occupy the foremost place in our search for perfection we should nevertheless follow others as well and even challenge him if necessary. The first part of this thesis is completely in keeping with Erasmus' philosophy. He believed in the value of non-Christian writers, notably those of the Platonic tradition, in the task of perfection. The second part of this statement is, on the face of it, harder to reconcile with his declared orthodoxy. While it was possible to suggest challenging Cicero the idea of challenging Christ was, at the very least, audacious. Erasmus was however at pains to emphasize the importance of experience in the process of attaining knowledge of the perfection process. He did not believe that any kind of coercion or imposition of faith was possible. In his preface to the edition of Hilary he wrote of the degeneration of the church that had resulted from a proliferation of superficial faith. He argued that any faith that was not based on a solid knowledge of Sacred Scripture was useless. In order to achieve Christ a person had to abandon the superficial imitation of Jesus and find his or her own Christ within. In order to tap this resource a person would have to give up the external Christ so that they could achieve a lasting inner transformation. A true transformation could only be achieved if an individual verified and experienced the truth of Christ for himself or herself. In this way testing and challenging Christ would lead to an inner transformation into Christ. The perfected individual would end up with a solid and personally verified faith rather than one that was defined and enforced superficially by others. Clearly, this would be stronger and nearer truth. There would be a true, all-pervasive transformation of the individual rather than an outer adherence to a set of given beliefs and rules. Erasmus could never have suggested in a straightforward way that Christ himself should be challenged; this would have been the highest heresy. The whole thrust of the *Ciceronianus* is that in order to emulate a truly great man one must study him from every perspective and read all others in the field and even challenge him. One must then practice the craft of this person oneself and deal with the difficulties inherent in this practice. Then, and only then, can one be transformed in an individual way and become what the great person was. This is the only true method of imitation. Cicero achieved the pinnacle of literary and human perfection by gaining an understanding of the literary and philosophical achievements of his predecessors and by then combining this knowledge with his own native talent to produce a new and unique eloquence. It is clear that Erasmus believed that Jesus consciously constructed his life and preaching in order to show us the way of perfection. Human beings can achieve Christ, but not by slavishly imitating the superficial elements of the life of Jesus or his words in Scripture. It is essential to delve into the hidden meaning of his life, death and resurrection to understand the true method. It is then necessary to put all we have learned into practice. Like Jesus and Cicero the point is that each individual must become fully himself or herself in order to achieve the pinnacle of human perfection. The inner transformation and individual genius that are elaborated here are the trademarks of Erasmus' Christian humanism.

Chapter 5

The Perfection Process in Scripture

The incorporation of Christ, then, was the way of perfection, and the full knowledge of the *Logos* of Christ required for this was available to us before the time when Christ appeared in human form in the man Jesus. This belief did not, however, in any way diminish the importance of Scripture for Erasmus. On the contrary, he believed that, in the account it contained of the life and teaching of the incarnate Christ, we had been given the most perfect exposition of the way of perfection. The manifestation of the *Logos* in the man Jesus was of absolutely central importance for him because this functioned as a visible representation of the truth. Sacred Scripture, which contained the words and deeds of the incarnate Christ, was, therefore, the fount of all truth but it was something more too, it was the very instrument of salvation. Its function was that it was the best and most efficacious means of discerning the method of perfection and as such it had the power to transform us. The aspiring Christian would achieve the knowledge required for perfection by deciphering the words and deeds of Jesus outlined in Scripture. Erasmus believed that Christ not only taught the way to perfection by means of verbal instruction, but that he had also consciously constructed his life as a paradigm of the process of perfection. He wrote that we must take account not only of

> Jesus' words, but also how he conducted himself throughout his life. None of this was done by chance but rather by a divine plan and for the instruction of mankind. For there is nothing that does not have an exemplary character displaying godliness for us, nothing that

> does not reflect ancient prophecy or express a figure by which, in a dark manner, the law had designated Christ or a meaning forecasting future events.[1]

As we have seen, Erasmus was aware that knowledge of the true nature of reality was impossible to communicate directly, thus he valued the dual method constructed by Christ to teach us the heavenly philosophy. We could, therefore, uncover the *philosophy of Christ,* which contained the wisdom of the way of perfection, by interpreting the layers of meaning in Scripture. When Erasmus published his New Testament he clearly outlined his views on the *philosophy of Christ* in its preface where he said that he prized Scripture, above all, for this power of transformation.[2] He believed that its transforming power would work on any aspiring Christian as long as they approached the texts with the right mindset. He said:

> if anyone should devoutly philosophize, praying more than arguing and seeking to be transformed rather than armed for battle, he would without a doubt find that there is nothing pertaining to the happiness of man and the living of his life which is not taught, examined, and unravelled in these works.[3]

This belief in the crucial importance of Scripture as an aid to the perfection of the human being was why Erasmus worked so hard to develop his own knowledge of biblical exegesis and philology. His determination to develop a new philology and a more precise exegesis was the means of achieving his main goal of transforming our hearts. He was certainly not interested in the discipline of theology for its own sake. His frequent, satirical and savage disparagement of that profession, most notably in the *Praise of Folly,* is testament to this. His study of the early Fathers of the church had led him to the belief that there had once been a better, truer theology but that it had now degenerated from this earlier golden age. He described the process of degeneration in a letter to Lorenzo Campeggi written in 1520. First he described the golden age of early Christianity when

> Christian philosophy was a matter of faith, not of disputation; men's simple piety was satisfied with the small oracles of Holy Scripture, and charity, a natural growth, had no need of complicated rules,

> believing all things and never coming to a stop.[4]

He then outlined how this happy state of affairs had not lasted because rhetoric and the philosophers, first Platonic then Aristotelian, were marshalled into the service of Christian philosophy. While this had seemed a natural progression in the beginning, it had gradually degenerated until 'theology began to be a form of skill, not wisdom; a show-piece, not a means towards true religion...the crystal springs of the old gospel teaching were choked with sawdust by the Philistines'.[5] In a letter to Jean Carondelet, which served as the preface to his edition of St Hilary, he described the same degenerative process and concluded that 'finally faith began to reside in the written word rather than in the soul, and there were almost as many faiths as men…articles increased, but sincerity decreased' and 'the teaching of Christ...began to depend on the support of philosophy'.[6] Erasmus thought this was a ludicrous situation and he told Jean that he would not be damned

> If you do not know whether the Spirit proceeding from the Father and the Son has a single or a double principle, but you will not escape perdition unless you see to it in the meantime that you have the fruits of the Spirit, which are charity, joy, peace, patience, kindness, goodness, forbearance, gentleness, faith, moderation, self-control and chastity.[7]

What Erasmus hated most of all was the scholastic dependence on Aristotle and it was partly this perhaps that prompted him to use the term *philosophy of Christ* as a description of the message of Scripture. He believed, as we have seen, that sacred letters did not require the assistance of any external and artificially imposed philosophy, rather, Scripture had its own inherent philosophy: the *philosophy of Christ.*[8] The scholastic use of Aristotelianism as a dialectical tool was rendered redundant for Erasmus by the *philosophy of Christ* which was superior in every way to any human philosophy. It alone had the power to transform human beings and lead them to perfection.

Scripture had value and meaning for Erasmus because it was useful. It had a function. He named his new version of Scripture the *Novum Instrumentum.* The primary meaning of *Instrumentum* is a tool or implement and this was consistent with his belief that it functioned as the tool or instrument of our salvation. All of Erasmus' writings are intended to function as aids to the process of perfection. From the early days of the *Enchiridion*, in which he tried to craft a handbook for the aspiring Christian to aid him or her in this struggle, to the end of his life, this was his aim. Sacred Scripture was his primary source in this task and he worked incessantly to bring the force of its salvific efficacy to all people. As early in his public career as 1504 he told John Colet that he had spent the last three years learning Greek and reading Origen and that 'hereafter I intend to address myself to the Scriptures and to spend all the rest of my life upon them'.[9] In 1518 his goal was still the same. He wrote to Justus Jonas and told him his only aim in writing was to help his readers to become better human beings.[10] He went on to say, again, that he intended to pursue this goal to the end of his life, and that is precisely what he did.

This goal is apparent across the whole spectrum of his Scriptural writings but it is in the *Paraphrases* that his own voice can be most clearly discerned. He interprets everything in them as relating to some part of the perfection process. His *Paraphrase on Mark* is the most allegorical of the synoptic paraphrases. In it, in particular, we get a clear view of his objective of elaborating the process of perfection through an allegorical interpretation of Jesus' words and deeds. Early on in the paraphrase he outlined the initial stages of the process that the aspiring Christian had to engage in thus:

> the first task is instruction; through instruction the catechumen begins to recognize both his own baseness and God's goodness and is wholly displeased with himself. Then realizing that hope of salvation is obtained from no other source, he takes refuge in the gratuitous kindness of God. To acknowledge one's disease is a large step towards regaining health; to recognize one's benightedness is a large step towards the light.[11]

So the first, and most important, part of the process was the conscious acknowledgement of one's state of utter imperfection. Without this vital step the process could never even begin. Erasmus believed that this was what the portrayal of the agony in the garden of Gethsemane represented. He described it as 'a valley at the foot of the Mount of Olives' and he went on to say that 'no-one can ascend to the cross of Jesus unless he first descends into this valley, unless he abases himself, renouncing all the resources of human pride'.[12] Christ had demonstrated this for us when he had trembled with fear and weakness in Gethsemane. It was essential for aspiring Christians also to descend into the depths of their own hearts and see the true weakness and abjectness of their nature. Erasmus' first major work, the *Enchiridion,* was written to help the reader to achieve this very insight. He said he wrote it in order to show us to ourselves. In the *Paraphrase on Mark* he said that at the outset: 'God, ... requires from us sinners neither burnt offerings nor gifts. Simply acknowledge your disease and have faith in the physician'.[13] Thus, having fully realized the true nature of one's being, which was no easy thing, the second step in the process was to have faith in the healing powers of Christ. Erasmus interpreted Christ's healing of a paralytic man as a metaphor for this part of the method. He said that when God

> has decided in his goodness to cure a man's paralytic spirit, he fills him with a wonderful dissatisfaction, such that he hates himself and even tires of his life. He sees in what darkness, in what vice he is entangled; he abhors himself; he would completely despair did not he who sent the vinegar of sorrow add the oil of good hope as well.[14]

Continuing the analogy with disease and healing he then said:

> when the potion administered by a trusted physician violently convulses the whole body, the more violent the convulsion the greater the hope of recovery, especially in a life-threatening illness. In the same manner the closer the repentant sinner is to salvation - Christ being the physician - the deeper his despair.[15]

This is a graphic exposition of the crucial Erasmian concept, taken from St Paul, in which strength is made perfect in weakness. The person who becomes fully conscious of himself or herself suffers despair because they see their faulty nature with great clarity. They also see that the entire apparatus of the world and the human condition itself conspires against their progress. The Christian soldiers are not left in this impossible state however, instead, they are given the grace to conquer their weaknesses and ultimately, after a long struggle with their lower tendencies, they are cured. When the paralytic was cured by Jesus he took his bed on his shoulders and went home. For Erasmus the bed represented the man's weaknesses. Erasmus interpreted this as meaning that 'he was now master of his desires whereas before he had been their slave. Note that the man did not simply abandon his bed but he now carried it. In the Erasmian system we do not annihilate our weaknesses we overcome them by subjecting them to our higher selves. This is what carrying the cross means. This is what "crucifying the flesh" with its vices and desires means.'[16] In his *Paraphrase on Romans* Erasmus explained that Christ's death and resurrection were a paradigm for this part of the process of perfection. He said that we must follow the example set by Christ and that in practice what this meant was that in imitating his death we must 'lose feeling for all our former desires' and, in fact, we must kill them.[17] This was not a prescription for severe asceticism. Erasmus did not believe that the monastic life of his day was in any way praiseworthy. Instead, what he described was a process that was equally accessible to lay and cleric alike. It is a process of leaving behind the values of the world while still living fully in the world. It is one in which experience and a proper way of seeing broadens knowledge of oneself and the true nature of reality rather than one in which the emphasis is laid on denying and punishing the fleshly desires. It is world-affirming rather than world-denying because without the world and its influences there would be no struggle and therefore no perfection. Having engaged in this proper way of seeing, the Erasmian Christian will then gradually be changed by this experience and will be less and less under the sway of the flesh and the world. Then he or she will eventually emulate Christ's resurrection by rising to pious living and will 'live together with the living Christ' and 'reproduce the image of Christ as far as possible'.[18] Erasmus believed that only in this indirect way could the Christian be transformed. It was a question of proper understanding and experience, from which transformation would follow naturally by some secret power of nature. God, of course, was the real agent of our transformation. He said that Jesus was happy that the unlearned people who watched his miraculous healing of the paralytic still saw him as a man but they marvelled at the divine power manifested before them:

> Let us be one of the simple crowd, glorifying God, and let us glorify God not only when by his mercy he takes away our spiritual disease, but also when we see others repent of their

former vices through the kindness of the same Jesus.[19]

The process, then, was a progressive one in which each step could only be achieved with active participation and great effort on the part of the aspiring Christian. Strength of will and accurate understanding, which would be the result of this effort, would be developed gradually. It was not at all a question of blindly following prescribed commandments and rules of behaviour. These would not produce the desired transformation. Erasmus, in describing the fact that the apostles also had to engage in this process, put the following words into the mouth of Jesus:

> When my disciples have reached that strength of mind in which they are now being trained, love will achieve more with them than the commandments of either the law or John are wrestling from you now. But they have not as yet attained this strength. they are still weak for the presence of this body stands in their way. But there will come a time when the physical presence of the bridegroom will be taken from them. Then they will have acquired more strength having drunk the Spirit from heaven, and they will not only fast and do so of their own accord, but will perform even braver and bolder deeds willingly and joyfully.[20]

Here Erasmus showed that the apostles themselves, as ordinary men, were subject to this process of perfection and, despite having the living Christ as their companion and teacher, they did not manage to reach the highest level of perfection while Jesus was alive. He described how, near the end of his life on earth, Jesus told them plainly about his coming suffering and death but he urged them to be mindful also of his coming resurrection. They could not bear it because 'they loved Jesus with great affection, but a human kind of affection. For they had not yet received the heavenly Spirit who would perfect in them what was still imperfect'.[21] Even Peter, the apostle chosen by Jesus to lead his church, is depicted as being all too human. In a state of fear, he warned Jesus of the impending danger but Jesus rebuked him.[22] When Erasmus described how Jesus gradually shaped the minds of his disciples so that they would become strong enough to withstand his death on the cross he made it clear that this was an image of the same process that must take place in each Christian heart. The incorporation of the spirit of Christ gradually accustoms the Christian to follow Christ even to the cross.[23] He said that it was 'a difficult journey to go up to Jerusalem. It needs strong and valiant men in whose hearts this world no longer has a place.'[24] The apostles were not yet strong enough to cope with this mystery. When the apostles did not understand this concept Erasmus explained that Jesus started from scratch and again explained that his life was a metaphor for the method of perfection. He asked them 'are you able to drink from the cup from which I am now preparing to drink? Are you able to receive the baptism which I am about to receive?'[25] Later he said 'let your only endeavour be to emulate me'.[26] Jesus then explained his mission on earth to save all humankind: 'Let anyone who follows me do as I do, just as I simply obey the commands of the Father right to the cross'.[27] Erasmus explained that this meant 'the freer a man is from all carnal affections the better prepared he is for the battle of the cross'.[28]

This inability of the closest companions of Jesus to understand the process of perfection indicated to Erasmus that the esoteric truth of Christianity was very difficult to communicate. It was startling indeed that even Jesus had encountered this problem. His closest companions were continually misinterpreting him. This happened because perfection was a matter of gradual change rooted in experience, and consequently the method of perfection could only be divulged gradually in conformity with the progress achieved by the aspiring Christian. Erasmus believed that St Paul was aware of this and provided us with a good example of how to overcome it. In his *Paraphrase on Romans* he said:

> Paul knew and saw certain things which it was unlawful for one to say, and he knew to what extent milk and to what extent solid food were needed. He knew the stages of growth in Christ, and what had to be applied to each one.[29]

In interpreting Jesus' method of teaching from a boat offshore as being an image of the best way to impart the Gospel truth, Erasmus advised the teacher of the gospel that he should adapt himself to the limited understanding of his hearers, 'for they cannot as yet follow you'.[30] He went on to say that 'at first the doctrine must be adapted to their uneducated minds until they have made progress'.[31] He believed it was for this reason that Christ taught in parables, that is in similes, because this is the simplest and most suitable way of teaching uneducated people.[32] He did, however, caution that it was essential that the hearer participated by doing his or her utmost to understand the lesson otherwise the parable could be completely misinterpreted. 'Unless one listens attentively it is a tale rather than a parable. Not everyone has ears to hear the evangelical parables, for under their lowly and laughable garb they conceal heavenly wisdom'.[33] It was essential that aspiring Christians should participate in the process to the best of their ability. They had to experience the truth of this process at each stage in order to progress. There is a great emphasis here again on the fact that experience is the key to understanding. Erasmus reported that Jesus wanted the disciples to 'hear and see' his words. In other words they had to experience the truth with at least two of the senses. The need for gospel preachers to take the spiritual state of their listeners into account is also revealed in his interpretation of the incident where the apostles who did not understand the parable of the sower, asked Jesus to explain it to them. Erasmus said Jesus warned them 'that we must not disclose everything to everyone, but that the gospel doctrine must be dispersed only at the appropriate time and according to the understanding of the listeners'.[34] Jesus told the apostles that they were allowed to know the truth but that for those people who were 'excluded from the inner circle, all is conducted in parables, whether I speak or act before them. For they do not have suitable ears or suitable eye's.[35] Erasmus did not, however, believe that the multitude would always be excluded from the full gospel truth because he depicted Jesus saying:

> do not think that it is my wish to keep always a secret what I now entrust to you in secret...At present I hide many things from the multitude because they are not capable of understanding, and even if they were capable, the time has not yet come. Truly, when the time comes, there is nothing so secret among us but it must be divulged; nothing so arcane but it must be openly preached to all.[36]

Jesus then told the disciples that everything must take second place to this. They must do it day and night. 'Woe to him who does not bring forth the good seed entrusted to him, who conceals the light given to him'.[37] In conformity with this precept Erasmus believed that nothing of Christ's message should be kept hidden but it was essential to bear in mind the stage of development of ones readers.

Throughout his *Mark,* Erasmus continued to reveal this hidden meaning of the actions of Jesus as a paradigm of perfection. He interpreted the account of the baptism of Jesus in this way, saying that 'in the Lord was expressed in corporeal form what happens spiritually to all men who in sincere faith receive the evangelical baptism. The body is bathed with water and the spirit is anointed with invisible grace.'[38] He went on to expound in the same way on Jesus' actions immediately after his baptism. 'Jesus, therefore, showing in his own person what he wanted us to do, was immediately after his baptism driven into the wilderness by the power of the Spirit.'[39] There he prayed and battled with Satan until finally he defeated him. In doing this Erasmus believed 'he showed that the new recruit must flee the common multitude until he has tamed the flesh, defeated Satan, and acquired the true strength of the Spirit by meditation on the divine law and by devout prayers'.[40] He saw Jesus' actions, not as a mere historical account, nor, in the usual way, as a model for imitation, but primarily as secret instruction to the Christian. The actions of Christ had to be deciphered and mined for their secret meaning and not copied slavishly and unknowingly. Again, here, Erasmus was not advocating that the reader should physically leave the world and go into a monastery or a desert, rather, he was suggesting an interior mental abandonment of identification with the values and cares of the world in order to see the spiritual reality more clearly. He argued that Jesus, by retreating to the wilderness in order to avoid the crowds he was attracting.

> teaches us what we must do. He who has the power to work evangelical miracles does not seek a large but an enthusiastic audience...No one follows Jesus unless he is burning with an ardent desire for him. He who has left behind the luxury of cities and follows Jesus through rough and pathless country follows him to his own great benefit. For he who loves truly follows the beloved through everything: through ignominy, famine, loss of substance, exile, prison, torture, and death.[41]

In this action of Christ the aspiring Christian learns the great difficulties that have to be overcome in the process of perfection. This scriptural example will then serve to strengthen the resolve when these difficulties arise because Scripture will have demonstrated that they are necessary and will pass. Later in the *Paraphrase* Erasmus interpreted a third retreat of Jesus in a yet different way. Jesus got into a boat to preach because the crowd of people wishing to hear him was too large. Erasmus saw this as a covert instruction to those who wish to teach the Gospel message to others:

> understand, O teacher of the gospel what this image means - flee the crowd - but still teach, if the crowd might overwhelm you withdraw to the boat of the gospel "which knows no earthly upheaval" and from where you can teach in peace.[42]

Again Erasmus himself heeded this lesson from Scripture. He lived as independently as he could, rejecting all offers of position and honours both civil and ecclesiastical which might have ensnared him in worldly affairs and interfered with his work. Moreover, despite the serious and potentially dangerous opposition of influential Catholic opponents he, nevertheless, continued until his last day to teach his version of the *philosophy of Christ.* He narrowly avoided extreme sanctions in his lifetime by using Scripture as his source for everything.

In his *Paraphrase on Mark,* Erasmus also explained his view of the process of perfection by interpreting a series of the miracles of Jesus as an allegorical description of it. He started this section by stating his familiar belief that: 'just as Jesus' words often take the form of a parable, so his actions, too, are frequently parables'.[43] He then demonstrated this idea by expounding on the miracles. First, in the case of the cure of a deaf-mute he said that 'these things were done apart from the crowd. For we must not make the profane crowd witness to the evangelical initiation, lest they mock what they do not yet understand.'[44] He then said that Jesus was anxious in case people would interpret the miracle as being an indication of his wonderful human powers rather than God's power working through him. 'Let man keep silent about whatever great deed he has done so that man's glory be kept hidden and God's glory be proclaimed!'[45] He argued that the spiritual element of the miracles was, in fact, far more miraculous than their physical manifestation. He said that although the people who experienced miracles thanked Jesus more for physical healing than spiritual healing, this was the wrong way around.[46] As a consequence of this view of the secret meaning of miracles he said that 'all the miracles worked by Jesus were to our benefit.'[47] The people who were healed in the flesh were not necessarily the true beneficiaries of Jesus' actions. He was performing miracles that would be effective, in the far more important spiritual realm, for all the future generations of humankind because they were physical demonstrations of spiritual realities. This was one important practical aspect of the way in which Jesus was the source of our salvation. Erasmus went on to interpret the miracle of loaves and fishes as meaning that the 'bread of the gospel is sufficient to our salvation'[48] and that

> perhaps the apostles will add some epistles, but this is insignificant and of very little importance compared to the provisions of the Gospel. This allowance has been made for the sake of certain fastidious people, but we must not ask for more.[49]

This was indicated by the fact that Jesus satisfied all and there were even seven baskets of food left.[50]

As we have seen Erasmus believed that a crucial element of the process of perfection was an examination of the inner self in order to become more conscious. In his exposition of the cure of a blind man he argued that this was precisely what Jesus was demonstrating for us in this miracle. He explained that in the process of the cure Jesus touched the man to show us that 'no one can seek salvation from the Lord Jesus unless he is first touched by him. For the first touch makes a man know himself.'[51] Here Erasmus is implying that when Christ has penetrated our psyche we begin to see ourselves in a new and real way. He went on to argue that Jesus could have healed the man by a word but he chose instead to 'show his disciples by a figure the struggle which was necessary in order to be able to lead men to the recognition of the truth when they have already grown old in their error'.[52] In other words it was more important for Jesus to demonstrate the way to spiritual life for all of us rather than simply cure one man of a physical ailment. There were several steps in the process. First, Jesus led the man out of the village to demonstrate that the aspiring Christian must reject the views of the majority of people. This, again, is leaving the world behind. Then Jesus spat on his eyes and touched them with his hands. At this stage the blind man still did not open his eyes so Jesus asked him what could he see and at the sound of Jesus' voice the man said he could see 'men, like trees, walking about'. Jesus touched him again until he could see clearly.[53] Erasmus interpreted this as meaning that people who are without the Gospel light see worldly things in a disproportionately large way but when they receive the light they realize the insignificance of those things that seemed huge to them when their sight was faulty.[54] This initial blindness is the reason why perfection must be taught by degrees until the students of Gospel philosophy reach the stage where 'great mysteries and a more solid doctrine must be communicated to them, which will make them discern everything more clearly'.[55] The *philosophy of Christ* will gradually transform the individual and conquer his or her blindness until they can absorb and fully understand the whole Christian mystery, which will result in them seeing everything as it truly is.

Erasmus' belief in the value of Jesus' life as a paradigm of salvation was the basis of a kind of practical Redemption process rather than one that was solely an unknowable cosmic mystery. On this level, the Redemption of humankind was effected by 'faith in the Gospel' in a practical functional sense. This, together with his belief that ordinary people could incorporate Christ and, in a way, actually become Christ and participate in the process of saving others, could be seen as a dilution of the redemptive mission of Christ. Erasmus, however, never denied the mystery of the Redemption in the sense of God sending his Son to redeem fallen humanity but there is a sense in which we are redeemed by the power of Christ's life and teaching as the raw material for the method of perfection. What Erasmus always emphasized as being of use were those elements of the perfection process that we could understand and participate in. He believed that if we could understand the hidden meaning of Scripture by reading Jesus' actions and words allegorically we would then recognize the truth of the process by putting it into practice. There is always a great emphasis in Erasmus' writings on living out the truth of Scripture. It is never enough to just know of a truth it must also be lived and verified.[56] This in turn would engender faith within our souls in the greater and more inaccessible mystery of Redemption. This faith in turn would lead us on to greater understanding and towards perfection. Faith, therefore, as an agent that dragged us forward, was an essential part of the quest for perfection.

The Perfection Process in Scripture

Continuing his interpretation of Jesus' miracles Erasmus commented on the cure of another blind man. This time a blind beggar was healed because despite his infirmity he had recognized Jesus as the Son of God. Erasmus explained that this was an example of Jesus expressing 'in a corporeal image' what his death 'would effect through faith in the Gospel teaching'.[57] The message being conveyed was that 'Jesus...grants salvation in return for faith, not works'.[58] The whole process of salvation was one of seeing properly. Ordinary people are blind and they see everything in a distorted way. They value the worthless and despise the precious.[59] Erasmus interpreted the blind-beggar incident thus:

> disregarding everything else, he wished nothing but vision to discern God and his Son, Jesus. To know him is to have eternal life. To know is to see. O truly evangelical prayer! How few words in it and how much faith! Indeed this is the short prayer that reaches heaven.[60]

Salvation was a process of knowledge and true vision. Knowing Jesus meant knowing everything he did and said and truly understanding the spiritual meaning of his life. The process was only completed, however, when Jesus was emulated in all that he did and was. 'It is not enough to know Jesus; you must follow him when you have recovered your sight.'[61]

> Unless you recover your sight you cannot follow Jesus on his journey. For who would follow a man who willingly surrenders his life to death unless he discerns by his faith that temporary ignominy is the way to eternal glory; corporeal torment is the way to eternal joy; death is the way to eternal life.[62]

This Erasmian view of Faith as an essential factor for salvation was not at all like the Lutheran *sola fide*. The crucial difference is in the word *sola*. For Erasmus faith *alone* did not effect salvation His essentially positive view of our capacities meant that he emphasized the human being's own role in the perfection process whereas Luther's essentially negative view of human capacities was in conformity with his view that we were powerless to effect our own salvation. Erasmus' view of the perfection process was not in perfect accord with the Roman Catholic tradition either. Again, the importance he placed on our own role in perfection tended to lessen or even negate the function of the sacramental system of the church in the process. Nor did he have any sympathy with the over-emphasis of good works as a crucial part of salvation either. While, for him, the proper incorporation of Christ would result in the true Christian acting in a moral way, simply acting out moral behaviour in a superficial way was useless to salvation. In the *Enchiridion* he said that some people were by nature attracted to certain virtues or repelled by some vices and that this caused them to behave in an apparently virtuous way but that in fact this was of no use whatsoever in the pursuit of perfection. He said that it was 'a great error of mankind to think that what is merely an instinct of nature is perfect piety'.[63] Taking the example of the vice of lust he said 'There are some who are never titillated by the pleasures of the flesh. They should not attribute to their own virtue something that is in itself indifferent. It is a virtue to conquer lust, not simply to be free of it'.[64] Struggle was the essential dynamic in the Erasmian view of perfection. Internal struggle produced internal transformation. If there was no struggle then there could be no transformation.

Perfection was achieved by a process of deeper and deeper knowledge of the true nature of reality. The principle barrier to this was the blindness caused by an adherence to worldly values, or, the flesh. Thus, the process had to start with each individual coming to know themselves so that they could recognize their faults and weaknesses and thereby begin to tackle their eradication. Erasmus found this part of the process expressed allegorically in another miracle of Jesus. He explained that the healing of a woman with an issue of blood was a metaphor for the way in which Christ loves the person who recognizes himself or herself as a sinner. He described how Jesus having felt someone touch him asked who it was and the woman, in response, shook off her shyness and told him everything about herself. 'She kept nothing secret, she did not cover up the long-standing disease, the frustrated skill of the physicians, the furtive touching of Jesus' garment, the faith she had in him.' Erasmus' view of this was that 'the Lord Jesus loves this kind of confession, which makes the sinner recognize himself and attribute all the glory for his restored health to God'.[65] Human beings had to acknowledge the abjectness of the state that proper self-examination revealed. Erasmus was aware that this was no easy task. Even the apostles and St Peter himself had experienced this difficulty. He said of Peter at the time of Gethsemane that he 'did not as yet know himself'.[66] This, however, was the *sine qua non* of Erasmus' concept of the perfection process. If aspiring Christians could not recognize their faults and their true nature then there was no possibility of achieving perfection.

Erasmus' reading of Scripture assured him that Jesus had used his life and teaching to give many examples of how this weakness was itself a useful, and, actually essential, part of the process. In this sense the weakness of the flesh was not to be shunned because it was actually essential for perfection. Erasmus interpreted the incident where Jesus was asleep in a boat when a storm blew up and the apostles were scared as an example of this mechanism in action. He said that Jesus was aware that there were many people who would oppose the spread of Gospel truth. 'To strengthen his disciples against such men and to teach them that no storm, however fierce, ought to terrify those who wholeheartedly believe in the Lord Jesus, he allowed his disciples to incur danger to the point of despair!'[67] They were terrified and woke Jesus who immediately calmed the storm. Erasmus said this showed that although they had faith in Jesus, their faith was not yet perfect. He thought that the deeper meaning, however, was that Satan provokes storms like this in our hearts and that when this happens the remedy for the troubled Christian was that they should arouse Christ within themselves and tranquillity would then return.[68] In this way they would train themselves to be strong in the face of temptation just as Jesus trained his apostles. He had allowed them to reach the very point of despair implying that the greater the weakness of the flesh the better the opportunity for overcoming it and thereby strengthening the better part of human nature. Erasmus explained how Jesus artificially created a situation of desperation for the apostles in order that they might achieve a higher level of awareness and thus strengthen themselves for the next attack. As if to underline the importance of this point he later reiterated it by using the example of a different storm where the apostles were again afraid. In this incident Jesus walked on water to calm them. 'He seems to desert them for a while to exercise them in adversity to teach them a firm faith in himself.'[69] Again, Jesus used a situation of difficulty to test and strengthen the apostles but in fact he never really deserted them. He consciously left them in danger because it was conducive to their perfection. Erasmus was here outlining his belief that we cannot always see the true value of seemingly bad life circumstances but in this situation our faith must be strong enough to enable us to hold on in the dark until we have reached a safe harbour. In so doing we will become stronger and better able to triumph over adversity in future.

By degrees, Erasmus used his paraphrase of Mark to approach the central point of this idea. He described the imperfection of Peter, the man chosen by Jesus to lead the church after his death, who, out of human fear, warned Jesus of the danger he was in. Jesus rebuked him saying:

> Take your place behind me. This task which I am carrying out is no human task. You are still harbouring human affections, you do not know God's plan. If you are to be my disciple you must emulate my death, not impede it.[70]

Erasmus commented that in this passage Jesus was calling everyone to participate in the same process; this message was for all men, not just Peter.[71] At this point, Peter represents the ordinary human reaction of a person who does not yet have the new way of seeing and who has not yet reached the understanding of the *philosophy of Christ*. If he had, he would have understood that Jesus had chosen to die in order to show all Christians that they must emulate him in his suffering and cross. All must be willing to abandon cherished beliefs and old ways of seeing the world. They must to die to their old lives for Christ. This was the ultimate weakness through which true strength would be achieved. 'But whoever exposes his life to the danger of death out of love for me and for the constant profession of the Gospel will through me save his life, which would otherwise be truly lost.'[72] This idea is epitomized for Erasmus in the central metaphor of the *cross*. He explained that the meaning of the crucifixion was that

> whenever the storm of persecution breaks loose, we must take up our cross; though even in peaceful times no one will be without his cross, for it is not easy to renounce one's natural emotions and the pleasures and enticements of this world, to castrate one's flesh, to refrain from excess, to suppress desire, to harness anger, and to dismiss feelings of revenge.[73]

These enticements of the world have to be killed in us. Erasmus believed that the person who embarked on the path towards true Christianity would be impeded by the world and its values at every turn. He paraphrased Jesus thus:

> the world will rise and use every war engine against those who proclaim my name, It will threaten them with disgrace and exile, imprisonment, torture, proscription, and death. For this nation is evil and will always have more bad than good men, and among them it will be considered the worst crime to profess my name.[74]

Thus Erasmus believed that we must read the mystery of the cross as a metaphor for the central aspect of the perfection process. Like Jesus, each human being also had to die to the world, that is, the inclinations of the flesh, and also to all worldly values and honours because they were utterly opposed to those of Christ. Anyone who did this could then be reborn with him to a new life forever. The word Erasmus used in his *Paraclesis* for this process of rebirth was *instauratio,* which means renewal.[75] It cannot have escaped the attention of this innovative philologist that the term contained the stem of the Greek word for cross: σταυροσ. This combined with the *ratio,* or philosophical system, contained in the mystery of the cross when incorporated by the human being would achieve a transformation that would lead to perfection. The power of the cross, for Erasmus, lay in the fact that it was a wonderfully powerful, but nevertheless plain, symbol of this interior method. Human beings are designed in such a way that they achieve spiritual strength by enduring weakness. In dying to the world and overcoming the ultimate weakness of crucifixion Christ demonstrated for all time the way of perfection.

Weakness of the flesh also functioned in another related way as an instrument of perfection. Erasmus pointed out that Jesus had consciously used 'the tenacious malice of Judas for our salvation'.[76] Without the worldly instincts of Judas the plan of salvation would have foundered. This is as near as Erasmus comes to having a worked-out concept of evil. He used precisely the same idea in interpreting the actions of the high priest Caiaphus. He said 'Caiaphus is Satan' and he is

> the source of this whole tragedy. All ignominy suffered by Jesus, every destructive act - if it be destructive came from Caiaphus; who carried out a most sacred thing without knowing it, For he

> presided over the sacrifice without which no man could attain salvation.[77]

In this way the Erasmian system envisioned all of God's creation participating in perfection. It was a perfectly functioning whole. As a dimension that God has allowed, even the evils of the world were vital components of the perfection process. He argued that the afflictions which beset all of our lives

> open up for us the way to immortality: Since, indeed, we have taken up this new example from Christ and received from him an excellent doctrine, namely, that the virtue of endurance is strengthened by bearing evils, we become, by endurance like gold from the fire, better tested and approved by God and men.[78]

Erasmus found this idea, also, in St Paul's letter to the Romans where he showed that Christ conquered sin through sin. He wrote that 'it was provided by the wonderful and secret plan of God that the way by which our well-being was restored would correspond to the way in which we had suffered ruin'.[79] He then explained that since sin had come into the world through the man, Adam, God's secret plan was that it would also be conquered by a man. 'The goodness of Christ altogether conquers the wickedness of Adam' because Jesus Christ was 'likewise a man'.[80] Erasmus' reading of Paul made it vital for him that Christ was truly a human being. It was absolutely central to his version of the salvific process. 'It was appropriate, furthermore, for flesh to destroy flesh, sin to conquer sin, and death to overcome death.' And so God sent his son down to our level and made him a lowly and weak man in order that he could save humankind. 'Even though he is a stranger to all contagion of sin, nevertheless he was dressed in the same flesh in which other sinners are clothed. For he assumed the nature common to all and lived as a sinner among sinners.'[81] Thus Christ was not merely a human being but he was also, crucially, a sinner. He had to take on sin in order to conquer it for the sake of humankind. This, of course, was more than the Paris theologians and their ilk could swallow and Erasmus was duly accused of blasphemy.[82] He was always aware of the dangers of stretching orthodoxy beyond its limits but it was crucial to his salvific thought that only sin itself could overcome sin therefore Christ had to be a sinner.[83] This is the secret of the mystery of the cross. In this way

Erasmus always emphasized the role of the flesh in salvation. Since it was only by overcoming the flesh that we could perfect ourselves, the flesh was, therefore, an essential part of the process. That apparently hopeless and impossibly weak event, the crucifixion, was, in fact, the wonderful and glorious act that effected the salvation of all humanity. When Christ died on the cross he demonstrated in the most graphic and simple way possible that we must die to the world in order to rise again to a new life. He also showed that Christ is crucified by the world because the world is opposed to the spirit of Christ. Flesh is transformed by enduring and therefore overcoming flesh: that is the process. The power of the cross lay in the fact that even the most unlearned human being could understand it. It was not necessary to learn any complicated system of theology or philosophy in order to understand its message. Anyone who engaged in proper introspection would find the truth of the cross in his or her own heart.

The opposition of the world meant that the process was not an easy one however. Erasmus saw it as a struggle, or even a war, to the death. He knew that the aspiring Christian had to fight with every fibre of his or her being in order to achieve victory.

> Victory does not come to the sluggish, you must take up arms lest the enemy who lurks everywhere find you unprepared and unarmed and overcomes you. Directly the world will assail you, Satan will assail you, your own flesh will assail you. You must go on fighting to go on winning. And the battle will not end until your life ends. Yet the more often you defeat your enemy, the weaker he will depart from the battlefield and the stronger you will be.[84]

This enemy is, above all, an enemy within. Again, Erasmus found his main source for this in *Romans*. His paraphrase of St Paul's description of his own inner struggle for perfection is a perfect example of his view of the nature of the struggle. Paul longed for good 'by mind and reason' but desire and obedience to the flesh prompted him to do what was shameful.[85] He perceived two people in himself: the external person prone to vice, and the internal one who loved goodness.[86] The struggle between these two parts of himself was manifest in Paul when he said: 'I do not seem to be the one doing what I do. For who would do what he does not wish to do?' He went on to say that we take our identity from our better part but despite this he was conscious that he could not actually do what his own reason dictated.

> If one does not seem to do what he does against his will, when I do what I do not wish to do according to the better part of man, it does not seem to me that I do what I do, but rather the power of sin itself implanted in the grosser part of me.[87]

The Law of Moses, as expressed particularly in the commandments, was not a sufficient remedy for this state of struggle. Erasmus paraphrased Paul thus: 'the law does not remove this baser self from me; nevertheless, if at any time I attempt to obey the law, it forces me to acknowledge that my evil is deeply implanted and impressed upon my mind.'[88] Despite his attraction to the goodness that was outlined in the law he was nevertheless unable to achieve it, torn in struggle between the opposites in himself. 'For the inclination to sin is so deeply fixed in the flesh, and the habit of committing wrong is so powerful, (as if now a part of my nature), that like some unwilling and struggling captive I am dragged into sin.'[89] The antidote to this negative situation was not the law but Christ. Erasmus, quoting Paul, said: Christ allows us to conquer sin the law does not.[90] The law performed the important function of revealing our sinfulness to us but it did not provide the remedy. Knowing the precepts of the law was not enough; we needed the *philosophy of Christ* to discern the full method of perfection.

While this process of struggle was explicit in St Paul, Erasmus also found evidence of it in the scriptural account of the life of Jesus himself. He interpreted the incident in which the apostles were unable to cast out a demon from a boy as being an example of how Jesus taught them what they needed to do in order to aid sinners in their struggle against personal evil and towards ultimate salvation. His interpretation rests on the fact that he saw the demon not as an evil spirit but as evidence of a spiritual struggle between the good and evil impulses within the soul of the young boy. This is not at all what the literal text of the Gospel says but it was Erasmus' own view of the spiritual or true meaning of the passage.[91] He wrote: 'tenacious is the evil to which the sinner is accustomed from tender years'.[92] The boy's peculiar behaviour was a demonstration of the fact that 'a struggle had begun between his spirit, wishing to repent, and his desire, recalling him to his old ways'.[93] To Erasmus, the manifestation of an apparent evil spirit represented the fact that 'the evil was fierce and had turned into second nature'. [94] Jesus cured the boy and told the disciples that in order to help sinners 'you must pursue their vice in such a manner that you are seen to take an interest in the victim's salvation but with the realization that human effort is nothing without Christ secretly lending his voice'.[95] As a result of Jesus' intervention the boy's soul was calmed and a new equilibrium was established. 'He is at rest and quiet who before was moved by tides of desire, ambition, wrath, envy, and avarice in turn and carried away as if by the impulse of an impure and violent demon.'[96] Here Erasmus showed that he believed the demon in question was not some mysterious metaphysical entity but rather the base and worldly passions that had to be eradicated in all of us. He then emphasised that the reason the apostles could not cure the boy was because they had not yet reached a state of perfection themselves. Jesus began to explain this to them by saying that the demon in question was a spiritual type which could only be expelled by 'prayer and fasting'.[97] The function of prayer was to strengthen faith, which was essential to the work. He said that 'by fasting, which includes abstinence from all carnal desires, the rebellion of the flesh is put down'.[98] Thus the spiritual state of the gospel preacher was intrinsic to his efficacy. 'The greater our self-confidence grows, the more our power of working miracles decreases. The more the power of the flesh is subdued in us, the stronger the power of the Spirit grows.'[99] This is the main theme of Erasmus' work on preaching, *Ecclesiastae sive de ratione concionandi.* He also alluded to it throughout the *Paraclesis* where he argued that the most important aspect of the theologian's work was the transformation of his or her own heart and that anyone who had truly incorporated Christ whether that person was a 'common labourer or a weaver' qualified for the title of theologian.[100] Here, as always, Erasmus' emphasis was on interior qualities rather than external ones. It was more important that a preacher had engaged in the perfection process than that he or she had been ordained, or elevated in the church, or had received a university education. Their efficacy did not depend on their office or worldly status but on the state of their own souls.

While Erasmus saw the perfection process as being a very difficult type of warfare, there was one aspect of the process that mitigated in favour of its success. He believed that once the seed of Christ had been properly sown in a person whose heart was well prepared to receive it, an irresistible hidden force of nature would then take over and ensure that it grew to full perfection. He said that this seed 'grows in fortune and misfortune, and at every opportunity provided by those who support it or fight against it. For what has been sown by him whose will no one can resist cannot fail to sprout.'[101] This was how Erasmus interpreted the parable of the sower. He said that the sower sows his seed and then he sleeps. The seed meanwhile grows without anyone's labour 'driven by the hidden force of nature'.[102] He believed that 'nature has its own steps and maintains them without the sower's effort after the seed has been sown'.[103] He described how the seed germinated and grew shoots and then fruit and he said that 'by these hidden advances nature takes care that no one notices the progress, though he notices that progress has been made'.[104] This optimistic view of creation in which nature itself is designed ultimately for perfection given the right conditions was also expressed in the *Antibarbari.* Here he said that Jesus had made a promise to humankind that when he reached heaven he would then draw everything in creation up to him. Erasmus interpreted this as meaning that 'all things, whether hostile or heathen or in any other way far removed from him, must be drawn, even if they do not follow, even against their will, to the service of Christ'.[105] This is the cosmic equivalent of his idea that at the individual level strength is made perfect in weakness. In this way even evil functioned as an aid to perfection. The whole of creation was designed by God for the purpose of perfection. Erasmus never expounded on the full implications of this idea, probably because if he had, it might have come too close to the heretical concept of *Apokatastasis* propounded by his favourite Origen, in which all beings even the devil will ultimately be saved. He nevertheless believed that the whole of creation tends towards the perfection of Christ. In this way, Erasmus thought that all of creation was made to benefit us. We are the centre of nature and our perfection is its purpose. Christ, by a process of attraction, draws all created things to serve his purpose and, as we have seen, even sin and weakness have their place in the grand Erasmian scheme of things. They too are drawn to serve the perfection process.

The perfection of humanity is Christ. The process is one of incorporating Christ and becoming a son of God with him. Erasmus likened this attractive transforming force to fire. In his

Paraphrase on Mark he called it the

> fire of the divine Spirit that takes away from and purges the mind of all carnal affections and somehow transforms into God whatever it seizes, so that those who before were concerned with earthly things now disdain them and are carried away to heavenly things. Whoever is seasoned with this salt cannot be turned away from the purity of the gospel spirit by any enticement. Whoever is purged by this fire will disdain all harmful designs of his persecutor.[106]

This is the state of near perfection in which a person could withstand the enticements of sin. Erasmus interpreted the description of the second coming of Jesus in scripture as an allegory of this state. The more usual interpretation of the second coming as a future historical event created an upsurge of eschatological expectance in the early sixteenth century. This fervour is absolutely absent in Erasmus. He frequently interpreted references to the kingdom of Christ on earth as a spiritual state achievable in the here and now and not a futuristic material kingdom. In his *Mark,* he portrayed Jesus promising his second coming and saying:

> the Son of Man whom you see humble now and whom you will soon see as the most abject of men will appear in the majesty of his Father with all the angels and his chosen disciples. Nor is this time very far off. There are men here who in their lifetime will see the coming of God's kingdom in its power.[107]

In interpreting this, Erasmus said that the apostles did not understand what Jesus' words meant

> because their meaning was not unequivocal. For only after his death, resurrection, ascension, only after the Holy Spirit had been sent from heaven, was it that the power of that mustard seed unfolded, that is, the power of evangelical teaching.[108]

Thus it was only after they had been transformed by the Holy Spirit that they then had personal experience of this spiritual second coming. Erasmus believed it was a metaphor for the stage of the perfection process that we would arrive at when we reached the point at which the slings and arrows of the world did not overwhelm us and we were then not subject to all the influences of Pharisees, scribes, kings and the worldly powers. This was the effective end of the world for the Christian who, from then on, having died to the world lived in a new and spiritual way. This was consistent with the fact that Jesus said some of his disciples would see the second coming before they died. What this meant was that some of Jesus' audience in Mark's Gospel would achieve the stage in perfection in which they would experience the second coming of Christ as the culmination of the process on earth. First, Christ opened a human being to the way of the cross. Then by slowly dying to his or her old view of the world the person would begin to be a new creature who knew the true nature of reality. In this way they would experience the second coming of Christ in glory within their own soul. In other words, they would incorporate the spirit of Christ fully, which necessitated a rejection of the values of the world. Erasmus stated that Jesus taught 'the beginnings of the Gospel in Christ then progress by means of the Holy Spirit and finally perfection again in Christ'.[109] So it was a process that started with a kind of first coming of Christ entering into the life of the aspiring Christian, then, through the Holy Spirit, he or she would progress in the way of the Gospel until they had achieved a point where they could receive the second coming of Christ in completion of the process. Continuing his exegesis of this theme, Erasmus interpreted the next verse of Mark, in which Jesus led three of his disciples to a high mountain and showed them a vision of his future splendour, as meaning that Jesus revealed to Peter, James and John 'even before his death a taste of his future majesty, as far as human nature can comprehend it!'[110] Again, Erasmus asserted that this was not a one-off event. He believed that 'even today Jesus considers some chosen men worthy of being carried off to the mountain of pure contemplation, of being given a taste of eternal bliss through secret inspiration'. It is possible, on account of this and other references to such a state, that Erasmus was describing a personal experience.[111] The apostles, who had not as yet experienced the personal second coming of Christ, misunderstood the vision he had shown them. Erasmus explained that when these disciples came down from the mountain they began to discuss how the glory of his kingdom would come soon after his resurrection. When they asked Jesus about this he

> gave an ambiguous reply to the question of his disciples, for they were not yet capable of understanding the whole mystery. For they

> shrank from the things that were of greater concern to themselves and dreamt only of the glory of the kingdom, of which they had had a taste.[112]

Thus, they saw the second coming in the traditional way of the end of days. However, Erasmus interpreted it as something that was of 'greater concern to themselves': that is, the perfection of Christ which they would soon each experience personally. It was an immediate personal second coming rather than the cosmic one to come. 'They did not understand that this too was the kingdom of God: that once the Gospel had been propagated the heavenly Spirit would subjugate the power of this world and of Satan'.[113] On the personal level this meant that the desires of the flesh would now be subject to the spirit of Christ in each of them. Jesus did not wish them to know when the kingdom would come. Because of their weakness he allowed them to dream it would be soon.[114] Erasmus gave a further example of how the apostles were not yet ready to understand the nature of the second-coming and Jesus' death when he again described their reaction to Jesus' account of his forthcoming death and resurrection.[115] 'They could not as yet conceive in their minds the mystery of the cross, nor could they conjecture the purpose of his death'.[116] Even at this point, having followed Jesus for years, they were clinging to worldly emotions.

> They still knew only human wisdom. For it was God's plan to be reconciled with mankind through the sacrifice of the "immaculate sacrificial lamb",[117] and to forgive all men's sins on account of their faith. But the disciples kept dreaming of some worldly kingdom.[118]

Because they could not understand the mystery of the second coming they argued among themselves about who would be chief among them in this new earthly kingdom. In Erasmus' estimation, Jesus was aware of their weakness in displaying this sin of ambition and he tried to correct it. 'To tear this emotion - by far the most fatal one - from their hearts' Jesus told them: 'the first shall be last'.[119] He explained to them that the kingdom of heaven was the opposite of the kingdom of the world and that those whom the world disdained would be the highest rank in the spiritual kingdom. Erasmus used this scriptural account of the confusion of the apostles in relation to the resurrection to expound his own view of the second coming. The gospel verses he was paraphrasing do not mention a personal second coming at all. He did not emphasize a more mysterious cosmic event, but rather, he construed the verses in a way that was amenable to personal experience and beneficial to perfection. This personal second coming of Christ, the transforming element and result of internal struggle, was far more important to Erasmus than a cosmic mystery because it was useful for the perfection process in the here and now. He always used Scripture in this way.

The role of Scripture in the perfection process was paramount for Erasmus because human beings could achieve perfection by means of faith in the *philosophy of Christ* that was expounded in it. This wisdom had to be studied and meditated on in order to discern the layers of meaning it contained. The letter of the 'law', as Erasmus termed it, 'has no power to make anyone righteous and innocent before God as judge'.[120] By 'law' Erasmus not only meant the precepts of the Old Testament but he also meant any reading of the New Testament that was literal and did not penetrate to the deeper spiritual meaning. He nevertheless agreed with St Paul and believed that the law had its place in the process of perfection. It was useful because it outlined the nature of sin: 'to understand one's own sickness is a considerable step on the road to health'.[121] It was a useful and necessary first step but it was not sufficient to perfection. For this the incorporation of Christ was needed. He argued that the letter of the law should be shunned in favour of the new spirit. 'The law revealed sin and did not add strength to enable us to fight back against our vices', it was Christ who did that.[122] The law did not confer the power to resist evil and cling to the good. For him, Christ is 'the central point of the whole law'.[123] We can see clearly here that for Erasmus both Christ and the law are eternal concepts. In his *Paraphrase on Romans,* when he condensed the argument of the piece, he said Paul teaches

> that the true sons of Abraham are those who imitate the faith of Abraham, and those are truly Jews who profess Christ, that true righteousness and perfect salvation are conferred on an equal basis upon all, without the help of the law, through the gospel in faith alone in Jesus Christ.[124]

Erasmus was at pains to show that the eternal Christ was the fulfilment of the law and that the law was never enough on its own. He argued that outward signs of righteousness such as circumcision were useless if a person did not live a good life. Conversely, he said that God would regard the heathen as circumcised if 'he achieves what is the essence and goal of the law, namely, a sound and pure life; and if he trusts and obeys Christ who is the fulfilment of all laws'.[125] Indeed the true Jew would be a follower of Christ: 'one becomes a true Jew only when his mind has been purged of sin and is inclined toward Christ'.[126] The law is not only perfected in Christ it is superseded by Christ. He quoted Paul who said 'I Paul...until recently subject to the Law of Moses, now freed from Moses, I have been made a servant of Jesus Christ'.[127] The law was that part of Scripture that pertained to the flesh; Christ, on the other hand, embodied the Spirit. The law is given to us for a time but then when we advance to the Spirit of Christ we are no longer under the law. This is not simply an historical phenomenon but it is part of the progression to perfection. 'We ceased to owe anything to the flesh after we began to be one with Christ.'[128] Thus Erasmus insisted on the allegorical sense of Scripture: the hidden meaning under the Silenus-like exterior story of ordinary men full of human frailties and the apparently terrible failure of the cross. This duality of the spirit and flesh was an all-pervading concept in Erasmus' thought. Its source was St Paul, transmitted through Origen in particular, who saw the spiritual and the carnal in all things particularly in human nature itself. Erasmus paraphrased the concept as he found it in St Paul thus:

> There are two kinds of Judaism, two kinds of circumcision, two kinds of descendants of Abraham. There are two parts of the Mosaic Law: one carnal, the other spiritual - the body and soul, as it were, of the law. Baptism is twofold. In the first kind, we are cleansed from our former sins by a sacred bath, and in the second we die with Christ, having renounced the passions of the world. There is a double burial: a bodily burial in which Christ was buried for three days; and a spiritual burial by which we are freed from the vices of the world and rest quietly in Christ. There is a twofold resurrection: one which preceded in Christ and will follow in man; and another in which we are restored to life from our former sins and progress from virtue to virtue, in this respect practicing as far as possible the future life. There is a double righteousness, that of God and that of men, There is a double judgement, that of God and that of men. There is a double glory or praise, one according to God, and another according to men.[129]

Erasmus' paraphrases breathe this concept of the dual nature of all creation. He saw everything in this way because of his particular reading of Scripture. He was in the world but not of it. His wonderful satirical *Praise of Folly* is, perhaps, the best exposition of this concept. It is an examination of the concept of Folly, first, as the base ridiculous impulse in us and the world and then, when he has expanded it and mined its depths, he shows it to be a sublime impulse that leads to the Cross and perfection because the kingdom of God is the opposite of the kingdom of the world and so what the world considers supreme folly is in fact supreme wisdom. Many of Erasmus' contemporaries misunderstood him on account of his view of reality. He infuriated his enemies on both sides of the religious divide and they accused him of ambiguity and worse. He lived in a tension of opposites, knowing that Nature and Scripture and life itself had to be interpreted in a spiritual way in order to know anything. His way of seeing things was undogmatic and open-ended and fluid. The little marginal doodles he sketched of himself as a Janus figure with two faces on one head looking in both directions at once, one face with a happy sardonic grin and the other with down-turned unhappy mouth, was more than a description of his own state of mind at the time; it was an accurate portrayal of the human condition on many different levels.

In the end Erasmus believed that full and ultimate perfection was not granted in this life because the human condition on earth meant that our soul was always bound by the body, which was still subject to death and sorrows.[130] He said that while

> we receive a pledge of our salvation from Christ, nevertheless he did not grant us full salvation here, but wanted us to wait for it in the age to come... In truth, our perfect salvation is dependent on future events.[131]

He thought that this fullness of perfection would come at 'the resurrection of our bodies when we will leave behind the pain of this whole mortal existence and reign forever with the immortal Christ'.[132] Erasmus' Platonism never led him into the Neo-Platonic heterodox position of denying the resurrection of the body and the unity of body and soul. The body was a vital component of perfection. It was by means of the senses that we were able to experience and thus verify the truth of Christ. He said that those who had experienced the truth of Christ on earth should then believe in this future fulfilment of the promise of salvation.

> There remains only the glory! And this glory has reached us now as well, in large measure, unless you think it is not magnificent enough to be free from sin, to flourish in the glory of innocence, to have pure affections, to be incorporated with Christ so as to be one with him, to have his Spirit as a pledge, to be the heir of God and the co-heir of Christ. When all this befalls us, how can we have doubts that the rest will be fulfilled in its own time?[133]

Here he was addressing the person who, having engaged in the perfection process, had therefore experienced the truth of Christ as portrayed in Scripture. The method of perfection in all its stages was verified through personal experience of the process. The partly perfected individual would then know that Scripture embodied the truth of existence and it would be a small step to accept the account, outlined in Scripture, of the time to come. Erasmus himself made this leap of faith when he accepted St Paul's view of the cosmic dimension of the perfection process. His own belief in the importance of the flesh in the process of perfection meant that he had no difficulty in accepting the doctrine of the resurrection of the body. Moreover, he also accepted the same idea on the macrocosmic scale. In paraphrasing St Paul he wrote of the end of time: 'the whole structure of the world awaits this time, as if longing for the day on which the glory of the sons of God will be brought to light after their number has been completed'.[134] He accepted that the end of time depended on all of the sons of God reaching perfection and so the human perfection process had cosmic implications. He believed that the same struggle for perfection that took place in us also occurred in the cosmos.

> For we see that all the elements of the world are altered by so many transformations and are subject to so many corruptions - that the sun and the moon, (apart from the fact that they labour almost in vain to restore things which are always transitory), feel their own defects, and the stars fight with the stars. Moreover, there can be no doubt that the whole crowd of angels, contemplating our calamities from above, are moved by a kind of pious compassion towards us and, as far as they can, grieve for us in our misfortunes. Thus, does not the whole cosmos groan with us and as though in childbirth desire an end to its labour and pains?[135]

This struggle will not end until all the sons of God have all been perfected. He argued that until then

> even the world itself seems to participate in some way in human misery...This is because earth, water, air, the very celestial bodies, and finally even the angels themselves were created especially to serve the requirements of men. Consequently the world itself is not going to be free until perfect freedom comes to the sons of God. In the meantime, the world endures servitude unwillingly. For even in things without a mind there is a certain native craving for perfection. It endures, however, out of obedience to him by whose will it has been given over to this servitude, and it endures more patiently because it understands that it has not been given over forever, but on the condition that as soon as the sons of God have been fully liberated from every taint of mortality, then even the world itself will cease to be subject to the inconveniences of immortality.[136]

St Paul in these verses of Romans did not make the liberation of creation dependent on the liberation of the sons of God, rather both events happen concurrently. It was Erasmus, who elevated human beings above all the rest of creation in such a way that the universe only really existed to serve our needs. Thus the perfection of creation was utterly dependent on the completion of the number of the children of God. Then like the fleshy element in us, the cosmos itself will become perfect. In this way Erasmus' thought was thoroughly humanistic; for him, the human being was always at the centre.

Chapter 6

Terminus/Iuventas: The Image of Perfection

Erasmus' belief that the true nature of all creation could only be discerned by penetrating deep beyond its material appearance to the true spiritual reality is perfectly expressed in the device he chose to be his personal emblem. This duality applied especially to the most important element of the creation: the human being. Every created thing was both material and spiritual. What was apparent to the senses was only a dim reflection of the true reality. Allegory, therefore, was no mere literary device for Erasmus. It was the primary way to understand all that was essential for the perfection of humanity. In keeping with this, when he chose an image for his own personal seal and emblem he chose a richly allegorical symbol that expressed the essence of his *philosophy of Christ.* What he used was an image of the god Terminus which, when it is deciphered, can be read as the sum of his beliefs.

In 1508 Alexander Stuart, son of the king of Scotland and a pupil of Erasmus, gave him an old Roman gem that had an image on it of a god which has now been identified as Dionysus but which Erasmus said an Italian expert identified as the god Terminus.[1] Erasmus added the words *cedo nulli*, which later became *concedo nulli*, (I yield to no-one) to it and made the image his seal and emblem. Terminus was the Roman god of boundaries and was thus also perceived as the god of Death: the ultimate boundary of human life. The god Terminus had been the subject of discussion by the Aldine circle in Venice around the time Erasmus was there and adopted it as his emblem. One of this group, Gyraldus, expounded on it in his *Aenigmata* in which he outlined how Terminus would not yield to Jove when the latter removed all the other gods from the Capitol in order to build a new temple for himself; Hence Erasmus' motto *concedo nulli.*[2] Clearly, in this context, the device and motto could have been seen as an act of defiance against the Roman pontiff. It may appear odd that Erasmus, the man who above all espoused the belief that peace, harmony and unity were the *sine qua non* of Christianity, should have adopted such a defiant motto and he was, in fact, later accused of arrogance on account of it. In 1528 he found it necessary to defend himself against these accusations by explaining the meaning of his Terminus. In a letter to Alfonso Valdes, a secretary of the emperor, Charles V, he said that the words were spoken by Death and not Erasmus. He explained that he used the device to remind himself to correct his life because Death was a boundary that did not yield to anyone.[3] In other words he claimed that it was a *memento mori*. While the device could be read in this way there were many less contentious devices that could have represented this idea. It is unlikely that Erasmus, who was not given to causing unnecessary offence, would have chosen this particular device if it was not important to him in some other way. He chose this motto because while on the surface it could function as a *memento mori*, a deeper analysis of it would reveal that it represented the essence of his belief system. His sincerely-held belief that every individual had to find his or her own way to perfection and its consequence that slavish and literal imitation, even of Christ, was useless in this quest meant that Erasmus believed we must yield to no one in our search for our own perfection.[4] Perfection was an individual quest in which each aspiring Christian had to use the *prima materia* of his or her own nature in order to find the *Logos* of Christ within. The words *concedo nulli* were also singularly appropriate for Erasmus himself because he never yielded to anyone in relation to his own deeply held convictions about the true meaning of Christianity. He never compromised the fundamental elements of these beliefs in any way. He guarded his intellectual liberty with ferocity and tenacity and at times he was prepared to forego even the basic necessities of life rather than submit to restrictive patronage He also believed that the true Christian should not yield even to death itself because Christ had conquered death for all of his followers. Perfection ensured immortality.

The true worth of an emblem, of course, was that it was a means of portraying hidden truths. In the same letter to Valdes,

Erasmus argued that the device appealed to him not only for its allusion to the story of the god Terminus but that he also valued it for its obscurity. He made the same point when he wrote a commentary on the Venice printer, Aldus' device of a dolphin wound round an anchor. He said that this was a symbol for the saying 'Make Haste Slowly' and he pointed out that this kind of pictorial symbol originated in Egypt where it had been called a hieroglyph. This, he explained, was the term used for

> enigmatic designs so much used in the early centuries, especially among the priest-prophets and theologians in Egypt, who thought it quite wrong to express the mysteries of wisdom in ordinary writing and thus expose them, as we do, to the uninitiated public. What they thought worth knowing they would record by drawing the shapes of various animals and inanimate things, in such a way that it was not easy for the casual reader to unravel them forthwith. It was necessary first to learn the properties of individual things and the special force and nature of each separate creature; and the man who had really penetrated these could alone interpret the symbols and put them together, and thus solve the riddle of their meaning.[5]

Here, again, is the Erasmian belief that deeper, hidden reality could not be communicated directly because a proper insight could only be gained by a process in which the individual participated actively in the process. In this sense, the method of deciphering an emblem was good practice for the method of reading the visible creation in order to see true reality. Clearly, Erasmus knew and expected that his own emblem would be examined by everyone in order to decipher its hidden meanings.

In one sense, Terminus the boundary god can be interpreted as a reference to the Erasmian idea that we must stay within the bounds of our own capabilities. He expounded on this concept in his exposition of the adage, 'You Move What Should Not Be Moved'.[6] Here he explained that the source of the adage was Plato's *Laws* in which the philosopher had outlined a law that he called 'the statute of Jove, god of boundaries, about not altering bounds or frontiers'.[7] Plato had added to this the epigram 'not Death himself grasps what may not be moved'.[8] Erasmus believed that stretching too far above one's abilities was dangerous because after a certain point there would be no way of verifying anything and as we have seen personal verification was essential to the achievement of true knowledge which was necessary for perfection. He thought that many theologians, notably the scholastics, suffered from this malady. The search for truth and knowledge always started, and indeed ended, with the individual human being. The purpose of true philosophy for him was to elucidate the nature and method of human perfection. This could only be achieved through personal verification in experience. The level of perfection that could be reached on earth was, however, simply a preparation for the life to come and, like Plato, he believed that philosophy was, in fact, a preparation for death.[9] In this respect, his emblem Terminus, the god of death, was a reminder of the true philosophy.

The device, however, is not simply a depiction of Terminus because Terminus, being the god of death, is usually depicted as an old man with a beard. However, Erasmus' device consists of the upper torso of a beardless youth with windswept hair embedded in a cubic base that looks like a block of stone. The image on the ring given to Erasmus by Alexander Stuart has the head of an old man with a beard. Thus when Erasmus commissioned the artist Quentin Metsys to make a medal for him in 1519 with his emblem on one side and a portrait of himself on the other the image he commissioned was quite different from the one on his ring. Erasmus' device is, in fact, an image of Terminus combined with Iuventus the god of youth. There is an ink doodle in Erasmus' personal copy of Aulus Gellius' Attic Nights in the margin beside a section on enigmatic writings which refers to Terminus.[10] This drawing is almost certainly the work of Erasmus himself because of the quality of the ink and his penchant for doodling. It is a small head on a cube but the face has no long beard. In this, it is similar to the later Metsys medal and his Antwerp seal. Perhaps when Erasmus drew this some time after 1509, he was already demonstrating his own view of the association of Terminus with Iuventas/Iuventus the god or goddess of Youth.[11] In his defence letter to Valdes he described his device as one in which the lower part was a stone and the top half was a youth with flying hair. Nevertheless, throughout this same defence he referred to his device only as Terminus. With true Erasmian ambiguity, however he then related the story of Terminus refusing to yield to Jove, as told by Livy, and drew attention to the fact that in this story there were, in fact, two gods who refused to yield to Jove: Terminus and Iuventas. He then paraphrased Livy and explained that the refusal of the two gods to yield was interpreted with much rejoicing as meaning that it foretold an eternal empire. Finally, and rather curtly, he said that the youth was useful for war and the Terminus was fixed.[12] Anyone who had ever read Erasmus at all would have known that he would never have chosen an emblem associated with war to be part of his own device. Thus within a letter which, on the surface, was designed to defend his device against charges of arrogance levelled at him by enemies, he overtly described it as an innocent *memento mori* while at the same time he pointedly identified the top half of the statue as a youth and he drew attention to the fact that Juventas the goddess of youth was intimately bound up with his Terminus. Clearly, this letter raised more questions about the Terminus than it answered. While it was written to a good friend and supporter at the Imperial court in an apparent attempt to silence his detractors, Erasmus also took the opportunity to alert his followers to the all-important deeper meaning of his device. The image is clearly a representation of the unity of opposites within which we are compelled to live on earth. The optimism, energy and innocence of youth embedded in the dead, limited, reality of stone is a perfect depiction of the Erasmian notion that we must ever strive to reach the limits of our capabilities while always living within those limits. It is the union of spirit and flesh. The young man with the wind flying through his hair is animated by spirit and the rock is a depiction of the flesh, in the Pauline sense of earthly solid material things. As we have seen, Erasmus believed that we were made up of opposite elements:

> man is a marvellous creature composed of two or three very diverse parts, a soul which is like a divinity and a body which is like a brute beast...If the body had not been added to you, you would be a divinity; if the mind had not been bestowed upon you, you would be a beast. These two divergent natures were joined together in happy concord by the supreme craftsman, but the serpent, the enemy of peace, split them apart again in unhappy discord, so that now they cannot be separated without the greatest torment or live together without incessant warfare.....Such is their confused turmoil and strife that they seem to be distinct from one another, although they are one.[13]

This is the state of ordinary humanity, an unhappy state of disunity of the warring factions of body and soul. He said of the body that 'since it is mortal, it pursues temporal things; since it is heavy, it sinks downward, On the contrary, the soul remembering its heavenly origin, strives upwards, with all its might and struggles against its earthly burden:'[14] this is the Terminus/Iuventas image. It is a depiction of human nature but, crucially, it is more. Erasmus believed that this disunity was only an illusion: the two natures were, in reality, one. Reality, for Erasmus, was always the unseen spiritual state. He thought that in a perfect state of existence the true human being would be someone in whom the two natures would be united in a state of pure harmony. In rather Platonic terms Erasmus believed in some prior state in which the two natures had been joined in this way, with the mind freely and willingly commanding the body.[15] This perfect state was destroyed by sin, or what Erasmus thought of as missing the target, which resulted in a state of warfare between the two natures in which the body tyrannized the reason.[16]

The Terminus/Iuventas is a symbol of the dynamic of the Christian struggle and as such it embodies the truth contained in the *philosophy of Christ*. Throughout Erasmus' writings this Platonic and Pauline opposition of spirit and matter is a constant theme. In *The Praise of Folly* there is a description of the real state of the human being that is very evocative of the Terminus/Iuventas emblem:

> Christians come very near to agreeing with the Platonists that the soul is stifled and bound down by the fetters of the body which by its gross matter prevents the soul from being able to contemplate and enjoy things as they truly are.[17]

Erasmus' Folly then goes on to say that Death is a liberation from the fetters of the body when the mind unshackled can see the true reality.[18] The Terminus/Iuventas image is, in fact, very similar to the devices used by two of Erasmus' printers: Aldus of Venice and Froben of Basle. Aldus' dolphin wound round an anchor and Froben's serpents coiled around a staff are clearly similar symbols of a harmony of opposites. In his exposition of the adage, *Festina lente,* Erasmus acknowledged that both Aldus and Froben had a common purpose, which was the restoration of ancient literature.[19] In this text he examined Aldus' device in order to expose its secret meaning. First he looked at the dolphin which he said was the fastest of all fish and asked 'what symbol could be more appropriate than the dolphin' to express 'that eager and tireless spirit?'[20] The anchor, clearly, represented the static earthbound element. Erasmus then interpreted the image as representing a dynamic union or harmony of opposites in us. He presented an example from the *Iliad* as an allegorical example of this internal human process. He described how Homer depicted Pallas standing behind Achilles restraining him when he was about to wield his sword. He says it is right 'to call those powerful impulses the dolphin, and the anchor the wisdom that controls them.'[21] He went on to say that

> some natures need the spur, others the rein, and so the ancients rightly curled the dolphin round the anchor, because one must be tempered by the other, and both united, so as to produce the kind of balanced character which Plato imagined resulting from a fusion of Music and Gymnastics, if both were practiced.[22]

Here, the union of opposites becomes the actual dynamic of the process of perfection. In this process the two parts must exist in an ongoing tension which always strives towards harmony. Erasmus believed that this union of opposites was a fundamental law of human existence. He said that 'just as life is nothing other than the union of the body and soul, so health is the harmony between all the parts of the body'.[23] Moreover, this harmony was an underlying law of all nature and not just applicable to us. He saw the universe, as an ordered entity in which there was perfect harmony among the celestial bodies and the elements.[24] In his *Complaint of Peace,* he described peace as the perfect expression of this cosmic harmony. He argued that the whole of nature was governed by this law of attraction; Animals, plants and even seemingly inanimate stones exhibited this attractive force.[25] Finally, he revealed that this attractive force, which underlies all harmony, was love. This, for Erasmus, was one of the central mysteries of Christianity. The distinguishing mark of Christians was that they loved one another.[26] Christ came to bring the precept of evangelical love to humanity.[27] The Christian law of love was the attractive force in the universe. Crucially, however, it functioned as the instrument of transformation. In the *Antibarbari,* when he was outlining the wonderful harmony of creation in which God is omnipresent and all-powerful, he then described how the law of attraction underlay all progress in creation. The purpose of the law of love was the transformation of creation. In Christian terms this meant that Christ, the *Logos*, continually perfected all of creation by means of the attracting power that united opposites and transformed them into a new and more perfect creation. This was the underlying harmony in a seemingly discordant world. 'There is a great discord in nature which is the completest concord'.[28] As we have seen Erasmus emphasized the attractive force of Christ in his commentary on Christ's promise that if he was 'lifted up from the earth', he would 'draw all' unto himself.[29] This is Christ as the attracting, transforming, perfecting power of creation.[30] For Erasmus the perfect human being, the perfectly functioning Christian society and indeed the cosmos itself operated in this way. Christ, the *Logos,* is at the centre of each of these perfect systems as the transforming perfecting force. This fundamental force is love, and love, for Erasmus, was synonymous with God: God was love. He wrote about this in the *Enchiridion* when he described the death of the soul. He believed that this could happen before the death of the body and that the person in this state while still physically alive was spiritually dead. He said that this happened 'because its life is not present, which is God. For where God is, there is love, God is love'.[31]

Erasmus, however, chose to call his device Terminus rather than Terminus/Iuventas. Terminus, the god of boundaries, was usually used to represent death and was not usually associated with the concept of the union of opposites. This was more commonly an attribute of the god Hermes or Mercury who was the messenger of the gods and the intermediary between the gods and humans. The union of opposites, in its ultimate sense of the uniting that which was above with that which was below was often associated with alchemy and the Hermetic writings during the Renaissance. The question then arises as to why Erasmus did not use Hermes as his symbol, since it would have been a more obvious reference to his important concept of the union of opposites. The answer is that if he had used Hermes he would have run the risk of being associated with the occult philosophy of the Hermetic writings. His attitude to the Hermetic, Neoplatonic and Cabbalistic philosophies which had experienced a resurgence from the time of Ficino in Florence was always to keep them at arm's length. Ever since the condemnation of Pico these trends in Italian humanism were fraught with difficulties, especially for someone like Erasmus who wanted to make Scripture the bedrock of his system.[32] His determination to avoid this association is apparent from a small incident which is portrayed in his letters. One of his correspondents, Zasius, had referred to him in 1514, as *Termaximus.* This was probably a Latin pun on his Terminus device. At that stage Erasmus had no problem with this title. Later, however, things had changed and he wrote to Zasius complaining about it. The problem was that *Termaximus* is the Latin for the Greek *Trismegistos* and, of course, this has connotations of the author of the *Hermetica, Hermes Trismegistos.* As far as we know Erasmus did not use his device as an official seal until after 1518 when he had a seal struck at Antwerp but he had the Terminus ring in his possession since 1509. In 1523 he complained to Zasius because he realized that Zasius had taken an impression of his seal-ring when Erasmus was visiting him and he asked him not to use it. He said that he had been laughed at and mocked by his clever critics as "thrice-greatest" for a long time[33]

The Mercurial association with Hermeticism meant that Erasmus did not want to adopt a straightforward Mercurial symbol as his device. Notwithstanding this, his famous, and centrally important, image of the perfecting process of the *Logos* of Christ which he outlined in his *Paraclesis* was probably modelled on a description he had read of the god Hermes and his followers. This was the image of the concentric circles with Christ at the centre like fire attracting and transforming everything in the surrounding circles. This bears a striking resemblance to a description in the writings of the Greek medical writer Galen, which Erasmus later translated, of the followers of Hermes who are ranged about the god in concentric circles just as the followers of Christ are in the Erasmian image.[34] There is a circle that contains

> all honourable professional men who do not run, shout, or jostle. The god is in their midst and his followers around him, each man in his station, none deserting the rank assigned him by the god. Some are very close to him and surround him in set order: geometricians, arithmeticians, philosophers, physicians, astronomers, and grammarians. These are followed by a second circle of painters, sculptors, writers, carpenters, architects, and stonemasons. Thereafter comes a third class comprising the representatives of the remaining arts, each arranged in order, but in such a way that all

> face their common god and equally obey his commands.[35]

Then Galen describes a fourth class of people selected by the god and standing apart from the others. Hermes chose these specially not on account of their

> career, ancestry, or possessions: he honours those who live a life of virtue and excel in the arts, those who follow his commands and practice their arts lawfully, Such men he cherishes and ranks above the others, keeping them his close associates forever.[36]

Erasmus commented that he thought Socrates, Homer, Hippocrates, Plato and their devotees were in this class.[37] The resemblance to his Christocentric society in which it is Christ who is at the centre of the three circles of people is remarkable. Although Erasmus published this translation of Galen in 1526 and his Christocentric image was published in 1518, he would have had access earlier to the Venice edition of Galen, which had been published in 1490.[38] Clearly, then, he thought that there was a symbolic affinity between Mercury, the god who united heaven and earth, and Christ. The most important aspect of Christ, for Erasmus, was that he embodied the ultimate opposites of humanity and divinity, flesh and spirit. He was the connection between heaven and earth.

Another Mercurial allusion is apparent in the Metsys medal, which depicts Terminus' cubic base emerging from a pile of earth. This was not a necessary iconographic attribute of the god Terminus who was more often depicted on a pillar. This is significant because the heap of stones, or *ερμειον,* was also used in depictions of Mercury. Cicero thought that the connection with the *ερμειον* was the root of Hermes name. The significant fact is that both Hermes and Terminus were ancient boundary gods and in that sense they were interchangeable. Erasmus made reference to this in his adage *Mercuriale* and in the same adage he also described the heap of stones, or *ερμειον* which were commonly laid out for the god. Moreover, Erasmus' depictions of Mercury in the *Adages* influenced Alciati in his famous emblem book. This Erasmian influence actually led Alciati to conflate Mercury and Terminus. In the 1546 version of the *Emblemata* Alciati's second Mercury emblem is simply called Terminus.[39] Clearly, then, Erasmus' followers could read his symbol as a Mercury or Hermes. Erasmus added ammunition to this interpretation when he translated the Galen treatise on the liberal arts and medicine. While this was certainly a suitable subject for a learned humanist, Erasmus was not particularly interested, or expert, in the field of medicine. Perhaps he wanted to alert those of his readers who did not speak Greek to the source of his own image. This treatise, in addition to the concentric depiction of Hermes' followers, also contained a description of Hermes that was practically identical to Erasmus' Terminus emblem. Hermes, 'the lord of reason and father of all the arts' was depicted as 'a graceful young man' whose 'countenance is cheerful, his glance spirited, and the base on which he stands is of all shapes the most solid and least moveable; a cube supported on all sides by its four corners'.[40] The only difference between this image and the Terminus image was that the Hermes was a complete body while the Terminus was an upper torso only. The similarities, however, are striking. The graceful spirited young man combined with the solid immovable cube is the same harmony of opposites that are represented by the Erasmian Terminus. Erasmus then changed Galen's interpretation of this image and said of the cube: 'Sometimes even the god himself is represented by this figure'.[41] Galen had written that sometimes the god was adorned with this figure.[42] The change is significant because Erasmus' closest readers would have been aware of his device and now he was drawing attention to the fact that, at least the cube, if not the whole image represented Hermes as well as Terminus. As boundary gods they could both be seen to represent the union of opposites inasmuch as a boundary is a point or line where two spaces or entities meet. Death is the boundary between the material world and the spiritual one. It is the point at which they meet. In sum, when Erasmus chose his device he needed one that would encapsulate the idea that is the key to his entire thought system: the *philosophy of Christ* which was the method for perfecting our human nature. The secret of the *philosophy of Christ* is that in uniting our two essential parts: the human and the divine, we can achieve perfection and ultimately immortality. In this way we then yield to no one, not even death.

Holbein drawing of Terminus for stained-glass window, commissioned by Erasmus as a gift for Basle University.

Quentin Metsys medal 1519 Erasmus

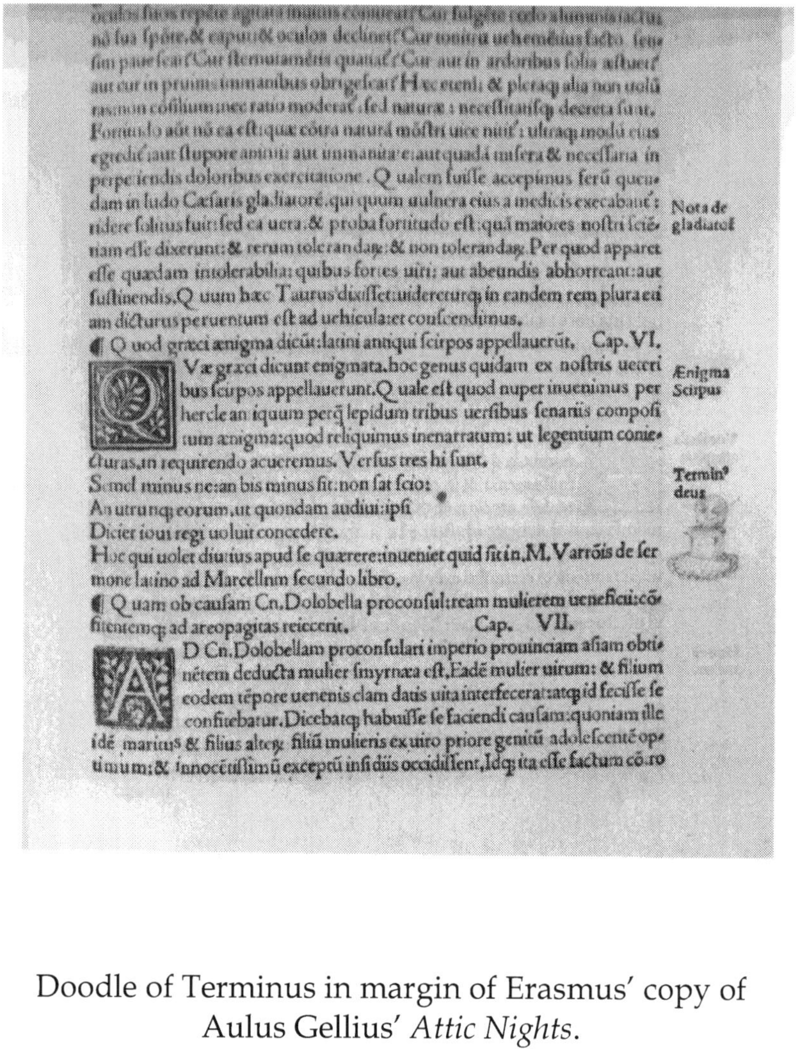

nõ sua spõte,& caput:& oculos declinet? Cur tonitru uehementius facto sensim pauescat? Cur sternutamẽtis quatiat? Cur aut in ardoribus solis aestuet? aut cur in pruinis immanibus obrigescat? Haec enim & pleraq; alia non uolũtas:non cõsilium:nec ratio moderat':sed naturae : necessitatisq; decreta sunt. Fortitudo aũt nõ ea est:quae cõtra naturã mõstri uice nitit': ultraq; modũ eius egredit':aut stupore animi: aut immanitate:aut quadã misera & necessaria in perpetiendis doloribus exercitatione. Qualem fuisse accepimus serũ quendam in ludo Caesaris gladiatorẽ,qui quum uulnera eius a medicis execabant': ridere solitus fuit:sed ea uera.& proba fortitudo est:quã maiores nostri sciẽtiam esse dixerunt:& rerum tolerandarũ:& non tolerandarũ. Per quod apparet esse quaedam intolerabilia:quibus fortes uiri: aut abeundis abhorreant:aut sustinendis. Quum haec Taurus dixisset:uidereturq; in eandem rem plura etiam dicturus peruentum est ad uehicula:et conscendimus.

Nota de gladiatoř

¶ Quod graeci aenigma dicũt:latini antiqui scirpos appellauerũt. Cap. VI.

QVae graeci dicunt enigmata.hoc genus quidam ex nostris ueteribus scirpos appellauerunt. Quale est quod nuper inuenimus per hercle antiquum perq̃ lepidum tribus uersibus senariis compositum aenigma:quod reliquimus inenarratum: ut legentium coniecturas,in requirendo acueremus. Versus tres hi sunt.

Ænigma Scirpus

Semel minus ne:an bis minus sit:non sat scio:
An utrunq; eorum,ut quondam audiui:ipsi
Dicier ioui regi uoluit concedere.

Termin' deus

Hoc qui uolet diutius apud se quaerere:inueniet quid sit in.M.Varrõis de sermone latino ad Marcellum secundo libro.

¶ Quam ob causam Cn.Dolobella proconsul:ream mulierem ueneficii:cõfitentemq; ad areopagitas reiecerit. Cap. VII.

AD Cn.Dolobellam proconsulari imperio prouinciam asiam obtinẽtem deducta mulier smyrnaea est,Eadẽ mulier uirum: & filium eodem tẽpore uenenis clam datis uita interfecerat:atq; id fecisse se confitebatur. Dicebatq; habuisse se faciendi causam:quoniam ille idẽ maritus & filius alter; filiũ mulieris ex uiro priore genitũ adolescentẽ optimum:& innocẽtissimũ exceptũ insidiis occidissent,Idq; ita esse factum cõ ro

Doodle of Terminus in margin of Erasmus' copy of Aulus Gellius' *Attic Nights*.

Erasmus' seal, Antwerp 1518
And the ring given to him by Alexander Stuart in 1509

Holbein drawing of Erasmus circa 1538.

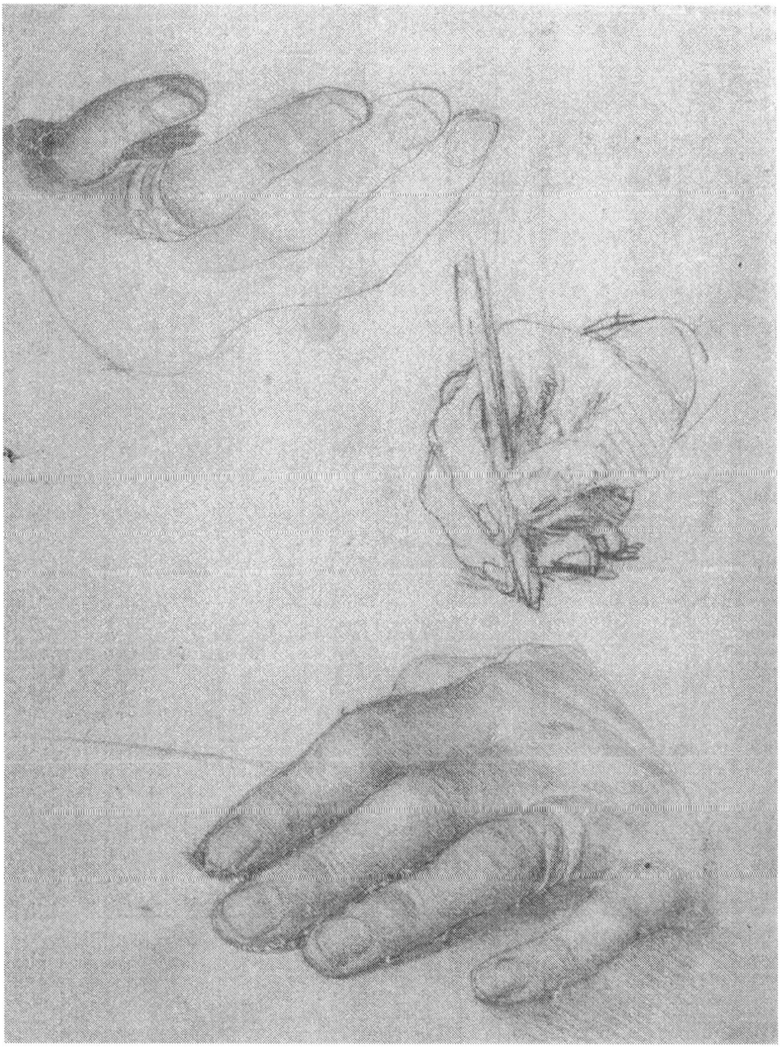

Holbein drawing of Erasmus' hands for the portrait called Erasmus and the Renaissance pilaster.

Quentin Metsys, portrait of Erasmus 1516.

Holbein portrait of Erasmus: simple version of Erasmus writing, in the style of St Jerome.

The Goddess Iuventas.

Chapter 7

The Perfect Human Being

The Terminus/Iuventus device functioned for Erasmus as an emblem that encapsulated the deepest meaning of his belief system for those of his followers who understood it, while simultaneously it could also be read as a simple *memento mori.* This was essential because it allowed him to signal his true beliefs while at the same time it protected him from potential accusations of heresy. As we have seen, there were many elements of Erasmus' view of Christianity that were unacceptable and not fully orthodox. His Christology, his view of human nature and his belief in the individual's role in the process of perfection, all of which were absolutely fundamental to his belief system, could not be accommodated within orthodox Christianity. Thus he never fully elaborated the implications of these concepts. His understanding of the individual's role in the perfection process, in particular, meant that his views were very close to those of the Pelagian heresy. Although Erasmus was very careful never to propound an overtly Pelagian argument there was, nevertheless, no known way in his day of reconciling his beliefs with a non-Pelagian theory of grace. Moreover, the centrality of this mechanism of perfection to his entire concept of the *philosophy of Christ* also functioned to lessen the role of the Church and its sacramental system in the process of human perfection. This, too, would have been utterly unacceptable and very dangerous for him had he outlined it clearly. Thus he had to employ whatever means he could to further his life's aim of expounding his view of true Christianity to as many people as possible. Even his enemies on both sides of the confessional divide understood that the enigmatic quality of his writings was hiding the unorthodox nature of his views. The methods that Erasmus employed to expound his views as fully as he dared while also avoiding censure and accusations of heresy demonstrate that he was completely aware of the fact that he was treading a fine line and that at any time he could have been silenced or worse.

His *philosophy of Christ* was based on his own interpretation of Scripture and here lay the problem for him. He had clearly decided that the existing scholastic system of theology, which depended on the use of dialectical disputation based on Aristotelian logic and the summaries and commentaries of medieval exegetes, would never allow him the freedom to interpret Scripture as he truly understood it. Instead he had to step outside the accepted theological norms and invent his own methodology. This led him to make use of a most daring strategy in this quest to elaborate the true *philosophy of Christ.* He decided to use the textual methodology of the *studia humanitatis* to produce a new version of Scripture. He claimed that, in doing this, he was not involved in formal exegesis but was simply correcting the grammar and language of the text and explaining textual obscurities. In fact, he used the new humanist approach to sources and language to circumvent centuries of scholastic domination of Scriptural interpretation. In this, he was part of a wider movement of humanists who were tentatively beginning to work outside the established system. These men, with the aid of the new medium of printing, were starting to challenge the hegemony of the university-based scholastically-trained professional theologians as they developed a new approach to scriptural exegesis.[1] Erasmus was the most daring and prolific of these early biblical humanists.

He went public with his new Scriptural programme in 1516 when he published his ground-breaking edition of the New Testament in Greek together with a new Latin translation which he called the *Novum Instrumentum.* Erasmus was very aware of the kind of opposition this audacious new edition of the New Testament would stir up. He knew that the existing Vulgate edition, which was credited to St Jerome, had been the bedrock of Catholic dogma and ceremonies since the late fourth century and as such it had achieved sacred status. Thus any alteration of its text would be construed as a direct threat to the authority of the Church. Moreover, most Christians believed that God continually directed the church and so any suggestion that the Vulgate was full of errors could easily be construed as blasphemy because God could not preside over error. Erasmus' fears were well-founded and he was, in fact, frequently attacked for much of the rest of his life on account of the implications of his New Testament writings and he was forced to spend a considerable amount of his time engaged in defending his work before he was finally formally censured.[2] He had tried to offset this opposition in advance. Prior to the publication of the *Novum Instrumentum* he had outlined a defence of his new programme in a scholarly debate with the Louvain theologian Martin Dorp. It has been proposed that the published correspondence of this debate about the objections of Dorp's colleagues to his *Praise of Folly* and his forthcoming New Testament was, in fact, a pseudo-quarrel orchestrated by Erasmus and his circle.[3] Whether this was the case or not, what was significant was that it allowed him to defend his New Testament in advance. His friend Thomas More clearly understood this when he wrote approvingly of Dorp to Erasmus shortly after the debate, in February 1516, saying that, having visited him, he found Dorp curiously attractive both on account of his scholarship and on account of the fact that his criticisms had allowed Erasmus to write his *Apologia*.[4] The prefatory materiel to the *Novum Instrumentum* forms the next part of this pre-emptive defence. He dedicated the work to the pope, Leo X, and throughout the prefatory material he presented his revision of the text of Scripture as an attempt to purify it and return it to its original state. He claimed that he was not innovating, simply correcting. He argued that the text had become corrupted by copyists down through the centuries and needed to be restored to its earlier pristine condition. The *Methodus* later enlarged to the *Ratio,* was one of the pieces usually published with the New Testament and in it he outlined his new Scriptural programme and argued that knowledge of the biblical languages was a basic requirement for the Scriptural exegete. This was a direct attack on the professional theologians of his day who carried out their work in Latin; Most of whom had no knowledge of all three biblical languages and therefore they could not even read his Greek New Testament.

He had one further and very important tactic in defending his work and this was to present himself as the *New Jerome*.[5] While he had been working on producing his *Novum Instrumentum* he had simultaneously been working on a new edition of the works of Jerome. In 1516, a few months after his *Novum Instrumentum* was published, he also produced the letters volumes of the Froben edition of St Jerome's writings together with a new *Life of Jerome.* The timing of this was no accident because these two great enterprises were linked. The publication of the new corrected Jerome was designed to legitimize his *Novum Instrumentum.* First, it enabled him to claim that he had done a great service to the venerable Church Father by restoring his writings which were

> not so much corrupted as virtually destroyed and defaced, and this partly by the fault of illiterate scribes whose habit it is to copy an accurate text inaccurately and make a faulty text worse to leave out what they cannot read and to corrupt what they do not understand.[6]

This, of course, is the very same argument he used in his revision of Scripture but it was also a masterstroke which made it more difficult for his opponents to claim that he was doing Jerome a disservice by supplanting his Vulgate with his own new Latin version. How could they accuse Jerome's champion of damaging Jerome? Moreover, he took great pains to construct a view of himself as having endured heroic labours in order to produce his *Jerome.*[7] He complained, at length, about the great difficulties he had encountered and the huge effort required in the revision of Jerome's letters and the clear implication was that it was only the fact that he held Jerome in such high esteem that provided him with the strength to complete the task. The second thing he achieved as a result of his edition of Jerome was the complete re-working of the image of Jerome. He decided to construct a life of Jerome using only Jerome's own writings. The new image of the saint that he then presented in his re-writing of the traditional hagiography allowed him to drop the centuries of myth and legend that had accrued to the saint. He presented Jerome, first and foremost, as a most learned and eloquent man: the very model of a Renaissance humanist. Moreover, he showed how Jerome had applied these skills of eloquence and vast erudition to the correcting and purifying of Scripture: precisely same thing that Erasmus was doing. In this way Jerome became at once a vital model for, and a bulwark of, his daring reworking of the New Testament. Erasmus' portrayal of Jerome in the new *Life* stripped

Jerome of many of the miraculous details of his traditional hagiography and made him less like a saint and more like the Erasmian version of the perfected human being who achieved this state by a process of inner transformation. In this way Erasmus' Jerome lost his cardinal's hat, his lion and some of the wilder stories about him. Erasmus could now claim that the original Vulgate had been written and compiled by a highly-evolved human being who had mined the *philosophy of Christ* from the Gospels and the Apostolic Letters.[8] Jerome's authority thus rested on his scholarship and the purity of his life rather than on divine inspiration. This was an important weapon for Erasmus' in his defence of his programme of using scholarship to correct the Vulgate. It was directly opposed to the views of the professional theologians who insisted that divine inspiration was the essential pre-requisite for biblical interpretation. Erasmus had first championed this cause, in 1505, when he published the manuscript he had found of Lorenzo Valla's attempt at this new kind of exegesis. In the letter that served as the preface to his edition of Valla's *Annotations* he had used Jerome's own words to defend this method. Here, he pointed out that Jerome had said that correcting a text did not require spiritual inspiration and thus it could be carried out by a scholar.[9] It must have tickled Erasmus' sense of irony that those words of Jerome were spoken to Jerome's friend Desiderius! Erasmus also pointed out at some length and with great vehemence in his *Life of Jerome* that many Christian writers had denied that Jerome was a theologian at all.[10] Here, again, he was aiming squarely at the scholastics who still ruled the theology faculties of his own day and who he knew would soon be his own greatest critics.[11]

When Erasmus portrayed himself as the *New Jerome* he was hiding behind this persona while remaining in plain sight at the same time. He continued to carry out his audacious programme and simultaneously protested his orthodoxy to the end of his life. As we have seen, he used his personal emblem to hide his deepest beliefs in plain sight also. His understanding of the potency of an image led him to commission several portraits of himself which show how the theme of the *New Jerome* and his Terminus/Iuventus emblem functioned in this way. He commissioned the first of these portraits in 1517 when he engaged Quentin Metsys, the foremost Flemish artist, to paint him. The timing of this first commission is very important. It was, of course, the year after the publication of his New Testament and his *Jerome*. In 1523 he also commissioned Hans Holbein to paint three more portraits of him. These culminate in a portrait that is the most enigmatic and detailed of all his portraits which now hangs in the National Gallery in London and is often referred to as *Erasmus with a Renaissance pilaster*. In this series of portraits, commissioned and designed by Erasmus, he inhabits the persona of the *New Jerome*. At a more profound level, however, he also encoded in them the deeper meaning of his writings.

The first portrait painted by Quentin Metsys in 1517 sets up this new persona.[12] It is a picture of Erasmus in his study writing. It contains clear references to the tradition of paintings of St Jerome of which the 1442 Van Eyck is, perhaps, the best example.[13] This tradition began in Italy in the second half of the fourteenth century. It flourished in the north and in Italy during the fifteenth and early sixteenth centuries and began to decline after 1530. Erasmus in his study surrounded by the paraphernalia of the scholarship would have been recognizable to his contemporaries as having a connection to the Jerome images. In the copy of this picture in the Royal Collection which is now considered to be the original, one of the books has the name Hieronymus written on it. Moreover, there is also a very particular reference to Jerome in the prominent position of the scissors, or rather, wick-trimmers hanging on the book-shelf beside Erasmus. These wick-trimmers were part of the iconography of Jerome. Metsys himself also included them in a picture he painted of Jerome in meditation. There are, however, some clues in this portrait of Erasmus that suggest the *New Jerome* had his own agenda. Erasmus is writing his *Paraphrase on Romans* in the picture. This text is a particularly rich source for the Erasmian version of the process of human perfection.[14] He is also wearing a ring that appears to be the one given to him by Thomas More which depicts the head of Lot's wife. The significance of this image for Erasmus was that it was a reminder to those on the path of perfection that they must not look back to the fleshpots of the world once they had abandoned them.[15] Perhaps the oddest thing of all is the fact that he is wearing a very large and conspicuous purse that rests at waist level. This is really very incongruous in a painting of a Christian scriptural scholar who is working on a paraphrase of St Paul, but it is clearly deliberate. As we have seen, the Terminus/Iuventas device that Erasmus later adopted as his seal and emblem was a symbol of transformation that had associations with the image of Mercury. One of the attributes of Mercury was a purse. Erasmus, then, may have been signalling to his close followers what his understanding of the real meaning of the *philosophy of Christ* was. In this context, it is also possible that even the wick-trimmers which are an overt reference to Jerome may also represent the central theme of the *New Jerome*. They are a unity of two opposite pieces of metal which separately are quite useless but when they are joined together they transform into something new and far more perfect and complete.

The three portraits of Erasmus painted by Holbein in 1523 are also depictions of Erasmus as the *New Jerome*. Two of them are straightforward portrayals of him writing at his desk with no extra Jerome iconography. The third painting, of Erasmus with the Renaissance pilaster, is quite different. This portrait is by far the most splendid and intriguing of the three. The most striking thing about the picture, on first viewing, is his face which is lit up and has an enigmatic expression that lies, very peculiarly, somewhere between the beginning of a very Erasmian sardonic smile and peaceful harmonious otherworldliness. It, too, is a picture of the famous scholar in his study. A closer examination, however, immediately reveals that all is not what it seems. Behind Erasmus and to his left is a shelf with some objects on it. The perspective of this shelf and the curtain that touches it do not make sense. The position of the shelf suggests that the wall it is attached to is at right angles to Erasmus but we can see from the top of the curtain that this wall is also parallel to him! The wall is continuous but the curtain pole and the shelf are seemingly at right angles to each other and yet each of these is positioned on the wall. The curtain disappears into the ceiling and it is not really possible to make sense of its perspective. Then, the light in the picture is also very odd. Erasmus' face is lit up so the light source is apparently somewhere above and in front of him but he is casting no shadow on the wall behind. Moreover although his face is lit up, his hat is not. There is more or less no light on it at all considering how much light is on his face. We can also see that at the top of the picture the wall behind the curtain is lit up in a way that defies explanation given that the curtain is between the light source and the wall. Clearly, then this picture was designed, like his emblem, to entice the viewer to decipher its real meaning. We are being told that not everything is as it seems. Erasmus, as he often did in his writings, is hiding in plain sight. This portrait, like the Metsys, displays a subtle interplay between Erasmus as the *New Jerome* and a depiction of the central emblem of Erasmus: his Terminus/Iuventus. Other than Erasmus himself the largest and most distinctive object in the picture is the Renaissance pilaster. This is a Terminus/Iuventus image. It resembles Erasmus' own gravestone which was erected by his close friends in 1536. The central roundel at the top of the gravestone encircles an image of Erasmus' Terminus/Iuventus symbol of the upper torso of a youth with flying hair encased in a stone cube. The top of the pilaster in the portrait has an image that is very similar. In this case, it is the upper torso of a girl with wings whose lower portion is rooted in an acanthus plant. The capital of the pilaster has mostly Corinthian attributes and thus the girl in the acanthus plant is a reference to Vitruvius' account of how the design for the Corinthian column came about. A young girl died in Corinth and her nurse put some favourite drinking-cups of hers in a basket on top of her gravestone and weighted them down with a tile. It happened, however, that there was an acanthus plant under the basket and it sprouted in spring and the tips of its leaves curled up under the weight of the tile into scroll shapes. The famous sculptor Callimachus saw this as he passed the gravestone and went home and chiselled the leaf shapes in marble and so the first Corinthian capital was made. This story had been recounted in a book by Cesare Casariano about Vitruvius which was published in 1521. This book also has an image of a Corinthian capital that contains a similar torso but it has no wings. The pilaster, therefore, refers to a grave monument and so in simple terms it represents Terminus the god of boundaries. However, because it is Erasmus' device it also contains a Iuventas reference. In this image, the figure representing the union of opposites is female. The wings have replaced the flying hair but it is clear that they both represent spirit. The cube of stone is replaced by the roots and leaves of an acanthus plant but the same message is apparent in both images: spirit is bound and rooted in matter. Here Erasmus is pointing out to his followers that his image is not simply a Terminus, but, as we have seen, it is really a Terminus/Iuventas image. The dual nature of the image is also alluded to by the fact that there is a second pilaster which is just discernible in deep shadow beside and behind the main pilaster. This is meant to alert the viewer to the hidden reality of the image. It is an allusion to Plato's cave in which the cave's prisoners mistake shadows cast on a wall for reality. Erasmus thought that we could only dimly see the real world and that this one was merely a shadow of it. What we think are shadows are reality and vice versa. Erasmus is thus hiding in plain sight. The female in the pilaster image is Iuventas. The young girl in the Vitruvius story had loved her drinking-cups and Iuventas was the cup-bearer of the gods. Moreover, there is yet another allusion to Juventas in the picture. On the shelf behind Erasmus there is a glass decanter. This is immediately identifiable as an attribute of Jerome and frequently appears in images of him. It refers to the Virgin Mary. Jerome wrote a famous praise of her virginity and because of this the decanter is always depicted with a seal or stopper. The decanter in this instance is uncorked and might refer to Erasmus' less than fulsome support for the concept of the Virgin birth. It is also likely that it is uncorked in order to draw our attention to the fact that it refers to something else. Right beside the decanter and partially hidden by a book there is what looks like an upturned glass cup or some kind of glass drinking vessel. Again, our attention is drawn to this item because it does not really rest on the book underneath it. It appears to float above it on one side and may even be protruding precariously so that it is really mostly unsupported. The decanter in Jerome iconography is not usually accompanied by a cup[16]. However, Juventas is usually represented as a young girl with a sleeveless dress carrying a decanter or flask and a cup. Thus the two vessels represent Iuventas.

The purpose and function of the Terminus/Iuventas emblem is that it represents the process of perfection. The portrait of Erasmus presents him as a man who has attained the level of perfection that is possible for the human being on earth. One of the clues to this is the light on his face. The lack of shadows behind him and the lack of light on his hat give the impression that the light is, in fact, coming out from his face. Erasmus related the idea of things shining or white with things divine.[17] In this portrait the shining white face may be an allusion to a letter in Erasmus's edition of Jerome in which the latter is writing to a young woman called Eustochium. This letter is a famous praise of virginity and there is a passage in it where Jerome describes what would happen to this young woman when she reached the peak of spiritual perfection. He says

> When once you desire the wisdom of the true Solomon and come to him, he will avow all his knowledge to you; he will lead you into his chamber with his royal hand; he will miraculously change your complexion so that it shall be said of you, 'who is this that goeth up and hath been made white?'[18]

Erasmus is related to the Terminus/Iuventas pilaster by his hair which flicks up like the curled edges of the acanthus leaves. He is embodying its attributes. He stands at what might be a desk but looks more like a stone slab which also alludes to the Terminus boundary stone. His hands are resting on a book that reads in Greek on one edge: *The Labours of Hercules* and on the other in Latin: *Erasmus of Rotterdam*. He is not busy writing as in all of his other portraits but instead he seems to have completed his task and the book on the slab in front of him is the result. The book has two ties which have been undone and so it is possible to open it and examine its contents. There is a third tie in the picture which is not undone. It has a knot in the shape of a crucifix which was part of the Jerome iconography. This tie is around Erasmus' waist and it is the kind of knot that can be undone with a simple tug. This suggests that we are being invited to undo the knot in order to see inside Erasmus to his soul. If we decipher the clues in the picture we will be able to see the real internal Erasmus. Erasmus referred to Hercules' knot in his *Adages* where he said that some people said Alexander the Great had cut it with a sword and that what it signified was that a very difficult task had been accomplished.[19] In another adage he related Hercules' knot to *Cassius' knot* which he said was used to denote a very close and inseparable friendship. He then went on to associate Hercules' knot with the idea of the union of opposites and he compared it to the Caduceus which he called Mercury's wand. He described the wand as having two serpents, male and female, twisted together in the middle of their bodies to make a Hercules knot. The parts above this knot embrace one another in such a way that as they curve they form a circle; the lower parts curve back in a similar way to the handle of the wand, and there again the two tails are united. He confirmed that this image had been adopted by Froben and that the knot had been consecrated to Mercury by the Egyptians. He then said that the Gauls and maybe the Egyptians too, identify Hercules with Mercury.[20] We have seen how Terminus acted as a cover for Mercury who would have been the more usual choice as a symbol of the unity of opposites. Here we can see that Erasmus was identifying Hercules with Mercury. In the picture then the Labours of Hercules can be read as another reference to the double nature of the Terminus/Iuventas symbol and, as such it represents the process of perfection.

This is actually clear, as we have seen, from the main source for the idea of the Labours of Hercules in Erasmus' writings which is his long essay on it in the *Adages*.[21] In this essay we find references to the two themes in our picture: Jerome and the process of perfection. In the essay Erasmus compares his struggles in relation to his edition of Jerome directly with those of Hercules. He also does the same thing in his letter-preface to the *Jerome* where he says:

> So I despised all the difficulties, and like a modern Hercules I set out on my most laborious but most glorious campaign, taking the field almost unaided against all the monsters of error.[22]

In both of these works he complains bitterly that the labours are of a kind that bring all the advantage to others and only harsh criticism to the author. This is echoed in the Latin inscription on the edge of the book on the shelf behind Erasmus that reads: 'I am that Johannes Holbein; someone could imitate me only with difficulty as well as he could criticise me'. This is a reference to the saying of the famous painter Zeuxis who had written under an image of an athlete that it was easier to criticize than to imitate it.[23] Again this is referring the viewer to Erasmus' *Life of Jerome* in which he quotes "a well known painter" as having said that "a person will find fault more quickly than he will imitate".[24]He also refers to this idea in his Hercules adage when he is describing how those heroic writers who are trying to restore good letters are attacked and criticized by people who 'couldn't hold a candle to them'. Quoting a Greek proverb he says they are like those who judge the Achaelans from the ramparts who 'if they had a try themselves, they would read the efforts of others with less squeamishness and more indulgence'. He was here referring to the theologians who had begun, at this stage to hurl very serious accusations and criticisms at him. The central meaning that Erasmus attached to the Labours of Hercules, however, was that it was an allegory for the difficulties that we encounter in the struggle for perfection. As we have seen this was the *sine qua non* of his view of the method of perfection. It is these very difficulties that are the dynamic of perfection and so the heroic Hercules, therefore, is centrally important to Erasmus in the allegorical expounding of his *philosophia Christi.* This is why Erasmus saw the significance of comparing him to Mercury: both are symbols of the transformative power of struggle. In the *Enchiridion,* he compared St Paul's personal inner struggle with that of Hercules.[25] In the twelfth rule of the *Enchiridion* he also outlined the method of perfection in terms of a Herculean struggle.

> when you do battle with the enemy, do not be satisfied with deflecting his blow or even repelling his attack, but bravely seizing the weapon, turn it back upon the attacker, cutting his throat with his own sword. This can be done if when you are tempted to evil you not only do not sin, but you make the temptation an occasion for the practice of virtue. And just as in the elegant imagination of the poets Hercules grew in courage and determination from the perils thrust upon him by Juno in her anger, so you also see to it that you not only do not become worse from the harassments of the enemy, but even emerge from the battle as a better man....there is absolutely no other method that is so effective in subduing and routing the enemy.[26]

There is also a Jerome link with this theme because the same idea that perfection is achieved as a result of trials and difficulties is expressed in his preface-latter to the 1524 edition of *Jerome.* Here Erasmus described all the trials and tribulations of Jerome and called him "our hero": the accolade of Hercules.[27] While Erasmus praised Jerome's eloquence and erudition he also praised the example he had given of the struggle for perfection. Erasmus' frequent and severe criticisms of contemporary monasticism and the way in which he valued the ordinary secular Christian have obscured this somewhat. What Erasmus objected to in contemporary monasticism was what he saw as a corruption of the monastic ideal of the early church and not the spiritual experience itself. He expressed great admiration for the inner struggles of Jerome by means of which he had strengthened his spiritual side and subdued his earthly instincts. In his *Life of Jerome,* he described Jerome's life work of purifying Scripture as one that he engaged in only after he had spent years in the desert purifying and perfecting himself.

> With dedication and with all his strength he carried out his aims so that he perfected for us that extraordinary model of Christian holiness. First there was the zeal to wash away in a flood of tears the faults of youth and by the severity of his labours as if with an abrasive cleansing agent, to wipe away the dirt collected through the thoughtlessness of youth. By fasting, vigils, and unbelievable austerity in his whole life he curbed the rebellious flesh and the lustful desires of youth that kept breaking out, teaching the body to serve the spirit lest the emotions work against him in his effort to reach the heavenly life. He was rigorous in imposing punishment on himself and was most pressing in demanding work of himself. He was a taskmaster, as he says elsewhere in short he offered himself, in the words of Paul, as a spiritual sacrifice to God, the form of worship by far the most acceptable to him. [28]

Erasmus was no ascetic. His praise of Jerome's struggle is not a traditional praise of the monastic practice of mortifying the flesh. What he was praising here was the inner process that Jerome engaged in order to transform himself into a more perfect being who could then complete his Scriptural writings with the pure heart they required. He castigated those theologians who would not admit Jerome to their ranks and asked:

> will the Scotists fulminate from their thrones on high? will Jerome be sitting at their feet in the lowest benches? And this because he preferred to give utterance to divine truth rather than to human nonsense, because he preferred to walk amid Scripture's verdant meadows rather than to struggle through the spiny thickets of these modern theologians, because he did not confuse everything with the most frigid of distinctions, but like a river of gold, as it were, he preferred to flow on carrying downstream with him much of value.[29]

Here, in the guise of a defence of Jerome, Erasmus engaged in a thinly-veiled defence of his own non-scholastic methods of Scriptural exegesis. Jerome fulfilled one more important function for Erasmus. He provided an important theological bulwark for the Erasmian system because he believed in free-will. This, as we have seen, was essential to the Erasmian view of perfection. The importance of Augustine in the middle ages was viewed by Erasmus as a serious error. He could not attack Augustinianism directly without being accused of heresy but he was often less than fulsome in his praise of the Doctor of Grace. In his *Life of Jerome* he said that Augustine was superior to Jerome only in his Episcopal office but in all other respects he was Jerome's inferior.[30] Luther understood the reasons for this from the beginning. As early as 1517 while discussing the fact that Jerome was inferior to Augustine, Luther remarked that Erasmus was 'of an absolutely different opinion on this. But the discernment of one who attributes weight to man's will is different from that of him who knows nothing else but grace'[31]

In the portrait, Erasmus has his hands resting on the Labours of Hercules. This is an indication that he has completed this spiritual struggle himself. His face glows with the light of spirit. The book looks like it is floating. It does not touch the bench in front of Erasmus and less than a quarter of it is placed over the bench. It would unbalance and fall under its own weight in a real situation. This is similar to the Iuventas glass behind him and is a link between the idea of the Labours of Hercules and his own emblem. In the *Adages* Erasmus expounded on the adage *to the Pillars of Hercules* and he explained that it had been used by Gregory of Nazianzus in his *Monodia,* where he said of St Basil that he had gone as far as the Pillars of Hercules. Erasmus said that this meant he had reached such a point of perfection that human nature was debarred from going further.[32]There is one last anomaly in the picture. The thumb on Erasmus' left hand is in an anatomically impossible position. On closer inspection it is not really a thumb at all. It is something Erasmus is holding that is flesh coloured. The clue to what it is lies in the iconography of Jerome. One of the most popular themes in Renaissance depictions of Jerome is Jerome in meditation. These pictures depict the struggles of Jerome in the desert alluded to above. He is often shown with a stone in his hand because he had written about beating his breast with one as part of his struggle. Some paintings show him with a bruise on his breast. Erasmus is holding a stone to show us that he too has engaged in this struggle. There is also a small joke in this which any of his friends would understand. Erasmus suffered from the stone, that is, kidney stones. He complained of this at regular intervals and once, after a visit to his friend Zasius had to be cut short on account of his ailment, he wrote to him to say that when he arrived home he 'produced with acute pain an incredible quantity of stones and gravel and one stone of enormous size'. He then described how it felt like being very close to death and that it was agony.[33] Erasmus, here, is alerting the viewer to the fact that he, like all aspiring Christians, has had to engage in the struggle to unite the opposites of spirit and flesh in himself. The fact that Holbein had some difficulty in executing what must have been a request from Erasmus to portray the stone in his hand while at the same time hiding it in full view is evident from a pair of drawings that have come down to us. They are drawings of Erasmus's hands that are clearly preparations for this portrait. The right hand is on one sheet of paper and is detailed but straightforward. The other sheet of paper is much more interesting. It shows three different drawings of hands. One of these is not related to our portrait and may be a sketch for one of the other portraits Holbein painted of Erasmus. The other two drawings are clearly depictions of Erasmus' left hand in our portrait. One of the hands is unfinished and the thumb is missing. This also has a very peculiar forefinger. It is unlikely that an artist as skilled as Holbein could have made such an odd attempt to portray a hand if he was simply attempting a realistic sketch of it. He clearly abandoned this attempt and turned the paper around 180 degrees and started again. The second hand is very similar to the first and has a thumb and looks like he gave a lot of care and attention to it. Like the 'thumb' in the portrait, however, the thumb in the drawing is not quite right. Given the fact that no other drawings by Holbein of preparatory hand sketches have survived it is reasonable to assume that he was trying to achieve some special effect with the hands of Erasmus in this portrait. The position of the hand is very similar to that of the portrait except that the 'thumb' in the portrait is even more exaggeratedly peculiar than in the drawing. This epitomizes the whole picture in which Erasmus is hiding in plain sight and all is not what it seems at first glance.

The enigmatic Erasmus' choice of the boundary god was also a suitable image for him in another way; this was because he chose to impose a limit or hermetic seal on himself and his writings. Balthasar Hubmaier, the Anabaptist, said of him that he wrote carefully but spoke liberally. This was because he was treading a very dangerous line because his views were complex and subtle and not completely orthodox. What we have in his writings and the details of his life is exactly what he wanted us to have. His letters are a rich source of information on his everyday life but they are also wholly unsatisfying. He tells us about his likes and dislikes with regard to food and lodgings and other trivia but we never really get to know the secrets of his heart. His true feelings about close friends and companions or his deeper thoughts about the momentous upheavals that surrounded him often remain shrouded beneath the measured comments of his writings. While the depth of his feeling about the abuses in society and the church is evident in his biting satire, he did not make personal attacks in these writings.[34] The precise nature of his *philosophy of Christ* has to be mined from his works despite the heroic dedication of the man who was so profoundly devoted to his task that he spent every waking hour furthering his goal. His Christianity was undogmatic, open and fluid. He wanted to encourage his readers to engage in their own quest rather than forcing a set of dogmas on them. Erasmus devoted his whole life and all of his energies to his goal He had no other hobbies or pastimes; he had no single close companion to whom he devoted time and emotion. He was rather Christlike in being above personal human attachments, and yet he so loved his fellow humans that he devoted all of his own life to a task whose sole end was to further the salvation of humankind. He expressed this best himself when he told his friend, Justus Jonas, in 1518: 'for praise of my learning or my literary skill I care nothing; one thing seriously gives me pleasure, if what I write makes anyone better, if my productions contribute to the glory of Christ'.[35] History decreed that the age that followed Erasmus' death was one that had little or no need for an undogmatic and reasonable voice such as his. The battle-lines were drawn with all sides fighting for dominance. Many lives have been lost since then on the bloody battlefield of dogma. This present age has seen a new resurgence of fundamentalist beliefs. Perhaps now, more than ever, we need to listen to the voice of a man who believed that all human beings of all ages races and cultures have the very same inherent ability to use their own discernment in order to see what they must do to achieve the ultimate goal of life which is human perfection.

Notes

Notes to Introduction

[1] For an excellent account of the recent historiographical trends in Erasmus Studies see Bruce Mansfield, *Erasmus in the Twentieth Century,* (Toronto, 2003).
[2] Recent biographies of Erasmus all present this view of him to one degree or another. See Cornelis Augustijn, *Erasmus, His Life, Works, and Influence,* (Toronto, 1996) reprint; L-E Halkin, *Erasmus,* (Oxford, 1994) reprint; RJ Schoeck, *Erasmus Grandescens: The Growth of a Humanist's Mind and Spirituality,* (Nieuwkoop, 1988); JK McConica, *Erasmus,* (Oxford, 1991).
[3] See Erika Rummel, *Erasmus' Annotations on the New Testament: From Philologist to Theologian,* (Toronto, 1986); Albert Rabil jr, *Erasmus and the New Testament: The Mind of a Christian Humanist,* (San Antonio, 1972) and also his article 'Erasmus' Paraphrases of the New Testament' in *Essays on the Works of Erasmus,* ed., Richard DeMolen, (London, 1978) 145-61; JB Payne, 'Towards the Hermeneutics of Erasmus' in *Scrinium Erasmianum* 11, 13-49 and Manfred Hoffmann, *Rhetoric and Theology: The Hermeneutic of Erasmus,* Erasmus Studies 12 (Toronto,1994).
[4] Anthony Levi in his introduction to the *Praise of Folly* said that 'Totally to understand the contours of his thought in so many different fields demands a rare and complex competence unlikely to be found in any individual modern scholar'. Betty Radice, trans., *Praise of Folly,* (London, 1986) 10.
[5] Bruce Mansfield, *Erasmus in the Twentieth Century,* (Toronto, 2003) 207.
[6] Erasmus said this in his letter to Martin Dorp, *CWE, Letters,* 3, 337:115.
[7] He argued this in his *Apologia ad Fabrum* which is in Jean Leclerc,

ed., *Desiderii Erasmi Roterodami Opera Omnia,* IX, 66B and translated in *CWE,* 83, *Controversies.* For a discussion of Erasmus' theological studies at Paris see JK Farge, 'Erasmus, the University of Paris, and the Profession of Theology' in *Erasmus of Rotterdam Yearbook* 19 (1999) 18-46. Farge has argued first, that Erasmus' time 'in Paris was clearly too short to earn any degree at all in theology and, second that during the time he did reside there Erasmus paid scant attention to the formal study of theology. Finally, Erasmus was in fact ineligible for a Paris degree. Every theology candidate was required to swear two solemn oaths attesting to his legitimate birth'. *Ibid.,* 25. On the veracity of his doctorate of Theology see PF Grendler, 'How to Get a Degree in Fifteen Days: Erasmus' Doctorate of Theology from the University of Turin' in *Erasmus of Rotterdam Yearbook* 18 (1998) 40-69. Nevertheless there is a growing acceptance in Erasmus studies that he was indeed a theologian albeit with some reservations.

[8] Yates Frances, *The occult philosophy in the Elizabethan age,* (London, 1985) reprint, 24.

Notes to Chapter 1
Erasmus' Concept of Christ.

[1] *Collected Works of Erasmus,* Toronto, 1974- hereafter *CWE,* 49, *Paraphrase on Mark,* 162.

[2] *CWE, 42, Paraphrase on Romans, 53.*

[3] Christological heresies abounded throughout church history but particularly in the early church. The main groups who diminished or denied the humanity of Christ were the Marcionites, the Valentinians and the followers of Appolinarius; those who diminished or denied his divinity included the Ebionites, the Theodotians, the Sabellians and, of course, the Arians. There was also a third category of heresy that differed from orthodoxy in its assessment of the precise way in which two nature of Christ co-existed. These included the Nestorians, the Monophysites and the Monothelites. The councils of Nicea, Constantinople and Ephesus defined Church orthodoxy. Finally in the year 451 the council of Chalcedon came up with a definition of the composite nature of Christ, which despite continuing heresies was universally accepted.

[4] *CWE,* 9, *Letters,* 1333: 242, also *CWE,* 31, *Adages,* 165-70. See

especially no. lii, 167.

[5] *CWE*, 9, *Letters*, 1333: 242.

[6] *CWE*, 9, *Letters*, 1333: 232-.

[7] *CWE*, 9, *Letters*, 1333: 232.

[8] *CWE*, 9, *Letters*, 1333: 232.

[9] *CWE*, 9, *Letters*, 1333: 243.

[10] *CWE*, 9, *Letters*, 1255: 9.

[11] *CWE*, 9, *Letters*, 1333: 243.

[12] *CWE*, 9, *Letters*, 1333: 233. Noël Beda was the syndic of the faculty of theology at Paris from 1520 until 1535. He spent those years pursuing and prosecuting both humanists and reformers. Erasmus was high on his list of heterodox writers. Beda wrote several works condemning aspects of Erasmus' writings and in 1527, despite Erasmus' efforts to defend himself, the faculty at Paris condemned the *Colloquies*, *Paraphrases* and several other works at the instigation of Beda. For an account of the Beda controversy see Erika Rummel, *Erasmus and his Catholic Critics*, vol 2, (Nieuwkoop, 1989) 29 ff.

[13] *CWE*, 8, *Letters*, 1202: 203.

[14] JC Olin ed., *Christian Humanism and the Reformation*, (New York, 1976) 100.

[15] *CWE*, 1, *Letters*, see introduction to 108: 202, and 109-11:208 *ff.*

[16] *CWE*, 1, *Letters*, 109: 208.

[17] *CWE*, 1, *Letters*, 109: 208.

[18] *CWE*, 1, *Letters*, 109: 209.

[19] This is echoed in the belief expressed throughout Erasmus' writings that every human being also has to struggle within him or herself until death. See especially *CWE*, 66, *Enchiridion*, 49.

[20] The seventh rule in the *Enchiridion* is that contemplation of the higher spiritual realm will necessarily bring with it repugnance for material transitory things, *CWE*, 66, *Enchiridion*, 104.

[21] See below Chapter 2: Erasmus' Concept of Human Nature.

[22] *CWE*, 66, *Enchiridion*, 51 ff. For a full discussion of this process see chapters 2 and 5 below.

[23] *CWE*, 1, *Letters*, 109: 209.

[24] *CWE*, 1, *Letters*, 109: 210.

[25] *CWE*, 1, *Letters*, 109: 210.

[26] *CWE*, 49, *Paraphrase on Mark*, 162.

[27] *CWE*, 49, *Paraphrase on Mark*, 162.

[28] *CWE*, 49, *Paraphrase on Mark*, 162.
[29] *CWE*, 46, *Paraphrase on John*, 23.
[30] *CWE*, 46, *Paraphrase on John*, 23-4.
[31] See, for instance, Eugene F Rice's article, 'Erasmus and the Religious Tradition', in *Journal of the History of Ideas*, 11 (1950) 393, in which he shows that Erasmus' emphasis of the primary importance of the didactic element in Christ's mission in his *De casa natalitia Jesu* meant that he left out the central mystery of the Incarnation.
[32] *CWE*, 32, *Adages*, 48.
[33] *CWE*, 32, *Adages*, 48.
[34] JD Tracy has argued that the position adopted by Erasmus on this issue was semi-Arian. See JD Tracy in *Catholic Historical Review* lxvii (1981) 1-10.
[35] *CWE*, 9, *Letters*, 1334: 261. AB Hall has pointed out that Erasmus, in several places, corrected the Vulgate in such a way as to undermine the value of the verses in question against Arianism. (Romans 5:12; Romans 9:5; Philippians 2:6 and Colossians 11: 9.) See 'Erasmus: Biblical Scholar and Reformer' in TA Dorey, ed, *Erasmus*, (London, 1970) 81-114.
[36] For an excellent account of the barrage of the criticism that Erasmus' New Testament scholarship provoked see Erika Rummel, *Erasmus and his Catholic Critics*, 2 vols, (Nieuwkoop, 1989).
[37] Lefèvre d'Étaples was educated in Paris and studied Greek there. He was greatly influenced by his three trips to Italy where he met , Ficino and Ermolao Barbaro. The latter was the inspiration for Lefèvre's humanist translations of, and commentaries on, the entire Aristotelian corpus. While he rejected Plato he nevertheless became intensely interested in the Pseudo-Dionysian writings and the Hermetic corpus both of which owed a debt to early neo-Platonism. Under the influence of Erasmus and Valla he turned to Scriptural studies. The first fruits of this decision were a critical study of the *Quincuplex Psalterium* in 1509 followed three years later by commentaries on the Pauline Epistles. In 1521 he was called on to assist in the reform of the diocese of Meaux. Over the next few years he gradually adopted reformist views on such matters as the priesthood, the efficacy of the sacraments, the real presence, the intercession of saints and many other disputed religious topics. Growing radicalism in Meaux prompted him to flee to Strasbourg in 1525. In early 1526, however, he was recalled by Francis I and

appointed as tutor to the royal children. One of his crowning achievements was the translation of the bible into French, which task he completed in 1530. His rejection of Plato and his interest in Aristotle were at variance with the views of Erasmus and it may well have been his Aristotelianism that lay at the heart of their Christological dispute. Lefèvre's Christ was far more distant from humankind than Erasmus' Christ; just as the Aristotelian creator is removed from his creation.

[38] Volume 83 of the *CWE* contains a comprehensive account of the dispute. Later Erasmus was also accused of diminishing the divinity of Christ by the Spanish monks, to which accusation of heresy he replied with the *Apologia adversus monachos quosdam hispanos adversos,* Leclerc ix: 1015-94. For an account of the accusation of Edward Lee in the same vein see Robert Coogan, *Erasmus, Lee and the Correction of the Vulgate: The Shaking of the Foundations,* Travaux d'Humanisme et Renaissance, 261 (Geneva, 1992).

[39] *CWE, 5, Letters,* 778: 310.

[40] *CWE, 5, Letters,* 778: 310.

[41] *CWE, 83, Controversies.*

[42] *CWE, 5, Letters,* 730: 225. Ludwig Baer was a theologian and native of Basel, who, despite his connections with the faculty of theology at Paris and his own predilection for the scholastic method in theology, was nevertheless valued as a friend and colleague by Erasmus. The latter often sought Baer's expert opinion on theological matters.

[43] *CWE, 5, Letters,* 731 and 732: 227-30. Wolfgang Faber Capito was a theologian and humanist who lived in the Upper Rhine region. From 1515 he was appointed preacher at Basel cathedral and at the same time he was appointed professor of theology at Basel. During this time Erasmus and he developed a relationship based on mutual respect for each other's scholarship. Ultimately he joined the reformers and with Martin Bucer he directed the reform at Strasbourg. This led to a break with Erasmus, which was never healed. Beatus Rhenanus was also a humanist who lived in the Upper Rhine region. He spent from 1507 to 1527 in Basel where he met and was befriended by Erasmus. The two worked closely together and from 1515 Erasmus appointed Beatus to take charge of his editorial and personal affairs whenever he left Basel. After 1525

Beatus' own burgeoning career as a classical scholar and historian left less time for collaboration with Erasmus but the two were friends to the end. He became the most outstanding German historian of his age and he wrote a biography of Erasmus, which is useful but rather cursory.

[44] Guillaume Budé was a new type of man of letters: a humanist and lay, married man. He became the foremost French scholar and had much influence at the court of Francis I. His friendship with Erasmus was based entirely on correspondence: the two never met. It began in 1517 and despite early promise and their common interests it gradually disintegrated into peevish quarrelling, possibly because Erasmus would not accept an invitation from Francis I to become a courtier.

[45] *CWE, 5, Letters,* 778: 307.

[46] *CWE,* 5, *Letters,* 778: 308.

[47] *CWE,* 4, *Letters,* 554: 286.

[48] Betty Radice, trans., *The Praise of Folly,* (London, 1986) 233.

[49] *CWE,* 3, *Letters, 337*: 126.

[50] *CWE,* 3, *Letters,* 337: 126.

[51] *CWE,* 3, *Letters,* 337: 126.

[52] Betty Radice, trans., *The Praise of Folly, (*London, 1986) 198-9. MA Screech has demonstrated that Erasmus pushed this idea far beyond its basic scriptural meaning and with evidence from Erasmus' manuscript he has convincingly concluded that Erasmus was so anxious to portray Christ as a fool that he consciously misinterpreted the text, see his *Ecstasy and the Praise of Folly,* (London, 1980) 149-50.

[53] 2 Cor. 5:21.

[54] *CWE,* 3, *Letters,* 337: 127.

[55] *CWE,* 25, *Letter Writing,* 33.

[56] *CWE,* 66, *Enchiridion,* 30.

[57] *CWE,* 66, *Enchiridion,* 57.

[58] *CWE,* 66, *Enchiridion,* 57.

[59] *CWE,* 66, *Enchiridion,* 57.

[60] Martin Lips was a priest at the priory of St Maartensdal at Louvain. He used its well-stocked library to further the cause of good-letters. He met Erasmus about 1516 and thereafter was of enormous help to the humanist in producing his edition of St Augustine: both in searching out manuscripts and preparing work

for the press. He also helped in the production of Erasmus' Ambrose, Hilary, and Chromatius as well as these he performed other tasks such as making indices for the Gospels and the Acts of the Apostles. In about 1525 he was moved by his order to the remote village of Lens-St-Remy. This was probably on account of the growing hostility to Erasmus at Louvain. Despite this deprivation, however, he remained a loyal helper of Erasmus until the latter's death. Edward Lee was an Englishman who became a serious opponent of Erasmus. In 1516 he went to Louvain to learn Greek and it was there he encountered Erasmus. Their relationship was cordial at first but when Erasmus rejected some notes he had submitted to him on his New Testament Lee took offence and a protracted dispute ensued. Lee, being younger and far less experienced was never a match for Erasmus. However, Erasmus was aware that Lee was ambitious and well connected and therefore he was protecting his reputation in England by taking Lee seriously and refuting each point. At the time of the dispute Erasmus may still have harboured hopes of living in England in the future. For a discussion of the other possible reasons Erasmus may have had for this dispute see the article on Lee by Marjorie O'Rourke-Boyle in PG Bietenholz, *Contemporaries of Erasmus,* vol 2 (Toronto, 1986) 311-4

[61] *CWE,* 6, *Letters,* 843: 24.

[62] *CWE,* 6, *Letters,* 843. 24.

[63] *CWE,* 66, *Enchiridion,* 29

[64] *CWE,* 66, *Enchiridion,* 29.

[65] *CWE,* 66, *Enchiridion,* 30.

[66] *CWE,* 42, *Paraphrase on Romans,* 45.

[67] *CWE,* 2, *Letters,* 262: 230. Andrea Ammonio was one of Erasmus' closest friends in England. He was secretary to Lord Mountjoy and in 1511 he became Latin secretary to Henry viii. He held several ecclesiastical posts and finally he was appointed subcollector of papal taxes in England. He was instrumental in securing the parish of Aldington in Kent for Erasmus, which provided the latter with much-needed financial security.

[68] *CWE,* 6, *Letters,* 858:80.

[69] *CWE,* 42, *Paraphrase on John,* 17.

[70] *CWE,* 66, *Enchiridion,* 38.

[71] *CWE,* 46, *Paraphrase on John,* 18.

[72] *CWE*, 46, *Paraphrase on John*, 20.
[73] *CWE*, 46, *Paraphrase on John*, 18.
[74] *CWE*, 46, *Paraphrase on John*, 18.
[75] *CWE, 46, Paraphrase on John*, 20-1.
[76] *CWE*, 46, *Paraphrase on John*, 20-1.
[77] *CWE, 66, Enchiridion*, 73.
[78] *CWE, 66, Enchiridion*, 73.
[79] *CWE, 66, Enchiridion*, 73.
[80] *CWE*, 66, *Enchiridion*, 73.
[81] *CWE, 66, Enchiridion*, 70.
[82] Betty Radice, trans., *The Praise of Folly*, (London, 1986) 205.
[83] *Dulce Bellum Inexpertis*, in MM Phillips, *Erasmus on his Times*, (Cambridge, 1980)
122.
[84] *CWE*, 8, *Letters*, 1202: 209. This has clear echoes of Erasmus' paraphrase of Romans 13: 8-10, 'Love is, as far as possible, helpful to all, even to evil men, and it harms no one.' *CWE*, 42, *Romans*, 76.
[85] *CWE*, 39, *The Godly Feast*, 192.
[86] For a full discussion of this theme see below Chapter 3.
[87] *CWE*, 46, *Paraphrase on John*, 25.
[88] *CWE*, 42, *Paraphrase on Romans*, 28-9.
[89] *CWE*, 42, *Paraphrase on Romans*, 54.
[90] *CWE*, 49, *Paraphrase on Mark*, 22. See also *ibid.*, 36.
[91] *CWE*, 42, *Paraphrase on Romans*, 22.
[92] *CWE*, 42, *Paraphrase on Romans*, 22.
[93] *CWE*, 46, *Paraphrase on John*, 20.
[94] *CWE*, 46, *Paraphrase on John*, 16.
[95] *CWE, 33, Explanatio Symboli, 370.*
[96] *CWE*, 46, *Paraphrase on John*, 17.
[97] *CWE*, 46, *Paraphrase on John*, 17.
[98] *CWE*, 46, *Paraphrase on John*, 13.
[99] *CWE*, 46, *Paraphrase on John*, 16. This theme is discussed in detail in Chapter 3.
[100] *CWE*, 46, *Paraphrase on John*, 16.
[101] *CWE*, 50, *Paraphrase on the Acts*, 109, footnote 37.
[102] For example: the Christological and Trinitarian criticisms levelled at Erasmus by Edward Lee. For an account of these disputes see Robert Coogan, *Erasmus, Lee and the Correction of the Vulgate: The Shaking of the Foundation*, Travaux d'Humanisme et

Renaissance, (Geneva: Librairie de Droz, 1992) 261.

103 For an analysis of this controversy see CAL Jarrott 'Erasmus' *In Principio Erat Sermo:* A Controversial Translation' in *Studies in Philology* 61 (1964) 35-40, and Marjorie O'Rourke Boyle, *Erasmus on Language and Method in Theology,* (Toronto, 1977) 3-31.

104 Jean Leclerc, ed., *Desiderii Erasmi Roterodami Opera Omnia,* IX, (Leiden, 1706) col.112d-113b.

105 Origen used *verbum* and *sermo* interchangeably in his commentary on the *Song of Songs which is Solomon's 2:9.* Thomas More also defended Erasmus on this point by referring to Gregory of Nazianzus; see Mc Conica, *Erasmus,* (Oxford, 1991) 65.

106 For the contrary argument that Erasmus made this change on the basis of philology see JK Mc Conica, *Erasmus,* (Oxford, 1991) 64-5, where he argues that Erasmus was unaware of the outcry he would provoke. This does not explain, however, why Erasmus insisted on defending himself so vehemently in the *Apologia* and why he did not change *sermo* back to *verbum* in subsequent editions when the outcry was deafening. Many other historians also believe that, in general, Erasmus made philological decisions rather than theological ones in his biblical writings. See HJ De Jonge, 'The Character of Erasmus' Translation of the New Testament, as reflected in his Translation of Hebrews 9' in *Journal of Medieval and Renaissance Studies,* 14 (1984) 81-7 and RD Sider, 'The Just and the Holy In Erasmus' New Testament Scholarship' in *Erasmus of Rotterdam Society Yearbook,* 11(1991)4. In general this view is underpinned by a belief that Erasmus was more or less orthodox in his theology and that, consequently, he would have had no theological reason to change a reading.

107 Jean Leclerc, ed., *Desiderii Erasmi Roterodami Opera Omnia,* IX, (Leiden, 1706) coll. 119-120.

108 Jean Leclerc, ed., *Desiderii Erasmi Roterodami Opera Omnia,* IX, (Leiden, 1706) coll. 119-120.

109 *CWE,* 49, *Paraphrase on Mark,* 57.

110 *CWE,* 49, *Paraphrase on Mark,* 56.

111 *CWE,* 49, *Paraphrase on Mark,* 56.

112 See his letter to Paul Volz, *CWE,* 6, *Letters,* 858:82. This view is also expressed in the *Paraclesis,* JC Olin, *Christian Humanism and the Reformation* (New York, 1976) 96.

113 My italics, *CWE,* 49, *Paraphrase on Mark,* 57.

[114] *CWE*, 49, *Paraphrase on Mark*, 129.
[115] *CWE*, 49, *Paraphrase on Mark*, 135.
[116] This is discussed in detail in chapter 5 below. See also JD Tracy, *Erasmus: the Growth of a Mind*, (Geneva, 1972) 217.
[117] See below, chapter 5.
[118] *CWE*, 49, *Paraphrase on Mark*, 57.
[119] *CWE*, 49, *Paraphrase on Mark*, 96.
[120] *CWE*,39 , *The Godly Feast*, 185.
[121] Paul Volz was abbot of the Benedictine monastery of Hugshofen, near Schlettstadt. He was associated with the humanist literary circle of Schlettstadt which included notable humanists such as Beatus Rhenanus and Jacob Wimpfeling. He was an ardent admirer of Erasmus and the two remained on cordial terms to the end despite the fact that Volz joined the reformers in 1526. Volz was appointed preacher and chaplain to the nuns of St Nicolaus in Strasbourg but he was strongly influenced by the spiritualism of Kaspar Schwenckfeld and refused to sign the Wittenberg Concord. On account of this he was removed from his pulpit. He recanted later, however, under the guidance of Jean Calvin and was reinstated and even allowed to preach at the cathedral. Erasmus, for his part, believed that Volz exemplified the Christian traits he had outlined in his *Enchiridion* and in 1536 he sent him a gold cup and bequeathed one hundred pieces of gold to him in his will as a token of his esteem.
[122] *CWE*, 6, *Letters*, 858:80.
[123] *CWE*, 6, *Letters*, 858: 80.
[124] *CWE*, 6, *Letters*, 858: 81.
[125] *CWE*, 6, *Letters*, 858: 80.
[126] *CWE*, 6, *Letters*, 858: 81.
[127] *CWE*, 6, *Letters*, 858: 81.
[128] *CWE*, 6, *Letters*, 858: 81.
[129] *CWE*, 6, *Letters*, 858: 81.
[130] *CWE*, 6, *Letters*, 858: 81.
[131] *CWE*, 6, *Letters*, 858: 82.
[132] *CWE*, 6, *Letters*, 858: 82.
[133] See the *Paraclesis* in JC Olin, *Christian Humanism and the Reformation* (New York, 1976) 100.
[134] *CWE*, 3, *Letters*, 327: 78.
[135] *CWE*, 4, *Letters*, 843: 24-5.

[136] *CWE*, 4, *Letters*, 843: 25.
[137] See Chapter 2 below for a full discussion of this theme.

Chapter 2
Erasmus' Concept of the Human Being

[1] *The Letters of Marsilio Ficino*, vol.1, Letter 123, (London, 1975) 189
[2] The *Enchiridion* was written in 1501 and published in 1503 but was not an immediate success. It became a best-seller only after Erasmus had become famous. In 1518, Froben produced what Erasmus himself described as an elegant edition. From this time onwards it was a best-seller with forty editions appearing in the next ten years. See *CWE*, 66, 1-7 for further details of its history.
[3] The dual division is elaborated in *CWE*, 66, *Enchiridion*, 41ff, the triple division follows at *ibid.*, 51ff. For a discussion of Erasmus' anthropology see JK McConica, *Erasmus*, (Oxford, 1991) 55.
[4] *CWE*, 66, *Enchiridion*, 41.
[5] *CWE*, 66, *Enchiridion*, 41. The unity of the three apparently disparate parts of the human being is a Platonic notion, see Plato, *Republic*, 443 d-e.
[6] *CWE*, 66, *Enchiridion*, 41.
[7] *CWE*, 66,*Enchiridion*, 41.
[8] *CWE*, 66, *Enchiridion*, 41-2.
[9] Plato, *Republic*, 444b.
[10] See Plato, *Republic*, 441 d-e.
[11] *CWE*, 66, *Enchiridion*, 42.
[12] Plato, *Phaedrus*, 248c.
[13] *CWE*, 25, *De conscribendis Epistolis*, 32.
[14] *CWE*, 66, *Enchiridion*, 42.
[15] *CWE*, 66, *Enchiridion*, 42.
[16] Plato, *Republic*, 440 b.
[17] *CWE*, 66,*Enchiridion*, 42.
[18] *CWE*, 66, *Enchiridion*, 42.
[19] *CWE*, 66, *Enchiridion*, 42.
[20] Plato, *Republic* 440b. See chapter 3 for Erasmus' description of the true church.
[21] *CWE*, 66, *Enchiridion*, 51
[22] *CWE*, 66, *Enchiridion*, 47.
[23] *CWE*, 66, *Enchiridion*, 51.

[24] *CWE*, 66, *Enchiridion*, 51.
[25] *CWE*, 66, *Enchiridion*, 51.
[26] *CWE*, 66, *Enchiridion*, 51.
[27] *CWE*, 66, *Enchiridion*, 51.
[28] *CWE*, 66, *Enchiridion*, 52.
[29] *CWE*, 66, *De Contemptu Mundi*, 158. See also *CWE*, 66, *Enchiridion*, 49.
[30] See above in chapter 1.
[31] *CWE*, 66, *Enchiridion*, 49.
[32] *CWE*, 66, *Enchiridion*, 49. See also *CWE*, 34, *Adages*, 168, where the same sentiment is quoted by Erasmus from Horace, *Epistles*, II. i, 10-11, with the exception that there it is envy which is last to be conquered.
[33] *CWE*, 34, *Adages*, 167 - 182.
[34] *CWE*, 34, *Adages*, 167-8.
[35] *CWE*, 34, *Adages*, 170-1.
[36] *CWE*, 34, *Adages*, 170.
[37] *CWE*, 34, *Adages*, 167-8. Cicero, *De Finibus*, II.i, 118. See also Erasmus' colloquy on the *Art of Learning*, in which he made his character argue that all learning, but especially sacred knowledge, was only achievable by dint of extreme toil. *CWE*, 40, *The Colloquies*, 933
[38] *CWE*, 25, *De Conscribendis Epistolis*, 87.
[39] *CWE*, 25, *De Conscribendis Epistolis*, 87.
[40] *CWE*, 25, *De Conscribendis Epistolis*, 87
[41] *CWE*, 25, *De Conscribendis Epistolis*, 88; See also *ibid.*, 95.
[42] *CWE*, 66, *Enchiridion*, 49-50.
[43] *CWE*, 66, *Enchiridion*, 50.
[44] *CWE*, 66, *Enchiridion*, 50; Erasmus is quoting from Genesis 32:36.
[45] *CWE*, 66, *Enchiridion*, 50.
[46] *CWE*, 66, *Enchiridion*, 50.
[47] *CWE*, 66, *Enchiridion*, 50. In the third rule of the *Enchiridion* Erasmus outlined his belief that despite the arduousness of the struggle for perfection, it was, nevertheless, the only way to happiness. See *CWE*, 66, *Enchiridion*, 58 ff.
[48] *CWE*, 66, *Enchiridion*, 126. See also *CWE*, 29, *Oration on the Pursuit of Virtue*, 3-4, in which Erasmus, in the dedicatory letter, told Adolph of Vere, that his intention in the piece was 'simply to show you to yourself as though in a mirror, so that you can know

yourself'. He then went on to speak of 'Socrates mirror'.

[49] *CWE*, 66, *Enchiridion*, 126.

[50] *CWE*, 66, *Enchiridion*, 125.

[51] *CWE*, 66, *Enchiridion*, 55.

[52] *CWE*, 66, *Enchiridion*, 54.

[53] *CWE*, 66, *Enchiridion*, 54.

[54] *CWE*, 66, Enchiridion, 54-5.

[55] *CWE*, 66, *Enchiridion*, 54.

[56] *CWE*, 66, *Enchiridion*, 54.

[57] *CWE*, 66, *Enchiridion*, 96. See also ibid., 15. This is Platonic see *Republic* 441d-e.

[58] The notion that the flesh is the largest and strongest part of the human being is also to be found in Plato, *Republic*, 442 a-b.

[59] *CWE*, 66, *Enchiridion*, 38.

[60] *CWE*, 66, *Enchiridion*, 38.

[61] *CWE*, 32, *Adages*, 56-63.

[62] *CWE*, 32, *Adages*, 62.

[63] *CWE*, 32, *Adages*, 57.

[64] *CWE*, 32, *Adages*, 57.

[65] *CWE*, 32, *Adages*, 57.

[66] *CWE*, 66, *Enchiridion*, 41.

[67] *CWE*, 66, *Enchiridion*, 40.

[68] *CWE*, 32, *Adages*, 47.

[69] *CWE*, 32, *Adages*, 62.

[70] *CWE*, 32, *Adages*, 63.

[71] *CWE*, 66, *Enchiridion*, 46.

[72] See 1 Cor. 3:19.

[73] *CWE*, 66, *Enchiridion*, 39.

[74] Plato, *Republic*, book 7, 514 ff. See also Plato, *Phaedrus*, 249 c-d.

[75] Betty Radice, *Praise of Folly*, (London, 1986) 202-3 and *CWE*, 66, *Enchiridion*, 86.

[76] *CWE*, 31, *Adages*, 230.

[77] *CWE*, 66, *Enchiridion*, 85.

[78] *CWE*, 66, *Enchiridion*, 85.

[79] *CWE*, 66, *Enchiridion*, 85.

[80] *CWE*, 66, *Enchiridion*, 85.

[81] *CWE*, 66, *Enchiridion*, 85.

[82] *CWE*, 66, *Enchiridion*, 38.

[83] My italics, *CWE*, 66, *Enchiridion*, 65; Erasmus' reference is to 45-

54.
[84] *CWE*, 66, *Enchiridion*, 65.
[85] *CWE*, 66, *Enchiridion*, 65. This has clear echoes of Pico's *Oration on the Dignity of Man.* See Ernst Cassirer, PO Kristeller and JH Randall, eds., *The Renaissance Philosophy of Man,*(Chicago,1948) 225.
[86] *CWE*, 66, *Enchiridion*, 51-4.
[87] *CWE*, 66, *Enchiridion*, 65.
[88] *CWE*, 66, *Enchiridion*, 65. Significantly, here we can see that Erasmus, unlike many of his Renaissance contemporaries, did not hold the usual astrological views. While he did believe the celestial bodies had an influence on the earth itself, he thought that it was God who exercised this power in the human heart.
[89] *CWE*, 66, *Enchiridion*, 66.
[90] *CWE*, 66, *Enchiridion*, 66.
[91] *CWE*, 66, *Enchiridion*, 66.
[92] *CWE*, 66, *Enchiridion*, 66.
[93] *CWE*, 25, *De Conscribendis Epistolis*, 32. The same idea is expressed in Betty Radice, trans., *Praise of Folly*, (London, 1986) 202. Erasmus is quoting Socrates in Plato's *Phaedo*, 67 d-68 b.
[94] *CWE*, 26, *De Pueris Instituendis*, 304.
[95] *CWE*, 26, *De Pueris Instituendis*, 304.
[96] *CWE*, 26, *De Pueris Instituendis*, 304-5.
[97] *CWE*, 25, *De Conscribendis Epistolis*, 33.
[98] JC Olin, ed., *Christian Humanism and the Reformation*, (New York, 1976) 100. For a recent discussion of the term *philosophy of Christ* see Cornelis Augustijn, *Erasmus, His Life, Works, and Influence*, (Toronto, 1996) 75ff. He points out that Louis Bouyer correctly identified the term as being patristic in origin and that it was probably first mooted as a concept (although not explicitly) by Erasmus in the adage, *Sileni Alcibiades.*
[99] JC Olin, ed., *Christian Humanism and the Reformation*, (New York, 1976) 100.
[100] *CWE, 42, Paraphrase on Romans*, 20.
[101] See *CWE*, 31, *Adages*, 80, where Erasmus said that everyone is searching for happiness. See also *CWE*, 66, *Enchiridion*, 58-61: the third rule of the *Enchiridion*, which is a discussion of how the Christian way is the surest road to happiness. The underlying implication being that all people seek happiness. This partially Epicurean theme is also discussed earlier in *CWE*, 66, *Enchiridion*,

46-7.

[102] *CWE*, 66, *Enchiridion*, 58.

[103] *CWE*, 66, *Enchiridion*, 58.

[104] *CWE*, 66, *De Vidua Christiana*, 91.

[105] See the dedicatory letter to Adolph of Veere which accompanied Erasmus' *Oration on the Pursuit of Virtue*, *CWE*, 29, *De Virtute*, 5.

[106] *CWE*, 9, *Letters*, 1334: 251.

[107] This colloquy and Erasmus' syncretism are discussed in detail in Chapter 3 below.

[108] *CWE*, 7, *Letters*, 1013: 72. Jacob de Voecht was a cannon lawyer from Antwerp who studied at Louvain and Orléans. He then returned to Antwerp in 1506 and remained there until his death in 1536. During that time he appears to have been engaged in several diplomatic missions including one to London in 1509 where he met Thomas More. He was also a friend of the close associate of Erasmus, and town clerk of Antwerp, Pieter Gillis. Erasmus met him in 1500 when he lodged with him at Orléans. They remained in contact thereafter and Erasmus, in this letter, dedicated his edition of Cicero's *De officiis* to him in 1519.

[109] *CWE*, 42, *Paraphrase on Romans*, 20-1.

[110] *CWE*, 26, *De Pueris Instituendis*, 311.

[111] *CWE*, 26, *De Pueris Instituendis*, 311.

[112] *CWE*, 26, *De Pueris Instituendis*, 311.

[113] *CWE*, 26, *De Pueris Instituendis*, 311.

[114] The term *Instrumentum* can also mean a written document but the primary sense of the term is a tool or implement and Erasmus was always concerned with the usefulness of Scripture as an instrument of salvation.

[115] Catholic theology disagreed with the excessive spiritualism of Platonic and Origenistic thought. Nevertheless its insistence on the essential unity of body and soul did not imply that the flesh was vital in the perfection process, on the contrary it was seen as a hindrance to the spirit. Protestant theology under the influence of Luther's *Two Kingdoms* doctrine made an even greater distinction between the superior spirit and the inferior flesh.

[116] *CWE*, 66, *Enchiridion*, 44.

[117] *CWE*, 66, *Enchiridion*, 44. The same idea is expressed in *The Praise of Folly*; see Betty Radice, trans., *Praise of Folly*, (London, 1986) 106.

[118] *CWE, 66, Enchiridion,* 44.
[119] *CWE, 66, Enchiridion,* 49.
[120] *CWE, 66, Enchiridion,* 49; See also *ibid.,* 107-8 and Betty Radice, trans., *Praise of Folly,* (London, 1986) 106.
[121] Betty Radice, trans., *Praise of Folly,* (London, 1986) 106.
[122] Betty Radice, trans., *Praise of Folly,* (London, 1986) 106.
[123] *CWE, 66, Enchiridion,* 97 and 126.
[124] *CWE, 66, Enchiridion,* 69. The reference is to John. 6:63.
[125] *CWE, 66, Enchiridion,* 69.
[126] *CWE, 66, Enchiridion,* 69-70.
[127] *CWE, 66, Enchiridion,* 70-84. For a full treatment of the theme of flesh being made perfect in weakness see below Chapter 5.
[128] Plato, *Gorgias,* 493 a.
[129] *CWE, 25, De Conscribendis Epistolis,* 32.
[130] *CWE, 39, The Godly Feast,* 189.
[131] *CWE, 39, The Godly Feast,* 189.
[132] *CWE, 31, Adages,* 203-6.
[133] *CWE, 31, Adages,* 204.
[134] *CWE,* 31, Adages, 204.
[135] *CWE, 31, Adages,* 206.
[136] *CWE, 31, Adages,* 206.
[137] Betty Radice, trans., *Praise of Folly,* (London, 1986) 152-163.
[138] Betty Radice, trans., *Praise of Folly,* (London, 1986) 155.
[139] *CWE, 32, Adages,* 48.
[140] *CWE, 32, Adages,* 48.
[141] Betty Radice trans., *Praise of Folly,* (London, 1986) 113.
[142] *CWE, 32, Adages,* 44.
[143] *CWE, 32, Adages,* 44.
[144] *CWE, 32, Adages,* 44.
[145] For a full exposition of the meaning of this device see below Chapters 6 and 7.
[146] See *CWE, 25,De Conscribendis Epistolis,* 32, where Erasmus highlights the similarity between the Greek words *soma* and *sema* i.e. body and tomb. This is a reference to the Platonic notion that the soul is entombed in the body, see Plato, *Cratylus* 400 c and *Gorgias* 493 a.
[147] *CWE, 66, Enchiridion,* 54.
[148] *CWE, 66, Enchiridion,* 49.
[149] *CWE, 66, Enchiridion,* 49.

[150] *CWE*, 66, *Enchiridion*, 49.
[151] Ficino in his work, *Five Questions Concerning the Mind*, argued something similar to this. He claimed that 'the greater the difficulty with which all the descendants of the first parent receive blessedness when placed outside the order of nature, the greater the ease with which they would receive it if restored to that very order'. See Ernst Cassirer, PO Kristeller & JH Randall, eds., *The Renaissance Philosophy of Man*, (Chicago, 1948) 209. He also argued that 'the more laborious it is for the celestial and immortal soul continually to follow its happiness, while fallen into an intemperate earthly destructible body, the more easily it obtains it when it is either free from the body or in a temperate immortal celestial body'. *Ibid.*, 211.
[152] *CWE*, 66, *Enchiridion*, 106.
[153] *CWE*, 66, *Enchiridion*, 49.
[154] *CWE*, 66, *Enchiridion*, 48.
[155] *CWE*, 66, *Enchiridion*, 48. The quote is from Genesis 3:15.
[156] *CWE*, 66, *Enchiridion*, 48.
[157] *CWE*, 66, *Enchiridion*, 68-9.
[158] See the adage *The Labours of Hercules in CWE*, 34, *Adages*, 167-182; also *CWE*, 66, *Enchiridion*, 68 where Erasmus said that the myth of Hercules reminds us that heaven is won by noble exploits and untiring effort.
[159] *CWE*, 66, *Enchiridion*, 41. This notion is discernable in Pico della Mirandola's, *Oration on the Dignity of Man*, see Ernst Cassirer, PO Kristeller, & JH Randall, eds., *The Renaissance Philosophy of Man*, (Chicago, 1948) 225. Another possible source of this notion for Erasmus was Lorenzo Valla's, *Sermo Laurentiae Vallae de Mysterio Eucharistiae*, printed in *Lactantii Opera*, Venice, 1521, 159.
[160] *CWE*, 66, *De Vidua Christiana*, 224.
[161] While it is true that angels could degenerate, as in the myth of the Fall, there is no notion of angels transforming into a higher entity.
[162] This concept of self-creation and the concept that man can achieve a state higher than the angelic one are both to be found in Pico della Mirandola's *Oration on the Dignity of Man*, see Ernst Cassirer, PO Kristeller & JH Randall, (eds.) *The Renaissance Philosophy of Man*, (Chicago, 1948) 225.
[163] *CWE*, 66, *Enchiridion*, 41, speaking of body and soul Erasmus

said: 'such is their confused turmoil and strife that they seem to be distinct from one another, although they are one'.

[164] *CWE*, 66, *Enchiridion*, 81.

[165] See Betty Radice, trans., *Praise of Folly*, (London, 1986) 207.

[166] See Betty Radice, trans., *Praise of Folly*, (London, 1986) 207. See also Ficino, *Five Questions Concerning the Mind*, where he said 'The condition of the everlasting soul which seems to be in the highest degree natural is that it should continue to live in its own body made everlasting. Therefore, it is concluded by necessary reasoning that the immortality and brightness of the soul can and must at some time shine forth into its own body and that, in this condition alone, the highest blessedness of man is indeed perfected'. Ernst Cassirer, PO Kristeller & JH Randall, eds., *The Renaissance Philosophy of Man*, (Chicago,1948) 211-2,

[167] See Betty Radice, trans., *Praise of Folly*, (London, 1986) 207.

[168] *CWE*, 6, *Letters*, 858: 82.

[169] *CWE*, 66, *Enchiridion*, 84.

[170] *CWE*, 6, *Letters*, 858: 80-82.

[171] *CWE*, 66, *Enchiridion*, 84. The references are to Plato, *Phaedrus*, 251 a ff and Gen 28:12, by using them both together Erasmus demonstrated his belief in the unity of truth regardless of its source.

[172] *CWE*, 66, *De Contemptu Mundi*, 166.

[173] *CWE*, 66, *De Contemptu Mundi*, 166.

[174] *CWE*, 66, *Enchiridion*, 88.

[175] *CWE*, 42, *Paraphrase on Romans*, 47.

[176] *CWE*, 42, *Paraphrase on Romans*, 47.

[177] *CWE*, 42, *Paraphrase on Romans*, 37.

[178] *CWE*, 42, *Paraphrase on Romans*, 47.

[179] *CWE*, 42, *Paraphrase on Romans*, 48.

[180] *CWE*, 42, *Paraphrase on Romans*, 50.

[181] *CWE*, 46, *Paraphrase on John*, 22.

[182] *CWE*, 25, *De Conscribendis Epistolis*, 33.

[183] *CWE*, 23, *Antibarbari*, 59. The biblical verse is John 12:32.

[184] Plato, *Republic*, 490 a-b. In Plato, this concept includes the idea of the pre-existence of the soul which is not Christian.

[185] *CWE, 50, Paraphrase on Acts*, 110.

[186] *CWE, 66, Enchiridion*, 44.

[187] See above Chapter 1 Christ as *logos*.

[188] *CWE, 27, Querela Pacis*, 303.

[189] *CWE*, 27, *Querela Pacis*, 293.
[190] *CWE*, 66, *Enchiridion*, 90.
[191] *CWE*, 27, *Querela Pacis*, 298-9.
[192] *CWE*, 66, *De Vidua Christiana*, 230.
[193] There is an obvious Platonic influence here. See *Enchiridion* where Erasmus said that we progress to heaven on the wings of love as Plato thought, *CWE*, 66, *Enchiridion*, 84. Erasmus may also have been influenced on this point by Ficino's commentary on Plato's *Symposium*.
[194] *CWE*, 66, *Enchiridion*, 47.
[195] See *CWE*, 39, *The Godly Feast*, 185-6 where Erasmus has the character Timothy expound on the meaning of the word 'king' in a Scriptural quotation, he said that 'king' could be 'understood as the perfect man who, with his bodily passions under control, is governed solely by the power of the Holy Spirit.'
[196] *CWE*, 27, *Querela Pacis*, 300.
[197] *CWE*, 27, *Querela Pacis*, 301.
[198] *CWE*, 27, *Querela Pacis*, 301.
[199] *CWE*, 27, *Querela Pacis*, 301.
[200] *CWE*, 27, *Querela Pacis*, 301, and see also *CWE*, 66, *Enchiridion*, 79.
[201] *CWE*, 27, *Querela Pacis*, 302.
[202] *CWE*, 27, *Querela Pacis*, 294-6.
[203] *CWE*, 27, *Querela Pacis*, 294.
[204] *CWE*, 27, *Querela Pacis*, 294.
[205] *CWE*, 27, *Querela Pacis*, 295.
[206] *CWE*, 27, *Querela Pacis*, 295.
[207] *CWE*, 27, *Querela Pacis*, 321.
[208] *CWE*, 46, *Paraphrase on John*, 22.
[209] *CWE*, 46, *Paraphrase on John*, 22.
[210] *CWE*, 46, *Paraphrase on John*, 25.
[211] *CWE*, 31, *Adages*, 114 5.
[212] *CWE*, 42, *Paraphrase on Romans*, 13; *CWE*, 66, *Enchiridion*, 69-70; and Erasmus' letter to Volz, *CWE*, 6, *Letters*, 858: 82.
[213] That is not to say that his view of church was individualistic. Erasmus believed in the unity of Christians and to that end he said he was happy to accept items of doctrine or discipline that had the imprimatur of consensus. See Augustijn on the importance for Erasmus of what he calls the *consensus ecclesiae* or the *magno*

consensu. Cornelis, Augustijn, *Erasmus, His Life, Works, and Influence,* (Toronto, 1996) 151-3.

214 For a good description of Erasmus' view of the true church see JD Tracy, *Erasmus: The Growth of a Mind,* (Geneva, 1972) 212-6. Tracy shows how Erasmus differentiated between the internal real church of the true Christians and the external church that was not the true church at all.

215 *Dulce Bellum Inexpertis,* in MM Phillips, *Erasmus on His Times,* (Cambridge, 1980) 122.

216 *CWE,* 66, *Enchiridion,* 79; *CWE,* 27, *Querela Pacis,* 301-3. Tracy has argued that Erasmus 'remained a Catholic only because he believed in public concord and in patience in the face of evil'; See *Erasmus: The Growth of a Mind,* (Geneva, 1972) 215. It was not simply public concord that interested Erasmus, however, but that more profound *concordia* which was an expression of the essence of Christianity.

217 *CWE,* 9, *Letters,* 1334:252. This statement was, not surprisingly, censored by the faculty of theology at Paris. The letter was addressed to Jean de Carondelet who was an influential Burgundian statesman and churchman. He was a councilor to both Duke Philip the Handsome of Burgundy and Charles V. Erasmus prized him as a close friend and reliable supporter at the Hapsburg court in the Netherlands.

218 *CWE,* 9, *Letters,* 1334: 257.

219 *CWE,* 6, *Letters,* 898: 181.

220 *CWE,* 6, *Letters,* 844: 35. This letter is a very clear statement by Erasmus on his preference for Jerome and Origen over Augustine. He said that Augustine did not know Greek but 'what book was there in the whole library of Greek literature that Jerome had not mastered'. He then told Eck that he was aware that Augustine was favoured in 'the schools'; his explanation for this was that 'every class of men has its common throng, and the best has always appealed only to the few'. In the introduction to the *CWE* volume on the *Paraphrases of Romans and Galatians* the editor, RD Sider, notes that 'the influence of Augustine on Erasmus' interpretation of Romans and Galatians is notable by its absence, especially in the light of the fact that these two letters deal with the contrast between letter and spirit, grace and law, and similar themes which were at the heart of Augustine's theology. Erasmus goes counter to Augustine's exegesis of original sin in Romans 5, his view of law in

Romans 7 as applicable not just to pre-Christian people but to Christians also, his understanding of grace and free-will (predestination) in Romans 9; his interpretation of the encounter between Peter and Paul in Galatians 2. *CWE*, 42, *Romans and Galatians*, xviii. See also Jacques Chomrat, *Grammaire et Rhétorique chez Erasme*, 2 vols, (Paris, 1981). For an interpretation of the alternative view that St Augustine had a considerable influence on Erasmus see Charles Béné, *Erasme et Saint Augustin ou L'influence de Saint Augustine sur l'Humanisme d'Erasme*, (Geneva, 1969). Johann Maier of Eck is best known for his sustained attacks on Luther and was an important champion of the Catholic cause in Germany against the reformers. He was also a serious adversary of Erasmus being notably critical of his New Testament. Erasmus both distrusted and disliked him but nevertheless advised his fellow-humanists not to provoke such a powerful enemy. This in the main was his own reaction to Eck's criticism and thus he managed to avoid serious censure from this element of the Catholic faction in Germany.

221 JB Payne in his article 'Erasmus and Lefèvre d'Étaples as interpreters of Paul' in *Archive for Reformation History*, 65 (1974) 54-83, has concluded that 'Erasmus' sentiments, which we might think of as typical of his brand of humanism were, however, not just humanistic but patristic, especially Origenistic - not, however Augustinian. Origen and others of the later Fathers, especially Ambrosiaster and Pelagius, interpreted Paul as denying only the ceremonial law when he talks about its abrogation, as not intending to undermine free-will when he describes original sin and grace'. (81-2) The Augustinian interpretation of Paul was directly opposed to Erasmus' view of the operation of the will.

222 Romans 5:12. Charles Trinkaus has argued that 'Erasmus' own position on free-will is seen by him as in agreement with pre-Augustinian orthodoxy, but not because of the authority of antiquity but rather because he finds a congruity with the position he has independently developed on the basis of his own thinking'; *The Scope of Renaissance Humanism*, (Ann Arbor, 1983) 278, see also 274ff. For an alternative view of Erasmus' use of philology in his exegesis see HJ De Jonge, 'The Character of Erasmus' Translation of the New Testament, as reflected in his Translation of Hebrews 9' in *Journal of Medieval and Renaissance Studies*, 14 (1984) 81-7; RD Sider,

'The Just and the Holy In Erasmus' New Testament Scholarship' in *Erasmus of Rotterdam Society Yearbook,* 11(1991) 1-26. Both authors conclude that Erasmus did not use philology to promote a novel theological view but in both studies the subjects of Erasmus' exegesis were not ones on which he held particularly novel stances.

[223] By Edward Lee and Frans Titlemans in particular. See *CWE,* 56, *Annotations on Romans,* 151-2, footnote 2.

[224] *CWE, 56, Annotations on Romans,* 142.

[225] *CWE, 56, Annotations on Romans,* 155, this is based on Souter see footnote 22.

[226] Erasmus may have been using the same tactic when he made a similar "error" of attribution when he published the *Commentarii in Psalmos* by Arnobius the Younger; He thought this author was the Arnobius who died circa 330 but it was, in fact, another Arnobius who had been a monk in Rome a century later; the real author had attacked Augustine's doctrine of predestination as being heretical. Erasmus found a kindred spirit in this Arnobius and was very generous in his praise of him. He said he wrote 'with so much brilliance, so much learning, such pregnant brevity and (last but not least) such true religious feeling!' See *CWE, 9, Letters,* 1304: 144 ff.

[227] The Franciscan, Titlemans, taught at Louvain. In 1529 he published *Collationes quinque super epistolam ad Romanos,* in which he defended the Vulgate against the emendations of Erasmus, Lefevre, and Valla. Erasmus replied in his *Responsio ad Gerontodidascalum,* which elicited an *Epistola apologetica,* from Titlemans in 1530. For an account of this dispute see Erika Rummel, *Erasmus and his Catholic Critics,* vol 2, (Nieuwkoop, 1989) 14-22.

[228] Erasmus believed that all human evils came about gradually by a process of degeneration, see his *Dulce Bellum Inexpertis,* where he said: 'every bad thing either finds its way into human life by imperceptible degrees, or else insinuates itself under the pretext of good', MM Phillips, *Erasmus on his times,* (Cambridge,1980) 123.

[229] *CWE, 56, Annotations on Romans, 140.*

[230] *CWE, 56, Annotations on Romans,* 141. See also his *Paraphrase on James* 1:15, *CWE,* 44, 141, in which he also states that it was an inclination to vice rather than sin itself that was passed on from Adam.

[231] *CWE,* 42, *Paraphrase on Romans,* 34. Noel Beda, the syndic of the faculty of theology at Paris, accused Erasmus of Pelagianism on

account of the Paraphrase of this verse.

[232] *CWE*, 26, *De Pueris Instituendis*, 321.

[233] See Augustine, *De Natura et Gratia*, iii, 3-iv, 4. JD Tracy has argued that, on the one hand, 'Erasmus' beliefs about the goodness and moral autonomy of human nature would be perfectly comprehensible to any seventeenth-century Deist, or to one of those eighteenth-century Sorbonne theologians whose optimistic view of nature so closely resembles that of the *philosophes* ', but, on the other hand, he treated the works of St Augustine with 'peculiar respect'; JD Tracy, 'Two Erasmuses, Two Luthers: Erasmus's strategy in Defense of *De Libero Arbitrio* ' in *Archive for Reformation History*, 78 (1987) 57. This apparent contradiction can be explained by the fact that Erasmus acknowledged the debt that theology owed to St Augustine and that although he disagreed with his interpretation of free-will he was also aware that it was a thorny question which had exercised the finest minds throughout the ages and had never been solved definitively. Tracy tries to show that Erasmus, in this debate, was conscious of the ambiguity of his position on free will.

[234] *CWE*, 9, *Letters*, *1324*: 205-8.

[235] This was always the kernel of their disagreement. See E. Kinowaki, 'Erasmus's *Paraphrasis in Epistolam Jacobi* and His Anthropology' in J Chomrat, A Godin and JC Margolin, eds., *Actes du Colloque international Erasme*, (Geneva, 1990) 153-60, the author shows how Erasmus and Luther differed over this letter on the basis of its view of the process of justification; Luther disliked it because it did not contain the concept of justification by faith and Erasmus liked it for the same reason.

[236] *CWE*, 9, *Letters*, 1265: 43.

[237] See Robert Coogan, *Erasmus, Lee and the Correction of the Vulgate: The Shaking of the Foundations*, Travaux d'Humanisme et Renaissance, 261 (Geneva, 1992), in which Coogan describes how Lee was the first of many on the Catholic side to attack Erasmus as a Pelagian on the basis of his annotations.

[238] *CWE*, 9 *Letters*, 1342: 399

[239] *CWE*, 9, *Letters*, 1342: 400.

[240] The latest edition of this dispute in English is in *CWE*, 76 and 77, *Controversies*, this has an excellent introduction by Charles Trinkaus; See also EG Rupp, ed., *Luther and Erasmus on Free Will*, Library of Christian Classics, 17 (Philadelphia, 1969); RH Bainton,

Erasmus of Christendom, (London, 1970) 227-36 is still a good readable account of the dispute.

[241] Jacob Burckhardt, *The Civilization of the Renaissance in Italy,* (London, 1990), Penguin edition, 229. This idea was first mooted by Michelet but Burckhardt was the major exponent of it.

[242] PO Kristeller, 'The Renaissance in the History of Philosophical Thought' in Andre Chastel, *et al., The Renaissance: Essays in Interpretation,* (London, 1982) 134.

[243] For a discussion of this theme see PO Kristeller, 'Erasmus from an Italian Perspective', in *Renaissance Quarterly,* 23 (1970) 1-14; he has argued that 'Erasmus was to a much greater extent than is usually realized, a student and disciple of the Italian Renaissance, of its humanism as well as of its Platonism'. Kristeller concluded that Erasmus' Platonism was very like that of Ficino. Similarly, see JB Payne, 'Towards the Hermeneutics of Erasmus' in *Scrinium Erasmianum,* (11) 17, and Anthony Levi's introduction to Betty Radice, trans., *Praise of Folly,* (London, 1986) 21-5. MA Screech, however, has argued that although Ficino may have had some influence on Erasmus, on the whole he took his Platonism directly from Plato. See MA Screech, *Ecstasy and the Praise of Folly,* (London, 1980) xxi and 76.

[244] PO Kristeller, 'The Renaissance in the History of Philosophical Thought' in Andre Chastel, *et al., The Renaissance: Essays in Interpretation,* (London, 1982) 143.

[245] For details of the Greek writings which were published in the West in the 15th and 16th centuries see PO Kristeller, 'Renaissance Humanism and Classical Antiquity', in Rabil, Albert, *Renaissance Humanism: Foundations, Forms, and legacy,* (Pennsylvania, 1988) vol. 1, 5-16.

[246] Plato, *Republic,* book 7, 514 a ff.

[247] See Denis Hay, 'Historians and the Renaissance during the last 25 Years' in Andre Chastel *et al., The Renaissance: Essays in Interpretation,* (London, 1982) 7.

[248] Jacob Burckhardt, *The Civilization of the Renaissance in Italy,* (London, 1990) 351.

[249] Eugenio Garin in his work *Italian Humanism,* has argued that the humanist's choice of Plato was 'in the very last analysis..a preference for the conception of an open world, discontinuous and full of contradictions, incessantly changing and hostile to any kind

of systematization'. (Connecticut, 1975) 10.

250 In the letter he dedicated his edition of Valla's annotations on the New Testament to Fisher and said: 'I have attempted, in a few words, to dispel the widespread dislike of Valla's name. Being an intelligent man, he did not fail to see that a disease so deeply established could not be cured by anything short of harsh medicines, cautery, and surgery, and that this must inevitably invoke great suffering for many people, He was well aware that even among good men one can hardly find anyone who is willing to listen to the truth.' *CWE*, 2, *Letters*, 182: 90.

251 PO Kristeller, 'The Renaissance in the History of Philosophical Thought' in Andre Chastel *et al.*, *The Renaissance: Essays in Interpretation*, (London, 1982) 136.

252 PO Kristeller, 'The Renaissance in the History of Philosophical Thought' in Andre Chastel *et al.*, *The Renaissance: Essays in Interpretation*, (London, 1982) 136.

253 PO Kristeller, *Renaissance Thought*, (New York, 1961) 99.

254 PO Kristeller, 'The Renaissance in the History of Philosophical Thought' in Andre Chastel *et al.*, *The Renaissance: Essays in Interpretation*, (London, 1982) 133.

255 PO Kristeller, 'The Renaissance in the History of Philosophical Thought' in Andre Chastel *et al.*, *The Renaissance: Essays in Interpretation*, (London, 1982) 133.

256 PO Kristeller, 'The Renaissance in the History of Philosophical Thought' in Andre Chastel *et al.*, *The Renaissance: Essays in Interpretation*, (London, 1982) 133.

257 PO Kristeller, 'The Renaissance in the History of Philosophical Thought' in Andre Chastel *et al.*, *The Renaissance: Essays in Interpretation*, (London, 1982) 131-2.

258 PO Kristeller, 'The Renaissance in the History of Philosophical Thought' in Andre Chastel *et al.*, *The Renaissance: Essays in Interpretation*, (London, 1982) 133.

259 PO Kristeller, 'The Renaissance in the History of Philosophical Thought' in Andre Chastel *et al.*, *The Renaissance: Essays in Interpretation*, (London, 1982) 143.

260 PO Kristeller, 'The Renaissance in the History of Philosophical Thought' in Andre Chastel *et al.*, *The Renaissance: Essays in Interpretation*, (London, 1982) 142-3.

261 PO Kristeller, 'The Renaissance in the History of Philosophical

Thought' in Andre Chastel *et al., The Renaissance: Essays in Interpretation,* (London, 1982) 131.

[262] PO Kristeller, 'The Renaissance in the History of Philosophical Thought' in Andre Chastel *et al., The Renaissance: Essays in Interpretation,* (London, 1982) 144.

[263] PO Kristeller, 'The Renaissance in the History of Philosophical Thought' in Andre Chastel *et al., The Renaissance: Essays in Interpretation,* (London, 1982) 133. Charles Trinkaus has asserted that 'it is ridiculous to argue as to whether Ficino was the philosophical fulfillment of humanism or not. The point is that contemporary humanists flocked to his ideas and his *academy* with no hesitation and great approval, understanding his philosophy or not.' *In Our Image and Likeness,* (Chicago, 1970) 773.

[264] PO Kristeller, 'The Renaissance in the History of Philosophical Thought' in Andre Chastel *et al., The Renaissance: Essays in Interpretation,* (London, 1982) 133.

[265] PO Kristeller, 'Changing views of the intellectual History of the Renaissance since Jacob Burckhardt' in *Studies in Renaissance Thought and Letters,* 2 (Rome, 1985) 27.

[266] PO Kristeller, 'Changing views of the intellectual History of the Renaissance since Jacob Burckhardt' in *Studies in Renaissance Thought and Letters,* 2 (Rome, 1985) 28.

[267] PO Kristeller, 'The Renaissance in the History of Philosophical Thought' in Andre Chastel *et al., The Renaissance: Essays in Interpretation,* (London, 1982) 127.

[268] *CWE,* 66, *Enchiridion,* 111.

[269] *CWE,* 66, *Enchiridion,* 111.

Chapter 3
The Godly Feast

[1] *CWE,* 39, *The Godly Feast,* 183.

[2] *CWE,* 39, *The Godly Feast,* 183.

[3] *CWE,* 39, *The Godly Feast,* 182.

[4] *CWE,* 66, *Enchiridion,* 71.

[5] This was a banquet given by Matthew for his low-life friends together with Jesus and the disciples. See *CWE,* 49, *Paraphrase on Mark,* 39.

[6] Betty Radice, trans., *Praise of Folly,* (London, 1986) 180-1

[7] *CWE,* 49, *Paraphrase on Mark,* 42.
[8] *CWE,* 66, *Enchiridion,* 70. See above chapter 1.
[9] Betty Radice, trans., *Praise of Folly,* (London, 1986) 205.
[10] *CWE,* 2, *Letters,* 187: 103. Richard Foxe born in Grantham, Lincolnshire, was a civil and cannon lawyer who gained ecclesiastical and political preferment in return for his support of Henry VII, most notably, at Bosworth Field. He held ecclesiastical offices such as Bishop of Exeter, Bishop of Bath and Wells and Bishop of Winchester. In the political sphere he was Henry VII's councillor, secretary and keeper of the privy seal and he carried out many important diplomatic missions including several to Scotland. In 1516 he proposed that Wolsey replace him as the keeper of the privy seal. He was well disposed towards Erasmus and according to Thomas More had said that Erasmus' New Testament was worth ten commentaries. This letter is the preface to a version of Lucian's *Toxaris,* which Erasmus had dedicated to Foxe.
[11] *CWE,* 3, *Letters,* 327: 78, to Beatus Rhenanus and, *ibid.,* 337: 130, to Dorp.
[12] Above Chapter 1.
[13] *CWE,* 39, *The Godly Feast,* 175; See Plato, *Symposium,* 211 b-c.
[14] *CWE, Paraphrase on John,* 16.
[15] *CWE,* 39, *The Godly Feast,* 176.
[16] *CWE,* 23, *Antibarbari,* 59.
[17] *CWE,* 39, *The Godly Feast,* 176.
[18] This is a recurring metaphor in the *Enchiridion* see *CWE,* 66, 42-5.
[19] *CWE,* 34, *Adages,* 273. See also *CWE,* 66, *Enchiridion,* 42.
[20] *CWE,* 39, *The Godly Feast,* 185.
[21] *CWE,* 39, *The Godly Feast,* 205.
[22] Plato, *Phaedrus,* 250 a-d. Shining is also referred to by Erasmus as an aspect of the process of spiritual illumination, see *CWE,* 46, *Paraphrase on John,* 18.
[23] *CWE,* 46, *Paraphrase on John,* 20.
[24] *CWE,* 39, *The Godly Feast,* 178-82. For a different perspective see Terence Cave's discussion of Erasmus' literary purpose in this rich depiction of the frescoes; Terence Cave, '*Enargia:* Erasmus and the Rhetoric of Presence in the Sixteenth Century', in *L'esprit créateur* 16 (1976) 5-19.
[25] The idea that we can come to know God through his creation can be found in Roms 1:19-20, as well as in Plato, notably, in *Timaeus,* 28

c-29 d.
[26] *CWE*, 50, *Paraphrase on Acts,* 109. This concept is also to be found in Plato, *Phaedrus,* and 250 a-d. For the notion that the mind is hampered in its task of understanding by the body see Plato, *Phaedo,* 65 a - 67 c, and 81 c.
[27] *CWE*, 42, *Paraphrase on Romans,* 48.
[28] *CWE*, 46, *Paraphrase on John,* 13.
[29] *CWE*, 6, *Letters,* 3. Helias Marcaeus who was born in Metz was rector and confessor of a convent of Benedictine nuns at Cologne which contained relics of the Maccabeans. He spent much time and effort in promoting the cult of the seven Maccabean martyrs and their mother. This letter was one that Marcaeus persuaded Erasmus to write. It served as a preface to a text on the Maccabees attributed to Josephus, which Marcaeus published.
[30] *CWE*, 27, *Querela Pacis,* 300. See also *CWE*, 27, *Institutio Principis Christiani,* 252, where Erasmus says 'the battles and carnage of the Hebrews and their savage cruelty to their enemies are to be interpreted allegorically; otherwise they make pernicious reading'.
[31] *CWE*, 66, *Enchiridion,* 68.
[32] *CWE*, 39, *The Godly Feast*, 177.
[33] *CWE*, 39, *The Godly Feast*, 177.
[34] *CWE*, 39, *The Godly Feast*, 206.
[35] *CWE*, 39, *The Godly Feast*, 206.
[36] *CWE*, 39, *The Godly Feast*, 206.
[37] *CWE*, 39, *The Godly Feast*, 192.
[38] Eusebius, *The History of the Church,* (Penguin classics, 1988) 46.
[39] See DP Walker, *The Ancient Theology,* (London, 1972) 40.
[40] *CWE*, 46, *Paraphrase on John,* 17.
[41] *CWE*, 39, *The Godly Feast*, 194; See Plato, *Phaedo, 62* b.
[42] *CWE*, 39, *The Godly Feast*, 194; Plato, *Phaedo, 69* d.
[43] *CWE*, 39, *The Godly Feast*, 194.
[44] *CWE*, 39, *The Godly Feast*, 194.
[45] *CWE*, 7, *Letters,* 1013: 72.
[46] *CWE*, 23, *Antibarbari,* 59.
[47] *CWE*, 23, *Antibarbari,* 60.
[48] *CWE*, 23, *Antibarbari,* 62.
[49] *CWE*, 23, *Antibarbari,* 57-8. While it is true that in the *Antibarbari,* Erasmus said that Christ reserved the highest good, 'the perfect gift' for his own time, this can only really be reconciled with Batt's other

statements about the spiritual perfection of pagans by the Erasmian concept of the eternal nature of Christ. Although people since the Incarnation now have the highest good at their disposal, those people who sought this goal before that time were also capable of perfection.

[50] *CWE*, 9, *Letters*, 1013: 302-3. Johann von Botzheim was a canon of the cathedral chapter of Constance. He was a firm supporter of the new learning and even showed some sympathy for the reformers. Erasmus valued him as a friend and left him a silver spoon that had an image of Saint Sebastian on it in his will. He also described his house as a 'real home of the Muses' and it bears a strong resemblance to the villa in *the Godly Feast* despite the fact that, as far as we know, Erasmus first visited it after he had written the colloquy.

[51] *CWE*, 42, *Paraphrase on Romans*, 17, (my italics).

[52] *CWE*, 42, *Paraphrase on Romans*, 18.

[53] *CWE*, 42, *Paraphrase on Romans*, 20.

[54] *CWE*, 39, *The Godly Feast*, 185. This is reminiscent of Plato, *Republic*, 443 d, when he says 'the just man does not permit the several elements within him to interfere with one another, or any of them to do the work of others, - he sets in order his own inner life, and is his own master and his own law'.

[55] *CWE*, 66, *Enchiridion*, 104. Erasmus also found this concept in Plato and he often mentioned it. See *CWE*, 2, *Letters*, 180: 82; *CWE*, 8, *Letters*, 1195: 173; CWE, 8, *Letters*, 1202: 205; *CWE*, 8, *Letters*, 1167: 113.

[56] See above in Chapter 2, and also Anthony Levi, introduction to Betty Radice, trans., *Praise of Folly*, (London, 1986) 23-28.

[57] *CWE*, 66, *Enchiridion*, 40.

[58] *Paraclesis*, in, JC Olin, *Christian Humanism and the Reformation*, (New York, 1976) 100.

[59] *CWE*, 50, *Paraphrase on Acts*, 110, where Erasmus wrote that God fashioned Adam out of clay but 'breathed into this mud image a tiny bit of celestial breath, through which we might resemble more closely our parent God himself and because of the similarity in nature might recognize him more easily'. See also *CWE*, 66, *Enchiridion*, 41 where Erasmus said that the soul, on account of its heavenly nature is drawn towards heavenly things because 'like is attracted to like'.

[60] *CWE,* 42, *Paraphrase on Romans,* 49.
[61] See above chapter 1.
[62] *CWE,* 66. *Enchiridion,* 61.
[63] *CWE,* 6, *Letters,* 858: 79.
[64] *CWE,* 31, *Adages,* 227-236
[65] *CWE,* 31, *Adages,* 230.

[66] *CWE,* 50, *Paraphrase on Acts,* 100.
[67] *CWE,* 66, *Enchiridion,* 69.
[68] *CWE,* 39, *The Godly Feast,* 206-7.
[69] Betty Radice, trans., *Praise of Folly,* (London, 1986) 202-3. The allusion is to Plato, *Republic,* book 7: 514 a ff.
[70] *CWE,* 66, *Enchiridion,* 66.
[71] *CWE,* 39, *The Godly Feast,* 188.
[72] *Dulce Bellum Inexpertis* in MM Phillips, *Erasmus on his Times,* (Cambridge, 1980) 123.
[73] *Dullce Bellum Inexpertis* in MM Phillips, *Erasmus on his Times,* (Cambridge, 1980) 123-4.
[74] *CWE,* 66, *Enchiridion,* 69. See also *CWE,* 3, *Letters,* 337: 124, where Erasmus asked Maarten Van Dorp ' What can Aristotle have to do with Christ?
[75] *CWE,* 66, *Enchiridion,* 54.
[76] *CWE,* 66, *Enchiridion,* 54.
[77] *CWE,* 66, *Enchiridion,* 35.
[78] *CWE,* 39, *The Godly Feast,* 186.
[79] *CWE,* 39, *The Godly Feast,* 186.
[80] *CWE,* 39, *The Godly Feast,* 201.
[81] This is central to Erasmus' notion that spiritual strength is achieved by overcoming the weakness of the flesh. See above in Chapter 2.
[82] *CWE,* 39, *The Godly Feast,* 189.
[83] *CWE,* 39, *The Godly Feast,* 194.
[84] *CWE,* 66, *Enchiridion,* 69-70.
[85] See the adage *Dulce Bellum Inexpertis* in MM Phillips, *Erasmus on his Times,* (Cambridge, 1980) 121. It was also likely that this was based on his recollection of meals he had at Colet's house in London. In a letter to Justus Jonas, Erasmus reported that Colet would have a boy read 'in a loud voice a chapter from the Pauline

Epistles or the Proverbs of Solomon...a passage from which was then discussed.' *CWE*, 8, *Letters*, 1211: 235.

[86] *CWE*, 39, *The Godly Feast*, 183. This is also a clear Eucharistic allusion.

[87] *CWE*, 66, *Enchiridion*, 32.

[88] *CWE*, 66, *Enchiridion*, 32-3.

[89] Proverbs 21:1-3.

[90] *Paraclesis*, in JC Olin, *Christian Humanism and the Reformation*, (New York, 1976) 96-7.

[91] *Paraclesis*, in JC Olin, *Christian Humanism and the Reformation*, (New York, 1976) 98.

[92] *CWE*, 39, *The Godly Feast*, 184.

[93] *CWE*, 39, *The Godly Feast*, 184.

[94] *CWE*, 39, *The Godly Feast*, 185. See also *CWE*, 66, *Enchiridion*, 42-5

[95] *CWE*, 39, *The Godly Feast*, 185-6.

[96] *CWE*, 49, *Paraphrase on Mark*, 42.

[97] *CWE*, 39, *The Godly Feast*, 196.

[98] *CWE*, 39, *The Godly Feast*, 196.

[99] *CWE*, 39, *The Godly Feast*, 196.

[100] For a recent discussion of Luther's view of Erasmus see Richard Marius, 'Martin Luther's Erasmus, and How He Got that Way' in *Erasmus of Rotterdam Society Yearbook* 18 (1998) 70-88.

[101] *CWE*, 49, *Paraphrase on Mark*, 43.

[102] *CWE*, 49, *Paraphrase on Mark*, 45.

[103] *CWE*, 49, *Paraphrase on Mark*, 45.

[104] *CWE*, 39, *The Godly Feast*, 189. The verse is Corinthians 1: 6.

[105] *CWE*, 39, *The Godly Feast*, 190. The theologians at Paris objected to this interpretation on the grounds that it was an attack on the practice of fasting. The gospel verse is Titus 1:15.

[106] *CWE*, 39, *The Godly Feast*, 190.

[107] *CWE*, 39, *The Godly Feast*, 191.

[108] *CWE*, 39, *The Godly Feast*, 198-9.

[109] *CWE*, 39, *The Godly Feast*, 199. Of course this proved to have been prophetic in England when Henry VIII instituted the dissolution of the monasteries.

[110] *CWE*, 39, *The Godly Feast*, 199.

[111] *CWE*, 39, *The Godly Feast*, 199.

[112] *CWE*, 39, *The Godly Feast*, 199.

Chapter 4
The Ciceronianus

[1] *CWE, 28, Ciceronianus,* 337.
[2] See *CWE, 28, Ciceronianus,* 327, for instance. The Greek *Nosoponus* is usually translated as Mr. Workmad, it could also be translated as diseased toil and could, therefore, be even more derogatory. Nosoponus, particularly in the early part of the piece, was also meant to be a caricature of Christophe de Longueil, 'who represents for Erasmus a gifted man spoiled by adherence to Ciceronianism'. See *CWE, 28, Ciceronianus,* 324-7.
[3] *CWE, 28, Ciceronianus,* 392.
[4] *CWE, 28, Ciceronianus,* 370-1.
[5] *CWE, 28, Ciceronianus,* 380-1.
[6] *CWE, 28, Ciceronianus,* 386.
[7] *CWE, 28, Ciceronianus,* 390-1.
[8] Cicero is the most quoted author in Erasmus' collections of adages. On Erasmus' respect for Cicero see G Vallese, 'Les Lettres-prefaces au *De Officiis* et aux *Tusculanes*', in *Colloquia Erasmiana Turonensia,* (Paris, 1972) vol 1: 241-6. See especially *CWE, 39, The Godly Feast,* 192.
[9] *CWE, 7, Letters,* 1013: 72.
[10] *CWE, 7, Letters,* 1013: 72.
[11] *CWE, 28, Ciceronianus,* 400.
[12] *CWE, 49, Paraphrase on Mark,* 57.
[13] *CWE, 28, Ciceronianus,* 369.
[14] *CWE, 28, Ciceronianus,* 356.
[15] *CWE, 27, Querela Pacis,* 303.
[16] *CWE, 8, Letters,* 1202:203.
[17] *CWE, 27, Querela Pacis,* 304.
[18] *CWE, 28, Ciceronianus,* 345.
[19] *CWE, 27, Querela Pacis,* 301. See John 13:35.
[20] P.S. Allen, *EE,* vii, no 1976. Hermann von Wied came from an aristocratic family and was Archbishop of Cologne from 1515 until his resignation in 1547. During the 1530s he tried to introduce reforms into his diocese but the failure of the religious colloquies of 1540-1 led him adopt the Protestant reform. As a consequence of this the pope deposed him in 1546. Erasmus' objective in this letter was that von Wied, as an eminent Catholic with a desire for reform,

might use his influence to mediate between the factions.
[21] *CWE*, 28, *Ciceronianus*, 386.
[22] *CWE*, 28, *Ciceronianus*, 387.
[23] *CWE*, 8, *Letters*, 1202:204.
[24] *CWE*, 8, *Letters*, 1202:203. This is also a major theme is the *Ratio Verae Theologiae.*
[25] *CWE*, 8, *Letters*, 1202:203.
[26] Mark 4: 33-4.
[27] John 20: 30.
[28] *CWE*, 8, *Letters*, 1202:203.
[29] JC Olin, *Christian Humanism and the Reformation*, (New York, 1976) 97.
[30] JC Olin, *Christian Humanism and the Reformation*, (New York, 1976) 97.
[31] For a discussion of this quality which Erasmus calls *prudentia* and which can be likened to the rhetorical principle of accommodation see Hilmar Pabel, 'Promoting the Buisness of the Gospel: Erasmus' Contribution to Pastoral Ministry', in *Erasmus of Rotterdam Society Yearbook* 15 (1995) 63ff. See also Manfred Hoffmann, 'Language and Reconciliation: Erasmus' Ecumenical Attitude' in *Erasmus of Rotterdam Yearbook* 15 (1995) 80-1.
[32] *CWE*, 28, *Ciceronianus*, 376.
[33] *CWE*, 28, *Ciceronianus*, 352.
[34] *Paraclesis*, in JC Olin, *Christian Humanism and the Reformation*, (New York, 1976) 96.
[35] *CWE*, 66, *Enchiridion*, 34.
[36] *CWE*, 28, *Ciceronianus*, 352.
[37] See *CWE*, 5, *Letters*, 809: 360-7.
[38] 1 Corinthians 7: 32-3.
[39] *CWE*, 28, *Ciceronianus*, 351.
[40] *CWE*, 49, *Paraphrase on Mark*, 35.
[41] *CWE*, 28, *Ciceronianus*, 351.
[42] *CWE*, 28, *Ciceronianus*, 352.
[43] Paracelsus treated Erasmus for a medical ailment but there is no record of any contact on religious or philosophical matters. See Letter from Erasmus in Allen *EE* no 1809. Agrippa was an admirer of Erasmus and they did correspond between 1531 and 1533 but Erasmus was very cautious in his dealings with him and never strayed into discussion of alchemy or cabbala.

[44] *CWE*, 39, *Colloquies*, 553.
[45] *CWE*, 28, *Ciceronianus*, 386.
[46] This idea has been most fully explored in modern times by CG Jung.
[47] This theme is also fully explored in Chapter 3.
[48] *CWE*, 28, *Ciceronianus*, 369.
[49] *CWE*, 66, *Enchiridion*, 34.
[50] JC Olin, *Christian Humanism and the Reformation*, (New York, 1976) 100.
[51] See for instance *CWE*, 42, *Paraphrase on Romans*, 33; *CWE*, 49, *Paraphrase on Mark*, 120; *CWE*, 25, *De Conscribendis Epistolis*, 33.
[52] *CWE*, 49, *Paraphrase on Mark*, 120.
[53] *CWE*, 6, *Letters*, 858: 80-82.
[54] *CWE*, 28, *Ciceronianus*, 352.
[55] See Chapters 6 and 7.
[56] *CWE*, 49, *Paraphrase on Mark*, 78.
[57] *CWE*, 28, *Ciceronianus*, 353.
[58] Erasmus' version of Christianity would have been impossible without St Paul. The *Enchiridion* in particular is suffused with Pauline concepts especially the spirit/flesh dichotomy. See especially *CWE*, 66, *Enchiridion*, 72, where Erasmus urges the reader to value St Paul's writings.
[59] 1 Corinthians 1:18-25.
[60] 1 Corinthians 2:6-7; 1 Corinthians 3:1-3; 1 Corinthians 9:19-23.
[61] 1 Corinthians 10:1-4.
[62] *CWE*, 28, *Ciceronianus*, 353.
[63] *CWE*, 28, *Ciceronianus*, 353.
[64] *CWE*, 28, *Ciceronianus*, 353.
[65] Exodus 16:31 and Numbers 11:7.
[66] *CWE*, 66, *Enchiridion*, 32.
[67] *CWE*, 66, *Enchiridion*, 32.
[68] *CWE*, 66, *Enchiridion*, 68-9.
[69] *CWE*, 66, *Enchiridion*, 69. See also the *Ratio Vera Theologica*, in Hajo and Annemarie, *Ausgewahlte Werke* (Munich, 1933) 280:30-3, where Erasmus showed that he was aware of the dangers in this method and urged moderation and said that it should not be used to support pronouncements on faith.
[70] For a discussion of Erasmus' influence on the radical reformers see GH Williams, *The Radical Reformation*, (London, 1962) 8-11 and

also Peter G Bietenholz, *Encounters with a radical Erasmus: Erasmus' work as a source of radical thought in early modern Europe,* (Toronto, 2009). It was also significant in this regard that the first vernacular translation of the *Enchiridion* was a Czech version produced by the Bohemian Brethren in 1519 who found the *philosophy of Christ* very attractive.
[71] *CWE,* 28, *Ciceronianus,* 355.
[72] *CWE,* 28, *Ciceronianus,* 40. Erasmus devoted a major section near the beginning of the *Enchiridion* to an exposition of the importance of the concept of self-knowledge for the acquisition of wisdom and hence perfection. *CWE,* 66, *Enchiridion,* 38ff. This notion is also Platonic see Plato, *Phaedrus,* 230 a.
[73] *CWE,* 28, *Ciceronianus,* 363.
[74] Mark 4: 33-4. John 20:30.
[75] *CWE,* 28, *Ciceronianus,* 363.
[76] *CWE,* 66, *Enchiridion,* 58.
[77] *CWE,* 28, *Ciceronianus,* 369.
[78] Betty Radice, trans., *Praise of Folly,* (London, 1986) 156.
[79] *CWE,* 28, *Ciceronianus,* 373.
[80] *CWE,* 28, *Ciceronianus,* 376.
[81] *CWE,* 28, *Ciceronianus,* 376
[82] *CWE,* 66, *Enchiridion,* 57.
[83] *CWE,* 66, *Enchiridion,* 34.
[84] *CWE,* 28, *Ciceronianus,* 392.
[85] *CWE,* 28, *Ciceronianus,* 447.
[86] *CWE,* 28, *Ciceronianus,* 447.
[87] See Chapter 3 on *The Godly Feast* for an analysis of the Erasmian concept that all truth is truth of Christ.
[88] *CWE,* 28, *Ciceronianus,* 396.
[89] *CWE,* 28, *Ciceronianus,* 393.
[90] *CWE,* 28, *Ciceronianus,* 396-7.
[91] *CWE,* 28, *Ciceronianus,* 397.
[92] *CWE,* 66, *De Contemptu Mundi,* 173.
[93] *CWE,* 28, *Ciceronianus,* 397.
[94] *CWE,* 28, *Ciceronianus,* 397.
[95] *CWE,* 28, *Ciceronianus,* 397.
[96] *CWE,* 66, *Enchiridion,* 45.
[97] *CWE,* 66, *Enchiridion,* 45.
[98] *CWE,* 28, *Ciceronianus,* 398.

[99] *CWE*, 28, *Ciceronianus*, 398.
[100] *CWE*, 28, *Ciceronianus*, 399.
[101] *CWE*, 28, *Ciceronianus*, 399.
[102] *CWE*, 28, *Ciceronianus*, 399.
[103] *CWE*, 28, *Ciceronianus*, 399.
[104] *CWE*, 42, *Paraphrase on Romans*, 37.
[105] *CWE*, 66, *Enchiridion*, 40-1.
[106] *CWE*, 66, *Enchiridion*, 110.
[107] *CWE*, 66, *Enchiridion*, 57.
[108] *CWE*, 66, *Enchiridion*, 30.
[109] This theme is discussed in detail in Chapter 5.
[110] *CWE*, 28, *Ciceronianus*, 401.
[111] *CWE*, 28, *Ciceronianus*, 402.
[112] *CWE*, 28, *Ciceronianus*, 402.
[113] *CWE*, 28, *Ciceronianus*, 403.
[114] *CWE*, 28, *Ciceronianus*, 407. Erasmus also used this idea of emulation rather than imitation in relation to Christ in the *Paraphrase on Mark*. See *CWE*, 49, *Paraphrase on Mark*, 130.
[115] *CWE*, 28, *Ciceronianus*, 407.
[116] *CWE*, 28, *Ciceronianus*, 408.
[117] *CWE*, 28, *Ciceronianus*, 408.
[118] *CWE*, 66, *Enchiridion*, 54.
[119] *CWE*, 66, *Enchiridion*, 55.
[120] *CWE*, 66, *Enchiridion*, 56.
[121] *CWE*, 66, *Enchiridion*, 40.
[122] *CWE*, 66, *Enchiridion*, 34.
[123] *CWE*, 66, *Enchiridion*, 34-5.
[124] *CWE*, 28, *Ciceronianus*, 438.
[125] *CWE*, 28, *Ciceronianus*, 443.
[126] *CWE*, 28, *Ciceronianus*, 438.
[127] *Paraclesis*, in JC Olin, *Christian Humanism and the Reformation*, (New York, 1976) 93.
[128] *CWE*, 28, *Ciceronianus*, 405.
[129] *CWE*, 28, *Ciceronianus*, 445.
[130] *CWE*, 10, *Letters*, 1390: 98. See also Betty Radice, trans., *Praise of Folly*, (London, 1986) 26-7.
[131] See *Paraclesis* in JC Olin, *Christian Humanism and the Reformation*, (New York, 1979) 100.
[132] *CWE*, 28, *Ciceronianus*, 445.

[133] *CWE*, 28, *Ciceronianus*, 445.

Chapter 5
The Perfection Process in Scripture

[1] *CWE*, 49, *Paraphrase on Mark*, 135.
[2] *Paraclesis*, in JC Olin, *Christian Humanism and the Reformation*, (New York, 1976) 100.
[3] *Paraclesis*, in JC Olin, *Christian Humanism and the Reformation*, (New York, 1976) 102.
[4] *CWE*, 7, *Letters*, 1062: 197.
[5] *CWE*, 7, *Letters*, 1062: 197. See also *CWE*, 9, *Letters*, 1334: 257 in which Erasmus outlined the same process of degeneration. He believed that in all human affairs evil entered into the world by degrees and the church and its theology were no different.
[6] *CWE*, 9, *Letters*, 1334: 257.
[7] *CWE*, 9, *Letters*, 1334: 252.
[8] This was one way in which Erasmus translated the humanist rejection of Aristotle into a purely theological milieu.
[9] *CWE*, 2, *Letters*, 181: 86.
[10] *CWE*, 6, *Letters*, 876:145.
[11] *CWE*, 49, *Paraphrase on Mark*, 16.
[12] *CWE*, 49, *Paraphrase on Mark*, 162.
[13] *CWE*, 49, *Paraphrase on Mark*, 36.
[14] *CWE*, 49, *Paraphrase on Mark*, 36.
[15] *CWE*, 49, *Paraphrase on Mark*, 36.
[16] *CWE*, 49, *Paraphrase on Mark*, 37. The reference is to Galatians 5:24.
[17] *CWE*, 42, *Paraphrase on Romans*, 37.
[18] *CWE*, 42, *Paraphrase on Romans*, 37.
[19] *CWE*, 49, *Paraphrase on Mark*, 38.
[20] *CWE*, 49, *Paraphrase on Mark*, 42. The Mark passage is 2. 19-21.
[21] *CWE*, 49, *Paraphrase on Mark*, 106.
[22] *CWE*, 49, *Paraphrase on Mark*, 106.
[23] *CWE*, 49, *Paraphrase on Mark*, 28.
[24] *CWE*, 49, *Paraphrase on Mark*, 128.
[25] *CWE*, 49, *Paraphrase on Mark*, 129.
[26] *CWE*, 49, *Paraphrase on Mark*, 130.
[27] *CWE*, 49, *Paraphrase on Mark*, 131.

[28] *CWE,* 49, *Paraphrase on Mark,* 132.
[29] *CWE,* 42, *Paraphrase on Romans,* 13.
[30] *CWE,* 49, *Paraphrase on Mark,* 55.
[31] *CWE,* 49, *Paraphrase on Mark,* 55. This is the special quality of *prudentia* that Erasmus thought was essential for the Christian preacher. It is far more than the humanist art of rhetoric. It requires a profound knowledge of the subject and the exact psycological/spitirual state of the audience. It is not, at all the same as that quattrocento discipline which Trinkaus identified as the *theologia rhetorica.* The emphasis the earlier humanists placed on the necessity for eloquence in the art of persuasion led them to value eloquence above all, but Erasmus was always more concerned with persuasion itself rather than eloquence. See Charles Trinkaus, *In Our Image and Likeness,* vol 2 (Chicago, 1970) 610 ff.
[32] *CWE,* 49, *Paraphrase on Mark,* 55-6.
[33] *CWE,* 49, *Paraphrase on Mark,* 56. This is clearly a Silenus image and Erasmus was the first European writer to adopt the Silenus image from Plato's *Symposium* and apply it to Christ and the Christian message. See JD Tracy *Erasmus: The Growth of a Mind,* (Geneva, 1972)214. See also *Sileni Alcibiades,* in *CWE,* 34, *Adages,* 262-282.
[34] *CWE,* 49, *Paraphrase on Mark,* 57.
[35] *CWE,* 49, *Paraphrase on Mark,* 57.
[36] *CWE,* 49, *Paraphrase on Mark,* 59.
[37] *CWE,* 49, *Paraphrase on Mark,* 59.
[38] *CWE,* 49, *Paraphrase on Mark,* 19.
[39] *CWE,* 49, *Paraphrase on Mark,* 20.
[40] *CWE,* 49, *Paraphrase on Mark,* 20.
[41] *CWE,* 49, *Paraphrase on Mark,* 30.
[42] *CWE,* 49, *Paraphrase on Mark,* 55.
[43] *CWE,* 49, *Paraphrase on Mark,* 96.
[44] *CWE,* 49, *Paraphrase on Mark,* 96.
[45] *CWE,* 49, *Paraphrase on Mark,* 96.
[46] *CWE,* 49, *Paraphrase on Mark,* 100. Erasmus was no lover of the idea of miracles. In the preface to his edition of the letters of St Jerome for instance he said 'miracles..are confected by fabulists to bamboozle the vulgar'.
[47] *CWE,* 49, *Paraphrase on Mark,* 97.
[48] *CWE,* 49, *Paraphrase on Mark,* 99.

[49] *CWE*, 49, *Paraphrase on Mark*, 99.
[50] *CWE*, 49, *Paraphrase on Mark*, 99.
[51] *CWE*, 49, *Paraphrase on Mark*, 102.
[52] *CWE*, 49, *Paraphrase on Mark*, 103.
[53] *CWE*, 49, *Paraphrase on Mark*, 103.
[54] *CWE*, 49, *Paraphrase on Mark*, 103.
[55] *CWE*, 49, *Paraphrase on Mark*, 104.
[56] *CWE*, 49, *Paraphrase on Mark*, 102.
[57] *CWE*, 49, *Paraphrase on Mark*, 133.
[58] *CWE*, 49, *Paraphrase on Mark*, 134.
[59] This, of course, is the theme of *The Praise of Folly*.
[60] *CWE*, 49, *Paraphrase on Mark*, 134.
[61] *CWE*, 49, *Paraphrase on Mark*, 134.
[62] *CWE*, 49, *Paraphrase on Mark*, 134.
[63] *CWE*, 66, *Enchiridion*, 53.
[64] *CWE*, 66, *Enchiridion*, 53.
[65] *CWE*, 49, *Paraphrase on Mark*, 70-1.
[66] *CWE*, 49, *Paraphrase on Mark*, 161.
[67] *CWE*, 49, *Paraphrase on Mark*, 63.
[68] *CWE*, 49, *Paraphrase on Mark*, 64-5.
[69] *CWE*, 49, *Paraphrase on Mark*, 86.
[70] *CWE*, 49, *Paraphrase on Mark*, 106.
[71] *CWE*, 49, *Paraphrase on Mark*, 106.
[72] *CWE*, 49, *Paraphrase on Mark*, 107.
[73] *CWE*, 49, *Paraphrase on Mark*, 107-8.
[74] *CWE*, 49, *Paraphrase on Mark*, 108.
[75] Leclerc, Jean, ed., *Desiderii Erasmi Roterodami opera omnia*, 10 vols, (Leiden, 1703-6) V 141f.
[76] *CWE*, 49, *Paraphrase on Mark*, 161.
[77] *CWE*, 49, *Paraphrase on Mark*, 170.
[78] *CWE*, 42, *Paraphrase on Romans*, 33. This concept is also in the *Enchiridion*, see *CWE*, 66, *Enchiridion*, 49-51. It is clear from his poems that Erasmus approved of this mechanism as early as 1499. See Erasmus' poem about the fall of man and its consequences in which he said that death would only be cured by death, pain by pain and wounds by wounds. *CWE*, 85, *Poems*, 110: 285ff.
[79] *CWE*, 42, *Paraphrase on Romans*, 34.
[80] *CWE*, 42, *Paraphrase on Romans*, 35.
[81] *CWE*, 42, *Paraphrase on Romans*, 45.

[82] *CWE,* 42, *Paraphrase on Romans,* 150. Noel Beda, of the faculty of theology at Paris, twice accused him of blasphemy on account of this.
[83] See also the *Praise of Folly,* in which Erasmus wrote of Christ, 'he assumed the nature of man and was seen in man's form: *just as he was made sin so that he could redeem sinners*'. (My italics). Betty Radice, trans., *Praise of Folly,* (London, 1986) 198-9; and *CWE,* 42, *Paraphrase on Romans,* 45.
[84] *CWE,* 49, *Paraphrase on Mark,* 21.
[85] *CWE,* 42, *Paraphrase on Romans,* 43.
[86] *CWE,* 42, *Paraphrase on Romans,* 44.
[87] *CWE,* 42, *Paraphrase on Romans,* 44.
[88] *CWE,* 42, *Paraphrase on Romans,* 44.
[89] *CWE,* 42, *Paraphrase on Romans,* 44.
[90] *CWE,* 42, *Paraphrase on Romans,* 44 - 45.
[91] Mark 9:17-29.
[92] *CWE,* 49, *Paraphrase on Mark,* 113.
[93] *CWE,* 49, *Paraphrase on Mark,* 113.
[94] *CWE,* 49, *Paraphrase on Mark,* 114.
[95] *CWE,* 49, *Paraphrase on Mark,* 114.
[96] *CWE,* 49, *Paraphrase on Mark,* 114.
[97] *CWE,* 49, *Paraphrase on Mark,* 115.
[98] *CWE,* 49, *Paraphrase on Mark,* 115.
[99] *CWE,* 49, *Paraphrase on Mark,* 115.
[100] *Ecclesiastae sive de ratione concionandi.* Jean Leclerc, ed., *Desiderii Erasmi Roterodami opera omnia,* 10 vols (Leiden, 1703-6) V, 767-1099. For the *Paraclesis* see JC Olin, *Christian Humanism and the Reformation,* (New York, 1976) 98.
[101] *CWE,* 49, *Paraphrase on Mark,* 61.
[102] *CWE,* 49, *Paraphrase on Mark,* 60.
[103] *CWE,* 49, *Paraphrase on Mark,* 60.
[104] *CWE,* 49, *Paraphrase on Mark,* 60.
[105] *CWE,* 23, *Antibarbari,* 59.
[106] *CWE,* 49, *Paraphrase on Mark,* 120.
[107] *CWE,* 49, *Paraphrase on Mark,* 108.
[108] *CWE,* 49, *Paraphrase on Mark,* 109.
[109] *CWE,* 49, *Paraphrase on Mark,* 61.
[110] *CWE,* 49, *Paraphrase on Mark,* 109.
[111] For a thorough and scholarly discussion of the concept of ecstatic

experience in Erasmus' writings see MA Screech, *Ecstasy and the Praise of Folly,* (London, 1980) For reference to this particular Gospel incident see 191 ff.

[112] *CWE,* 49, *Paraphrase on Mark,* 111.

[113] *CWE,* 49, *Paraphrase on Mark,* 111.

[114] *CWE,* 49, *Paraphrase on Mark,* 111.

[115] *CWE,* 49, *Paraphrase on Mark,* 116.

[116] *CWE,* 49, *Paraphrase on Mark,* 116.

[117] 4 Peter 1:19.

[118] *CWE,* 49, *Paraphrase on Mark,* 116. Many of the radical reformers adopted this concept of a worldly kingdom which was contrary to Erasmus' interpretation, and although there is some evidence that a number of them were influenced by Erasmus' emphasis of the spirit, rather than the letter, of Scripture it is clear that they were mistaken in their interpretation of his position as a whole. See Peter G Bietenholz, *Encounters with a radical Erasmus,* (Toronto,2009), for the latest survey of Erasmus' thought as a source for the radical thinkers of the early modern period.

[119] *CWE,* 49, *Paraphrase on Mark,* 116.

[120] *CWE,* 42, *Paraphrase on Romans,* 24.

[121] *CWE,* 42, *Paraphrase on Romans,* 24.

[122] *CWE,* 42, *Paraphrase on Romans,* 43.

[123] *CWE,* 42, *Paraphrase on Romans,* 22.

[124] *CWE,* 42, *Paraphrase on Romans,* 10.

[125] *CWE,* 42, *Paraphrase on Romans,* 22.

[126] *CWE,* 42, *Paraphrase on Romans,* 22

[127] *CWE,* 42, *Paraphrase on Romans,* 13.

[128] *CWE,* 42, *Paraphrase on Romans,* 47.

[129] *CWE,* 42, *Paraphrase on Romans,* 11.

[130] *CWE,* 42, *Paraphrase on Romans,* 48.

[131] *CWE,* 42, *Paraphrase on Romans,* 49.

[132] *CWE,* 42, *Paraphrase on Romans,* 48.

[133] *CWE,* 42, *Paraphrase on Romans,* 50-1.

[134] *CWE,* 42, *Paraphrase on Romans,* 48.

[135] *CWE,* 42, *Paraphrase on Romans,* 48-9.

[136] *CWE,* 42, *Paraphrase on Romans,* 48.

Chapter 6
Terminus/Iuventas: The Image of Perfection

[1] The gem which Erasmus had set into a ring survives and is in the Basel museum.
[2] See Edgar Wind, *'Aenigma Termini'* in *Journal of the Warburg and Courtauld Institutes* 1 (1937-8) 66-9. The *locus classicus* is Livy, *Ab Urbe Condita,* book 1, 55, 3-6, and book 5, 54, 7.
[3] *EP* 2018, *CWE* 14. Alfonso de Valdes was a nobleman from Cueneca in Castile. He began his career as a member of the secretarial staff of Charles V and by 1526 he was imperial secretary. He became Erasmus' staunchest supporter at the imperial court and defended him against the attacks of the friars in 1527. In 1530 when Gattinara died Valdes took over his role of mediator between Catholics and Protestants at the Diet of Augsburg. Despite the failure of this effort he never lost hope of a re-united Christendom. When he died of plague in 1533, Erasmus lost a valuable friend in the Spanish court.
[4] See above in Chapter 4 on *the Ciceronianus.*
[5] *CWE, 33, Adages,* 6. Erasmus was probably influenced in this matter by Ficino who in the *argumentum* before his *Pimander* attributed the invention of the hieroglyph to Hermes.
[6] *CWE,* 32, *Adages, 44.*
[7] *CWE,* 32, *Adages, 44.* The Plato reference is to *Laws, 8*: 843 a.
[8] *CWE,* 32, *Adages, 44.*
[9] Betty Radice, trans., *Praise of Folly,* (London, 1986) 202. This commonplace is from Plato, *Phaedo,* 67 e.
[10] Aulus Gellius, *Noctes atticae,* (Venice,1509) LXXIX, Cap.VI. This is in the Erasmus collection of the Bibliotheek Rotterdam, 94 D 6.
[11] The god of Youth could be depicted as either male or female.
[12] Livy, *Ab Urbe Condita,* book 1, 55, 3-6, and book 5, 54, 7.
[13] *CWE,* 66, *Enchiridion,* 41.
[14] *CWE,* 66, *Enchiridion,* 41.
[15] The pre-existence of souls is a Platonic commonplace; see for instance, *Phaedrus,* 249 c. This concept was opposed to the church doctrine of creationism and therefore heterodox.
[16] *CWE,* 66, *Enchiridion,* 41-2.
[17] Betty Radice, trans., *Praise of Folly,* (London, 1986) 202.
[18] Betty Radice, trans., *Praise of Folly,* (London, 1986) 202.

[19] *CWE*, 33, *Adages*, 14.
[20] *CWE*, 33, *Adages*, 9.
[21] *CWE*, 33, *Adages*, 16.
[22] *CWE*, 33, *Adages*, 17.
[23] *CWE*, 27, *Querela Pacis*, 294.
[24] *CWE*, 27, *Querela Pacis*, 294.
[25] *CWE*, 27, *Querela Pacis*, 294. The stone in question is the loadstone or magnet.
[26] *CWE*, 27, *Querela Pacis*, 301-3.
[27] *CWE*, 42, *Paraphrase on Romans*, 58 and 76.
[28] *CWE*, 23, *Antibarbari*, 61.
[29] *CWE*, 23, *Antibarbari*, 59, the verse is John 12:32. This concept of Christ drawing all things good and bad to himself is also reminiscent of Origen's view that in the end even the devil will be saved: the *Apokatastasis*, which is based on Acts 3:21.The clearest statement of this Origenistic concept is in Jerome *Ep. ad Pammachium et Oceanum*, 7. This doctrine was condemned by the Council of Constantinople and, thus, Erasmus would never allude to it overtly.
[30] *CWE*, 66. *Enchiridion*, 14. Erasmus may have found this concept of perfection through attraction in Plato's *Republic*, 490 b, where Plato describes how the philosopher ever strives after true being 'until he has attained the knowledge of the true nature of every essence by a sympathetic and kindred power in the soul, and by that power drawing near and mingling and becoming incorporate with very being, having begotten mind and truth, he will have knowledge and will truly live and grow; and then and not till then will he cease from his travail.' Jowett , version, 269.
[31] *CWE*, 66. *Enchiridion*, 28.
[32] Lisa Jardine in *Erasmus man of letters*, has argued that Erasmus and his circle had worked to show that their leader was Rudolphus Agricola in order to legitimise their northern movement. This may not have been a matter of prestige, as she argues, but rather part of this need to appear quite separate from the less acceptable developments in Italian humanism.
[33] See G. Clutton, '*Termaximus* a humanist jest' in *Journal of the Warburg and Courtauld Institutes*, 2 (1938-9) 266-8. The 1514 letters are 317 and 319. The 1523 letter is 1353. Johann Ulrich Zasius was born at Frieburg im Breisgau. He was both clerk of the court at

Frieburg and a lecturer on law at the university. He was a humanist of note and was in written contact with a very wide circle of the leading humanists of Europe. One of his most outstanding achievements was the Frieburg law code of 1520 which cogently fused the law of Frieburg with Roman law. This later influenced other German codifications and remained in force until the 19th century. His talents were not confined to the law and Erasmus called him 'the only German who knows how to express himself'. (*CWE, Letters,* 3, 408) The two were on friendly terms and Zasius admired Erasmus as a Catholic reformer but in the end he thought Erasmus too cautious in his dealings with the protestant reformers. There are no recorded letters between the two in the period 1524-9 and this might reflect some difficulty between them.

[34] *CWE*, 29, *Ex Galeno versa,* 217-48.

[35] *CWE*, 29, *Ex Galeno versa,* 227.

[36] *CWE*, 29, *Ex Galeno versa, 227.*

[37] *CWE*, 29, *Ex Galeno versa,* 227.

[38] *CWE*, 29, *Ex Galeno versa,* 226 ff. Erasmus actually used the 1525 Aldine edition of Galen for his translation but he was very likely to have had access to the earlier, 1490, edition of Pincio de Cuneto.

[39] BC Bowen, 'Mercury at the Crossroads in Renaissance Emblems' in *Journal of the Warburg and Courtauld Institutes* 48 (1985) 222-8. The adage is iv. vii,4.

[40] *CWE*, 29, *Ex Galeno versa,* 226.

[41] *CWE*, 29, *Ex Galeno versa,* 226.

[42] *CWE*, 29, *Ex Galeno versa,* 226; The Greek verb at issue is κοσμουσιν, see, *ibid.*, footnote 17, 467.

Chapter 7
The Perfect Human Being

[1] For an excellent account of his movement see Erika Rummel, *Biblical humanism and scholasticism in the age of Erasmus,* (Leiden, 2008).

[2] This censure was published in 1531 by the Paris theologians led by Beda but it stopped short of an accusation of heresy.

[3] Lisa Jardine, *Erasmus, Man of Letters*. 111-22 and 180-7.

[4]*CWE, 2, Letters,* no 388.

[5] Lisa Jardine, in her *Erasmus, Man of Letters,* has argued that Erasmus carefully controlled his image but her study concentrates on the premise that Erasmus' aim was to portray himself as the head of the northern group of scholars who championed the *studia humanitatis* which, of course, is fundamentally an educational and literary movement. In her view Erasmus' portrayal of himself as the new Jerome was primarily an attempt to elevate the role of the scholar and the *bonae litterae* in which a kind of secularizing of Jerome led to the sanctification of the humanist scholar. See particularly her chapter 2. This emphasis on his undoubted interest in educational and literary fields neglects his most central aim which was the purification of Christianity in order to disseminate the *philosophy of Christ* as widely as possible.

[6] *CWE, Jerome,* 7.

[7] Both in his letter preface to the *Jerome* and in the adage, *The Labours of Hercules.*

[8] *CWE, Jerome,* 33.

[9] *CWE,2, letters,* 94.

[10] See especially *CWE,* 61, *Jerome,* 52-4.

[11] For a synopsis of the theologians objections to Erasmus see Erika Rummel, *Erasmus,* (New York, 2004) chapter on biblical humanism.

[12] This was a diptych the other sitter being Peter Gillis of Antwerp who was friends with Erasmus and Thomas More, to whom the portraits were given as a present. The original belongs to Her Majesty the Queen and is displayed regularly as part of the royal collection.

[13] Detroit Institute of Arts, inv. 25.4.

[14] See above Chapter 5

[15] *CWE* 66, *Enchiridion,* 56.

[16] There is one painting which has a cup by Joos van Cleve but it was painted in 1528 and was probably influenced by Holbein's Erasmus. It has a stopper in the decanter which accompanies it.

[17] *CWE,* 39, *The Godly Feast,* 205

[18] *CWE,* 61, *Jerome,* 156

[19] *CWE,* 31, *Adages* 54.

[20] *CWE,* 33, *Adages,* no 34, 257.

[21] *CWE,* 34, *Adages,* 167 - 182 See above chapter 2.

[22] *CWE,* 61, *Jerome,* 10.

[23] Pliny, *Naturalis Historia,* XXXV, 36.63.

[24] *CWE*, 61, *Jerome*, 61.
[25] *CWE*, 66, *Enchiridion*, 68.
[26] *CWE*, 66, *Enchiridion*, 107.
[27] *CWE*, 61, *Jerome*, 102.
[28] *CWE*, 61, *Jerome*, 33.
[29] *CWE*, 61, *Jerome*, 53.
[30] *CWE*, 61, *Jerome*, 45.
[31] See *CWE*, 61, *Jerome*, xxxvi. *Luther's Works* 48.
[32]*CWE*, 35, *Adages*, 79.
[33]*CWE*, 9, *Letters*, no 1353, p.442.
[34] The one exception to this is the *Julius Exclusus*, which he always denied publishing.
[35] *CWE*, 6, *Letters*, 145: 876.

Bibliography

Printed Sources

Editors various, *Collected Works of Erasmus,* Toronto, 1974-
Editors various, *Opera Omnia Desiderii Erasmi Roterodami,* Amsterdam, 1969-
Leclerc, Jean, ed., *Desiderii Erasmi Roterodami Opera Omnia,* 10 vols Leiden, 1703-6.

Secondary Works

Augustijn, Cornelis, *Erasmus, His Life, Works, and Influence,* Toronto, 1996.
Bainton, RH, *Erasmus of Christendom,* London, 1970.
Béné, Charles, *Erasme et Saint Augustin ou L'influence de Saint Augustine sur l'Humanisme d'Erasme,* Geneva, 1969.
Bietenholz, Peter G, *Encounters with a Radical Erasmus,* Toronto, 2009.
Bouyer, Louis, *Erasmus and the Humanist Experiment,* London, 1959.
Bowen, BC, 'Mercury at the Crossroads in Renaissance Emblems' in Journal of the Warburg and Courtauld Institutes 48 (1985) 222-8
Burckhardt, Jacob, *The Civilization of the Renaissance in Italy,* London, 1990. (reprint)
Cassirer, Ernst, Kristeller, PO & Randall, JH, eds., *The Renaissance Philosophy of Man,* Chicago, 1948.
Cave, Terence, '*Enargia:* Erasmus and the Rhetoric of Presence in the Sixteenth Century' in *L'esprit créateur* 16 (1976) 5-19.
Chastel, Andre, et *al., The Renaissance: Essays in Interpretation,* London, 1979.
Chomrat, Jacques, *Grammaire et Rhetorique chez Erasme,* 2 vols, Paris, 1981.

Clutton, G, 'Termaximus a humanist jest' in *Journal of the Warburg and Courtauld Institutes* 2 (1938-9) 266-8.
Coogan, Robert, *Erasmus, Lee and the Correction of the Vulgate: The Shaking of the Foundations,* (Travaux d'Humanisme et Renaissance, 261) Geneva, 1992.
De Jonge, HJ, 'The Character of Erasmus' Translation of the New Testament, as reflected in his Translation of Hebrews 9' in *Journal of Medieval and Renaissance Studies* 14 (1984) 81-7.
Dorey, TA, ed., *Erasmus,* London, 1970.
Farge, JK, 'Erasmus, the University of Paris, and the Profession of Theology' in *Erasmus of Rotterdam Yearbook* 19 (1999) 18-46.
Garin, Eugenio, *Italian Humanism,* Connecticut, 1975.
Gleeson, JB, *John Colet,* Berkeley, 1989.
Godin, André, *Érasme Lecteur d'Origene,* (Travaux d'Humanisme et de Renaissance, 190) Geneva, 1982.
Grendler, PF, 'How to Get a Degree in Fifteen Days: Erasmus' Doctorate of Theology from the University of Turin' in *Erasmus of Rotterdam Yearbook* 18 (1998) 40-69.
Gundersheimer, WL, 'Erasmus, Humanism, and the Christian Cabbala' in *Journal of the Warburg and Courtauld Institutes* (26) 38-52.
Halkin, L-E, *Erasmus,* Oxford, 1994. (reprint)
Hall, AB, 'Erasmus: Biblical Scholar and Reformer' in TA Dorey, ed., *Erasmus,* London, 1970, 81-114.
Hay, Denys, 'Historians and the Renaissance during the last 25 years', in Chastel, André, *et al., The Renaissance: Essays in Interpretation,* London, 1979.
Headley, JM, 'Gattinara, Erasmus, and the Imperial Configurations of Humanism', in *Archive for Reformation History* 71 (1980) 64-92.
Hoffmann, Manfred, *Rhetoric and Theology: The Hermeneutic of Erasmus,* (Erasmus Studies 12) Toronto, 1994.
 - 'Language and Reconciliation: Erasmus' Ecumenical Attitude' in *Erasmus of Rotterdam Yearbook* 15 (1995) 71-95.
Huizinga, Johan, *trans.*, F Hopkin, *Erasmus,* Haarlam, 1924.
 - *Erasmus and the Age of Reformation*, New York, 1957.
Hyma, Albert, *The Life of Desiderius Erasmus,* Assen, 1972.
Jardine, Lisa, *Erasmus, Man of Letters: The Construction of Charisma in Print,* Princeton University Press, 1993.
Jarrott, CAL, 'Erasmus' *In Principio Erat Sermo:* A Controversial Translation' in *Studies in Philology* 61 (1964) 35-40.
Jowett, Benjamin, trans., *The Dialogues of Plato,* vols 1-4, London,

1970.
Kinney, Daniel, 'Erasmus's *Adagia:* midwife to the rebirth of learning' in *Journal of Medieval and Renaissance Studies* ii, 2 (Fall, 1981) 169-91.
Kinowaki, E, 'Erasmus's *Paraphrasis in Epistolam Jacobi* and His Anthropology' in Chomrat, J, Godin, A, and Margolin, JC, eds., *Actes du Colloque international Érasme,* Geneva, 1990, 153-60,
Kray, Jill, ed., *The Cambridge Companion to Renaissance Humanism,* Cambridge, 1996.
Kristeller, PO, 'Renaissance Humanism and Classical Antiquity' in Rabil, Albert, ed., *Renaissance Humanism: Foundations, Forms, and legacy,* vol 1, Pennsylvania, 1988.
- 'The Renaissance in the History of Philosophical Thought' in Chastel, André, *et al., The Renaissance: Essays in Interpretation, London,* 1982, 127-52.
- 'Erasmus from an Italian Perspective' in *Renaissance Quarterly* 23 (1970) 1-14.
- *Studies in Renaissance Thought and Letters,* 4 vols, Rome, 1969-96.
- *Renaissance Thought,* New York, 1961.
Luck, George, *Arcana Mundi,* London, 1987.
McConica, JK, *English Humanists and Reformation Politics,* Oxford, 1968.
- *Erasmus,* Oxford, 1991.
McGrath, AE, *Reformation Thought,* Oxford, 1994.
- *The Intellectual Origins of the European Reformation,* Oxford, 1987.
McSorley, HJ, 'Erasmus and the Primacy of the Roman Pontiff: between Conciliarism and Papalism' in *Archive for Reformation History* 65 (1974) 37-54.
Mansfield, Bruce, *Phoenix of His Age,* Toronto, 1979.
- *Erasmus in the Twentieth Century,* Toronto, 2003.
Margolin, JC, *Érasme dans Son Mirroir et dans Son Sillage,* London 1987.
- *Douze Années de Bibliographie Érasmienne, 1950-61,* Paris, 1963.
- Quatorze*Années de Bibliographie Érasmienne, 1936-49, Paris,* 1969.
- Neuf*Années de Bibliographie Érasmienne, 1962-70,* Paris, 1972.
Marius, Richard, 'Martin Luther's Erasmus, and How He Got that Way' in *Erasmus of Rotterdam Society Yearbook* 18 (1998) 70-88.
Nauert, CG, *Humanism and the Culture of Renaissance Europe,* Cambridge, 1996.
Minnich, Nelson H, 'Some Underlying Factors in the Erasmus-Pio

Debate' in *Erasmus of Rotterdam Society Yearbook* 13 (1993) 1-43.
Muller, Christian, *et al., Hans Holbein the Younger the Basel Years,* Munich, 2006.
Oberman, HA, *The Roots of Anti-Semitism,* Philadelphia, 1984.
- The Impact of the Reformation, Edinburgh, 1994.
Olin, JC, *Christian Humanism and the Reformation,* New York, 1976.
- *Six Essays on Erasmus,* New York, 1979.
O'Rourke-Boyle, Marjorie, *Erasmus on Language and Method in Theology,* Toronto, 1977.
- *Christening Pagan Mysteries,* Toronto, 1981.
- 'Erasmus and the Modern Question: Was he Semi-Pelagian? in *Archive for Reformation History* 75 (1984) 59-77.
Pabel, Hilmar, 'Promoting the Business of the Gospel: Erasmus' Contribution to Pastoral Ministry' in *Erasmus of Rotterdam Society Yearbook* 15 (1995) 53-70.
- And Vessey, Mark, eds., *Holy Scripture Speaks: The Production and Reception of Erasmus' Paraphrases on the New Testament,* Toronto, 2002.
Panofsky, Erwin, 'Erasmus and the visual arts' in *Journal of the Warburg and Courtauld Institutes* 32 (1969) 215-6.
Payne, JB, 'Erasmus and Lefèvre D'Étaples as Interpreters of Paul' in *Archive for Reformation History* 65 (1974) 54-83.
- 'Towards the Hermeneutics of Erasmus' in *Scrinium Erasmianum* 11, 13-49.
- *Erasmus: His Theology of the Sacraments,* Richmond, 1970.
Phillips, MM, *Erasmus and the Northern Renaissance,* Suffolk, 1981.
- *Erasmus on His Times,* Cambridge, 1980.
Rabil, Albert jr, *Erasmus and the New Testament: The Mind of a Christian Humanist,* San Antonio, 1972.
- *Renaissance Humanism: Foundations, Forms, and legacy,* 2 vols Pennsylvania, 1988.
- 'Erasmus' Paraphrases of the New Testament' in DeMolen, Richard, ed., *Essays on the Works of Erasmus,* London, 1978, 145-61.
Radice, Betty, trans., *Praise of Folly,* London, 1986. (reprint).
Reedijk, Cornelis, *The Poems of Desiderius Erasmus,* Leiden, 1956.
Reeve, Anne, ed., *Erasmus' Annotations on the New Testament,* London, 1986.
Rice, E F, 'Erasmus and the Religious Tradition' in *Journal of the History of Ideas* 11 (1950) 387-411.
- 'The Renaissance idea of Christian Antiquity: Humanist Patristic

Scholarship', in Rabil Albert, *Renaissance Humanism: Foundations, Forms, and legacy,* vol 1, Pennsylvania, 1988.
- Saint Jerome in the Renaissance, Baltimore, 1988.

Rummel, Erika, *Erasmus and His Catholic Critics,* 2 vols, Nieuwkoop, 1989.
- *Erasmus' Annotations on the New Testament,* Toronto, 1987.
-*The Humanist-Scholastic Debate in the Renaissance and Reformation, Cambridge,* Mass., 1995.
- *Erasmus,* New York, 2004.

Rupp, EG, ed., *Luther and Erasmus on Free Will,* (Library of Christian Classics, 17), Philadelphia, 1969.

Schoeck, RJ, *Erasmus Grandescnens,* Nieuwkoop, 1988.

Screech, MA, *Ecstasy and the Praise of Folly,* London, 1980.

Sider, RD, 'The Just and the Holy In Erasmus' New Testament Scholarship' in *Erasmus of Rotterdam Society Yearbook* 11 (1991) 1-26.

Spitz, Lewis, *The Religious Renaissance of the German Humanists,* Cambridge Mass., 1963.

Thompson, DFS, *Erasmus and Cambridge,* Toronto, 1963.

Thompson, Geraldine, *Under Pretext of Praise,* Toronto, 1973.

Tracy, JD, *The Politics of Erasmus,* Toronto, 1979.
- *Erasmus: The Growth of a Mind,* Geneva, 1972.
- 'Two Erasmuses, Two Luthers: Erasmus's strategy in Defense of *De Libero Arbitrio* ' in *Archive for Reformation History 78* (1987) 37-59.

Trevor-Roper, HR, 'Erasmus and the Crisis of Christian Humanism', in *Renaissance Essays,* London, 1985, 59-75.

Trinkaus, Charles, *In Our Image and Likeness, 2* vols, Chicago, 1970.
- *The Scope of Renaissance Humanism,* Ann Arbor, 1983.
- 'A Humanist's Image of Humanism: the Inaugural Orations of Bartolommeo della Fonte' in *Studies in the Renaissance* 7 (1960) 90-147.
- 'Themes for a Renaissance Anthropology' in Chastel, André, *et al., The Renaissance: Essays in Interpretation,* London, 1979, 83-125.

Vallese, G, 'Les Lettres-prefaces au *De Officiis* et aux *Tusculanes*', in *Colloquia Erasmiana Turonensia,* vol 1, Paris, 1972, 241-6.

Vredeveld, Harry, 'The Ages of Erasmus and the Year of his Birth', in *Renaissance Quarterly* 46 (1993) 754-809.

Walker, DP, *The Ancient Theology,* London, 1972.

Weiss, JM, 'Ecclesiastes and Erasmus the Mirror and the Image' in *Archive for Reformation History* 65 (1974) 83-108.

Williams, GH, *The Radical Reformation,* London, 1962.
Wind, Edgar, '*Aenigma Termini*' in *Journal of the Warburg and Courtauld Institutes* 1 (1937-8) 66-9.
Yates, FA, *Giordano Bruno and the Hermetic Tradition,* London, 1982.
- *The Occult Philosophy in the Elizabethan Age,*

Index

Adages, 15, 25, 42, 47, 48, 59, 73, 104, 188, 208, 209, 212, 216, 218, 226, 227, 228, 230, 231, 233, 241, 244, 252, 256, 257, 259, 260
Adolph of Veere, 229
Adrian VI, 78
Agricola, 257
Agrippa, 5, 126, 247
alchemy, 126, 127, 128, 133, 186, 247
Alciati, 188
Aldus, 181, 184
Alexander Stuart, 179, 182
Alfonso Valdes, 180
allegorical, 31, 44, 60, 62, 93, 106, 125, 132, 146, 151, 158, 175, 179, 185, 210
allegory, 42, 63, 88, 94, 104, 112, 118, 124, 127, 128, 144, 171, 209
Ammonio, 21, 221
Antibarbari, 68, 91, 97, 170, 185, 232, 241, 242, 254, 257
Apokatastasis, 170, 257
Arian, 8, 16, 18, 218
Arianism, 16, 73, 218
Aristotle, 104, 150, 219, 244, 251
Augustine, 20, 76, 80, 122, 127, 211, 220, 234, 236, 237, 261
Aulus Gellius' Attic Nights, 182
Basel, 219, 256, 264
Batt, 98
Batt, Jacob, 242
Beatus Rhenanus, 18, 33, 219, 224, 241
Beda, 10, 217, 236, 254, 258
cabbala, 247
Cabbalism, 5
Capito, 18, 219
ceremonies, 33, 74, 109, 110, 200
Charles V, 180, 234, 256
Christian humanism, 8, 145, 147
Christocentric image, 188
Christology, 11, 17, 18, 199
Cicero, 26, 43, 55, 97, 114, 115, 116, 117, 118, 119, 121, 122, 124, 128, 133, 134, 135, 136, 138, 139, 140, 141, 142, 144, 145, 146, 188, 226, 229, 246
classics, 5, 83, 102, 242
Colet, 1, 11, 15, 151, 244, 262
colloquies, 126
Complaint of Peace, 93, 119, 185
Complutension Polyglot, 17
concedo nulli, 60, 179
consensus, 2, 97, 233
council of Trent, 107
De Conscribendis Epistolis, 226, 228, 230, 232, 248
De Contemptu Mundi, 66, 137, 226, 232, 249
De Pueris Instituendis, 52, 228, 229, 237
De Vidua Christiana, 229, 231, 233
Dionysius the Areopagite, 80
Dorp, 201, 241, 244
Dulce Bellum Inexpertis, 222, 234, 236, 244

ecclesia, 32, 39, 88, 113, 119, 120
Ecclesiastae sive de ratione concionandi, 169, 254
Ecclesiastes, 124, 265
Eck, Johann, 76, 234
Edward Lee, 20, 34, 219, 222, 236
emblem, 179, 180, 181, 182, 184, 188, 199, 203, 204, 205, 207, 212
Enchiridion, 3, 13, 17, 20, 21, 24, 32, 37, 38, 42, 43, 45, 46, 47, 48, 50, 54, 56, 57, 62, 68, 70, 86, 90, 94, 100, 101, 103, 105, 106, 121, 125, 128, 131, 133, 134, 136, 138, 140, 143, 144, 151, 152, 162, 186, 210, 217, 220, 221, 222, 224, 225, 226, 227, 228, 229, 230, 231, 232, 233, 234, 240, 241, 242, 243, 244, 245, 247, 248, 249, 250, 253, 256, 257, 260
Ex Galeno versa, 258
exegesis, 3, 18, 105, 149, 172, 200, 203, 211, 234, 235
Festina lente, 184
Ficino, 5, 36, 84, 96, 186, 218, 225, 231, 232, 233, 238, 240, 256
fire, 33, 43, 65, 68, 69, 104, 126, 128, 129, 144, 166, 171, 187
fire, transformation process likened to., 170
Fisher, 81, 239
Francis I, 218, 220
Franciscan, 34, 236
free will, 47, 64, 75, 78, 79, 237
Froben, 184, 202, 208, 225
Galen, 187, 188, 189, 258
Gethsemane, 11, 13, 14, 15, 21, 42, 151, 163
Gillis, 229, 259
Gospel of John, 9, 29, 58, 123
Greek, 17, 20, 22, 29, 33, 77, 83, 94, 98, 102, 116, 119, 151, 165, 187, 200, 208, 209, 218, 221, 230, 234, 238, 246, 258
harmony, 4, 13, 55, 59, 69, 70, 71, 74, 75, 119, 121, 122, 137, 180, 184, 185, 189
Helias Marcaeus, 242
Hercules, 42, 43, 208, 209, 210, 212, 231
heresy, 2, 8, 10, 16, 24, 34, 73, 81, 146, 199, 212, 216, 219, 258
Hermann von Wied, 121, 246
Hermes, 186, 187, 188, 256
Hermeticism, 5, 91, 187
Hieronymus Dungersheim, 19
Holbein, 204, 205, 209, 213, 259
Incarnation, 27, 30, 72, 73, 218, 243
Italy, 204, 218, 238, 261
Jacob de Voecht, 55, 116, 229
Jerome, 17, 44, 77, 201, 202, 203, 204, 205, 207, 208, 209, 210, 211, 212, 234, 257, 259, 260
Johanine Comma, 16
Johann von Botzheim, 98, 243
Julius Exclusus, 260
Justus Jonas, 120, 122, 151, 214, 244
Lee, 20, 34, 219, 221, 222, 237, 262
Lefèvre d'Étaples, 5, 17, 218, 235
Leo X, 201
Livy, 94, 182, 256
logos, 7, 8, 9, 22, 25, 26, 27, 28, 29, 30, 32, 35, 36, 69, 70, 89, 90, 91, 92, 95, 96, 101, 118, 129, 142, 144, 148, 180, 186, 187, 232
Luther, 2, 25, 75, 78, 79, 82, 110, 120, 121, 123, 161, 212, 229, 235, 237, 245, 260, 263, 265
Manna, 131, 132
Martin Dorp, 19, 201, 215
Mercury, 145, 186, 188, 205, 208, 210, 258, 261
Metsys, 182, 188, 203, 204, 206
microcosm, 39, 50, 80, 85, 91, 92
monasteries, 111, 245
monasticism, 137, 210
Mountjoy, 221
Neoplatonism, 65, 91

Index

Novum Instrumentum, 16, 56, 150, 200, 201
Origen, 40, 76, 151, 170, 175, 223, 234, 235, 257
Paracelsus, 126, 247
Paraclesis, 10, 53, 107, 123, 125, 128, 145, 165, 169, 187, 223, 224, 243, 245, 247, 250, 251, 254
Paraphrase on Acts, 102, 232, 242, 243, 244
Paraphrase on John, 14, 22, 27, 28, 67, 90, 93, 218, 221, 222, 232, 233, 241, 242
Paraphrase on Mark, 49, 88, 89, 108, 110, 118, 125, 128, 129, 151, 152, 158, 171, 216, 217, 218, 222, 223, 224, 240, 241, 245, 246, 247, 248, 250, 251, 252, 253, 254, 255
Paraphrase on Romans, 21, 27, 53, 55, 67, 77, 78, 98, 99, 100, 128, 139, 153, 155, 166, 167, 174, 178, 204, 216, 221, 222, 228, 229, 232, 233, 236, 242, 243, 244, 248, 250, 251, 252, 253, 254, 255, 257
Paris, 2, 10, 110, 166, 216, 217, 218, 219, 234, 235, 236, 245, 246, 254, 258, 261, 262, 263, 265
peace, 33, 44, 54, 69, 70, 71, 72, 74, 75, 122, 124, 150, 158, 180, 183, 185
Pelagian, 78, 199, 237, 264
Pelagianism, 73, 76, 77, 236
Pelagius, 77, 235
Phaedo, 97, 228, 242, 256
Phaedrus, 48, 92, 225, 227, 232, 241, 242, 249, 256
philology, 3, 149, 223, 235
philosophy of Christ, 4, 6, 7, 26, 36, 39, 52, 53, 54, 61, 79, 86, 98, 100, 107, 114, 115, 117, 123, 128, 130, 131, 134, 145, 149, 150, 158, 160, 164, 168, 174, 179, 184, 189, 199, 200, 203, 205, 214, 228, 249, 259
Pico della Mirandola, 5, 84, 231
Plato, 5, 34, 36, 38, 39, 40, 48, 52, 54, 58, 60, 61, 66, 68, 79, 80, 84, 90, 91, 92, 104, 181, 182, 185, 188, 218, 219, 225, 227, 228, 230, 232, 233, 238, 241, 242, 243, 244, 249, 252, 256, 257, 262
Platonism, 37, 56, 80, 82, 84, 86, 176, 218, 238
Poems, 253, 264
Praise of Folly, 3, 17, 19, 25, 34, 48, 57, 60, 64, 103, 121, 134, 149, 176, 184, 201, 215, 220, 222, 227, 228, 229, 230, 232, 238, 240, 241, 243, 244, 249, 250, 253, 254, 255, 256, 264, 265
prayer, 161, 169
prudentia, 122, 247, 252
Querela Pacis, 69, 232, 233, 234, 242, 246, 257, *See* Complaint of Peace
Ratio, 201, 247, 248
Redemption, 10, 15, 19, 20, 26, 72, 73, 99, 100, 160
Reformation, 1, 4, 79, 107, 111, 217, 223, 224, 228, 235, 237, 243, 245, 247, 248, 250, 251, 254, 262, 263, 264, 265, 266
Republic, 39, 48, 80, 225, 227, 232, 238, 243, 244, 257
Reuchlin, 5
Rome, 32, 87, 117, 135, 236, 240, 263
scholasticism, 5, 115, 134, 258
Scotists, 134, 211
secret teaching, 123, 130, 133
Seneca, 57
Sileni Alcibiadis, 91
sin, 19, 21, 34, 38, 40, 42, 45, 46, 61, 74, 76, 77, 78, 89, 124, 126, 133, 137, 143, 166, 168, 170, 171, 173, 174, 175, 177, 184,

210, 234, 235, 236, 254
Socrates, 4, 16, 49, 55, 60, 84, 97, 145, 188, 227, 228
sola fide, 75, 121, 161
Solomon, 106, 128, 208, 223, 245
St Hilary, 16, 75, 150
St Jerome, 200, 202, 204, 252
St Paul, 19, 22, 24, 27, 40, 42, 46, 48, 55, 58, 62, 66, 77, 97, 98, 102, 105, 110, 111, 122, 125, 130, 152, 155, 166, 167, 168, 174, 177, 178, 204, 210, 248
Symposium, 233, 241, 252
syncretism, 96, 102, 118, 229
The Labours of Hercules, 208, 231, 259
theologians, 16, 17, 19, 53, 60, 107, 110, 144, 166, 181, 182, 200, 201, 203, 209, 211, 237, 245, 258, 259
Thomas More, 3, 17, 201, 204, 223, 229, 241, 259
Timaeus, 241
Titlemans, 77, 236
traho, 68
transformation, 5, 33, 41, 43, 56, 63, 64, 65, 66, 74, 76, 95, 101, 102, 107, 127, 128, 142, 146, 149, 153, 154, 162, 165, 169, 185, 203, 204
transforming, 68, 75, 118, 119, 127, 128, 129, 149, 170, 174, 186, 187, 231
Trinity, 9, 16
Turin, 216, 262
Turks, 123
Tusculan Disputationes, 145
union of opposites, 185, 186, 189, 206, 208
Valdes, 180, 182, 256
Valla, 83, 203, 218, 231, 236, 239
Venice, 179, 181, 184, 188, 231, 256
Virgil, 43, 97
Virgin Mary, 22, 207
Volz, 32, 101, 223, 224, 233
Vulgate, 29, 76, 81, 200, 202, 218, 219, 222, 236, 237, 262
war, 38, 43, 47, 69, 85, 100, 140, 165, 167, 183
Zasius, Ulrich, 187, 212, 257
Zwingli, 110

Printed in Great Britain
by Amazon

85034997R00157